BLACKBERRY WINTER

The History
of
Leta Oesch
and Her Family

1899-1945

Olivia Dee Clancy

HERITAGE BOOKS
2016

HERITAGE BOOKS
AN IMPRINT OF HERITAGE BOOKS, INC.

Books, CDs, and more—Worldwide

For our listing of thousands of titles see our website
at
www.HeritageBooks.com

Published 2016 by
HERITAGE BOOKS, INC.
Publishing Division
5810 Ruatan Street
Berwyn Heights, Md. 20740

International Standard Book Numbers
Paperbound: 978-0-7884-2569-1
Clothbound: 978-0-7884-6282-5

To my grandmother and her seven children.

ACKNOWLEDGMENTS

I want to thank my grandmother for the many long hours she spent with me telling the stories and events that made up the years of her life.

I also want to thank Bill Mackay, Curator of the RCMP Museum in Regina, SK, for sending me all the information I requested on the Royal Canadian Mounted Police.

The Blessing and The Homesteader were reprinted by persmision from the book *Our Harvest of Memories*, published by Shell River North Book Committee, Shellbrook, Saskatchewan, Canada.

Chapter One

Myrtle angrily twisted her waist length coffee brown braids onto the top of her head. Quickly jabbing long hairpins in the thick coil to hold it in place, she barely had time to wash up and change into her favorite blue gingham dress. "Of all days for George to dawdle," she hissed. "I've had to do half of his chores as well as mine. Again. All he wants to do is sit and daydream and Mama lets him. He's just spoiled rotten." Her brother had been a pain in the neck to her since the day he was born.

"Myrtle," her mother called from the kitchen. "We'd best hurry or we'll be the last to get there."

Ramming the last hairpin into place, Myrtle grabbed her shawl and hurried down the narrow hall into the kitchen. Her new blue satin hair ribbon lay untouched on her small vanity table. There was no time to braid it into her hair as she had planned.

"We wouldn't be so late if Papa would have made George get up earlier so he could get his chores done," Myrtle muttered through clenched teeth as she wrapped a white cloth over a large platter of fried chicken. She felt old and plain and it was all George's fault. She was already seventeen and would probably end up an old maid taking care of her aged parents. There was a young man at church she had her eye on and she wanted to look especially pretty today so maybe, just maybe, he would finally notice her. "But who would notice a plain-Jane like me," she said to herself.

1

"Now Myrtle, it doesn't do any good to fuss. George is still just a boy and you know he's delicate."

Delicate, thought Myrtle, *you mean spoiled*. George was his mother's pet and he knew it. It irritated Myrtle to no end that he got away with anything and everything. If only her parents paid as much attention to her as they did to their precious George. He was small for his age but at twelve she felt they shouldn't still be treating him like a baby.

Hearing Allison, her father, kicking the dust off his boots as he came up the back porch steps - Sara would not tolerate anyone tracking up her floors - Myrtle thought better of saying any more. She knew how quick tempered her father was. Taking a deep breath, she turned her thoughts to the events that lay ahead. She had been looking forward to this day for months.

"Sara, we'd best get a move on." Allison was a stickler about punctuality.

"It's all ready to put in the wagon." Sara effortlessly handed him the large hamper laden with fried chicken, a smoked ham, potato salad, baked beans and three jars of bread and butter pickles as well as two apple pies. At five-foot-two and one hundred-sixty pounds, Sara was nearly as strong as Allison.

"Where's George?" Rolling down the sleeves of her white muslin blouse, Sara removed her apron and smoothed the front of her long dark skirt.

"He's in the wagon."

After everything was loaded, Myrtle climbed into the wagon behind her parents giving George a hard look. Accustomed to her ill temper he just looked away. He knew it made her angrier to be ignored. He was safe as long as Mama was close. He also knew it was best to stay away from his sister today.

Turning her back to him, Myrtle was determined not to let George spoil this day for her. Dew glistened on the grass and not one cloud interrupted the deep blue sky. The sweet smell of wild flowers floated around them. It was a perfect summer morning. August 12, 1899, to be exact. Myrtle would remember this date all the days of her life.

The family rode in silence as the wagon jostled along the rutted dirt road. This year the local community church had chosen the Logan River for the site of their annual picnic. Shortly after moving to Lyons, Nebraska, the Little family had joined the church.

Sara had not wanted to leave Missouri. She had lived in Tarkio most of her life. Her nine children by her first husband, James Dennis Murphy, had been born there, and he had been buried there. She had known James most of her life. They were married in 1862 when she was fourteen. The Murphy children were grown now with lives of their own.

James had died tragically in 1875 when a sand bank caved in on him. Sara felt it was the end of her own life. Two boys had dug him out with their bare hands. He had lived three days, never regaining consciousness. Sara struggled to make a living for herself and her nine children. She had to turn her modest home into a boarding house and never planned to re-marry until she met Allison seven years later. He rented a room from her and, it seemed to her, he started courting her immediately.

Allison and Sara had been married four years when he decided to move his family to Omaha, Nebraska. He bought a pig farm there but they lost everything when he contracted typhoid fever. In less than a year they moved up to Bert County.

Breaking the silence Allison called to the team, "Whoa. Whoa, there." Pulling the wagon to a stop in a grove of oak trees beside the Logan River he added, "Myrtle, help your mother unload."

Several families had already arrived. Women in homespun and gingham were busy spreading their patchwork quilts on the ground and arranging large food baskets on them. Men in overalls and dungarees were unhitching their teams and tethering the horses in the meadow near by. Children were laughing and squealing and running through the trees. A game of 'hide and seek' was being formed.

After helping Sara from the wagon, Allison lifted the bulging hamper down and began unhitching his team. George immediately ran off with a group of boys. Myrtle unloaded the quilts and her mother carried the hamper to a grassy spot under a large oak tree.

Soon the entire congregation had arrived. The small grove of trees between the meadow and the river was swarming with women and children busy settling in for a long enjoyable day. Large hampers stuffed with a variety of foods waited on patchwork quilts ready for the noon meal. Allison, along with most of the men, disappeared down river to do some fishing. Myrtle discreetly watched her coveted young man go off alone and secretly wished she could go with him but it was not proper for a young lady to be in the company of a young man unchaperoned. Instead she sat with her mother and the other women under the shade of a large oak working on the quilt squares Sara had brought. The women chatted as they each busied themselves with their individual handwork.

The sun was high overhead when the men began returning from the river carrying strings of fish cleaned and ready to fry.

Setting their handwork aside, women began uncovering the food. Small fires were started to cook the catch of the day. Mothers called to their children to come and eat. In no time most of the food was devoured. Babies were soon put down for a nap. A ball game was already in progress in the meadow. The boys wanted to go swimming immediately but were made to wait. "It is too soon after eating," their mothers warned. The boys raced toward the river as soon as they were allowed.

As the sun dipped toward the western horizon the women and older girls returned to their handwork under the shade of the ancient oak. Some worked on fancy embroidery, others were knitting. Others, like Sara and Myrtle, sewed quilt squares together with tiny even stitches. The younger children were noisily playing their pretend games close by. Allison and the other men lounged on the river bank fishing and smoking their pipes. As harvest time approached, it would be the last quiet restful day they would have for some time.

The still of the afternoon was broken by loud youthful voices and laughter. The boys were returning from their swim down river. With hair and clothes still damp, they all raced toward the left-over food and began devouring it greedily as only boys can. No one noticed that two of the boys were missing.

Allison and the other men decided that they could hold a little more fried chicken and maybe some blueberry pie. Dousing pipes and reeling in fishing lines, they joined the boys in another feast.

"Mr. Little? Mr. Little?" A small boy tugged at Allison's sleeve.

"Yes, Robert?" Looking down at the shinny up-turned face, Allison knew he was one of the last to get out of the water.

"Where's George? He said he would play ball with me."

"I'm sure he's around here somewhere. Let's take a look." Robert followed close behind as Allison checked the woods and meadow, asking the other boys if they had seen George. No one had. "You stay here, Robert." Allison hurried toward the river. Cold fear gripped him like a vise.

Several yards down river Allison found George's shirt and trousers neatly folded on top of his shoes. "George! George!" Allison tried in vain to keep the alarm out of his voice. No answer. Leaving the small pile of clothing as it lay, Allison raced toward the meadow. For the first time in his life, he felt sheer terror.

A search party was quickly formed. The men and older boys spread out along both sides of the river. Sara stood on the bank with arms wrapped around herself, staring unblinkingly down river where the men had disappeared. She had a terrible sense of foreboding.

"They'll find him, Mama," Myrtle said reassuringly. "You know what a good swimmer George is. He's probably under a tree somewhere, daydreaming like he always does." Sara did not hear Myrtle's words. She did not see the magnificent Nebraska sunset. All she could see was a group of men coming toward her along the river bank. Allison was carrying a small limp body wrapped in someone's shirt. Everything was distorted. They moved in slow motion. The voices were garbled. Sara crumpled to the ground. Myrtle stood frozen to the spot.

Three days later they buried George in the small church cemetery. Surrounded by their neighbors, Sara and Allison stood desolately beside the mound of dirt that covered the small casket. His face a mask of pain, Allison tried vainly to comfort Sara as the tears streamed down her face. Myrtle stood behind her parents dry-eyed. She had not cried. Not once. She didn't know why she could not cry. She felt the loss, the pain, and the empty place in her heart. Even though he had been a real nuisance to her all his life, she did love her brother and missed him terribly. But she could not cry.

The simple service ended and people began to drift away. Sara fell to her knees and began to moan. The terrible pain-racked sound came from deep within her. Allison knelt beside her, trying desperately to keep his emotions in check. The pastor and Myrtle stood beside the small wooden grave marker Allison had stayed up all night to finish. On it he had carved the words...

> Beloved Son George Allison Little
> Born March 20, 1887
> Died August 12, 1899
> "Remember me as you go by;
> For as you are now, so once was I."

The day after young George was buried, Sara's chocolate brown hair began turning gray. In less than a week her beautiful hair had turned completely snow white. Most days she was too ill to leave her bed. Allison became alarmed and called for the doctor who diagnosed Sara as having dropsy. Dropsy, the doctor explained, was a heart condition that had been aggravated by the extreme grief Sara was experiencing and she would need plenty of bed rest. As well as nursing her mother, Myrtle had taken over all the household duties. All her fanciful youthful thoughts of love and marriage were extinguished. Rising well before dawn each morning her day did not end until long after dark.

One season blended into another. In April 1901, Allison sold the farm in Lyons and moved his small family up to Gross. He believed that Sara would get well in new surroundings. There were too many unpleasant memories in Lyons.

Allison had thought of trying to homestead, but with Sara's poor health he now decided against it. He knew that until 1895, when the state line was finally determined, settlers living on the South Dakota and Nebraska "three mile strip" were not sure which state they lived in. In order to survey your claim you tied a rag on a wagon wheel and counted how many times it went around. To homestead, the rules stated you had to be at least twenty-one and prove up on your surveyed 160 acres by building a house, living it for five years and paying a $40.00 fee.

Instead of homesteading, Allison rented a small four room house in town and leased a few acres of land just outside Gross to raise corn and a few pigs. The land had a "soddie" on it but Allison did not want Sara to live in a house made of dirt, or sandstone, or chalk rock. She would have a real house to live in. A house made of wood with a stone fireplace and a small cast-iron cook stove.

Sara argued against the extra expense of renting in town but Allison was adamant that she have a comfortable home. Since gold was now the sole standard of currency, Allison believed this would stabilize the economy and he could a make comfortable living for them. So the argument was settled. Sara would have her house. But, despite all his hopes, her health did not improve.

To augment the family income, Myrtle went to work as a waitress in Grace Brunner's restaurant. At first her father was against her working in public, but agreed when Myrtle assured him it would only be temporary. They did need the extra money. The hours were irregular so she would still be able to keep up with her household duties and care for her mother.

The Littles lived so close to the restaurant all Grace had to do was step out the back door and yell for Myrtle when she needed help.

Early one morning just as she took the bread out of the oven, Myrtle heard Grace call from her back door. "Myrtle. Myrtle. Need your help." Quickly covering the hot bread with a cloth, Myrtle checked on her sleeping mother, grabbed a clean apron, and hurriedly put it on as she rushed out the door.

"How is Sara?" Grace was putting pies in the oven as Myrtle entered the small kitchen. Large platters of steaming food waited on the back of the huge cast-iron cookstove to be served to a roomful of diners.

Balancing two platters on one arm and grabbing a third, Myrtle answered over her shoulder as she went out of the kitchen, "She just sleeps most of the time." It still amazed Grace the amount of work Myrtle could do and the heavy loads she could carry. She was such a tiny person. Myrtle was only four-foot-eleven and didn't weigh a hundred pounds soaking wet.

When everyone had been served and the empty tables had been cleaned, Myrtle began to wash the mountain of dishes she had stacked on the sideboard. One table of diners lingered, slowly sipping their coffee. She would clean up after them later. Hearing the front door open, she quickly dried her hands and began to roll down her sleeves. "Tell them there's only roast beef and potatoes left," Grace said as Myrtle re-entered the dining room.

A young man stood quietly beside one of the empty tables. He quickly removed his hat as Myrtle entered the room. He was tall and thin with unruly sandy brown hair that was badly in need of a cut. His clothes were shabby but clean.

"You can sit anywhere. All we have left is roast beef and potatoes."

"Don't have any money, but I can chop wood, scrub floors, or do whatever you might be needin' to be done in trade for a meal." There was a hint of desperation in the softest brown eyes Myrtle had ever seen.

Allison had entered the restaurant and overheard the young man asking for work. "Well, young man, if it's work you need, I have plenty you can do. Myrtle, bring us two plates of whatever you have. By the way, what's your name?"

"Claude Smith, Sir."

After the two men had eaten their fill, Myrtle began clearing their table. Allison leaned back in his chair and announced, "Claude's agreed to stay with us, Myrtle. We can fix up a place for him to sleep in the woodshed."

Myrtle was stunned. Her mind raced. Had he lost his mind? Her father had never taken in a stranger before. And she wasn't sure she wanted a stranger around the house. After all, they knew nothing about this man.

Her first impression and misgivings were soon forgotten by Claude's gentle manner. The two quickly became friends. He was as hard a worker as Myrtle. When he was through in the fields and had finished feeding the hogs, he would help Myrtle with her chores. Many times he scrubbed the floors in the small house while she was hanging out laundry. He would also carry Sara out on the porch when she wanted to sit in the sun. By now Sara was so thin and frail she seemed to have shrunk like a wool shirt washed in boiling water. Myrtle did not mind that Claude seemed to fill the void Allison and Sara felt from the loss of their beloved son George. She liked him as much as they did.

Fall had turned to winter and the February wind howled around the small frame house. As usual, Myrtle was up before daylight, stoking the fire in the cookstove as well as the stone fireplace in the tiny parlor. When she had both fires blazing she opened the door to her parent's room. As soon as the door creaked opened, Allison was awake.

After Claude and Allison had eaten and left for the fields, Myrtle prepared a plate of scrambled eggs for Sara and put it in the warming oven. She would let her mother sleep a while longer on this cold wintry morning. Busying herself with household tasks it was nearly time to go to Grace's when she looked in on Sara.

"Mama. Mama." Myrtle touched Sara's face to rouse her. Her skin was stone cold. "No...No. Don't leave me, Mama," she whispered. For the first time in her seventeen years she felt the cold, total emptiness of loss. Her mother was gone.

When Myrtle did not show up for work, Grace knew something was terribly wrong. Coming to investigate, she found Myrtle, her face ashen, her eyes dry, standing motionless at Sara's bedside.

The blowing sleet stung their faces the day they buried Sara in the small church cemetery in Gross. Allison had had a simple gravestone carved which read...

> Beloved wife and mother
> Sara Elizabeth Athen Murphy Little
> Born May 18, 1845
> Died February 18, 1902

After the brief ceremony, Allison stood staring down at the half frozen mound of earth that covered his beloved Sara. Myrtle stood stiff and dry-eyed beside her father.

Allison began to change after Sara's death. The best part of him seemed to have died with her. He no longer tried to control his quick temper. He became obsessed by work. Each morning he would leave the house long before Myrtle was up and did not return until well after dark. Claude could not keep up with the pace that Allison set.

"He's killing himself, Myrtle," Claude told her as he finished his breakfast one morning. "He can't keep going like this."

"That's what he wants. He feels he has no reason to live now that Mama is gone. If George were alive he would want to live. He would want to live for George, but not for me." Myrtle's chin quivered slightly as she spoke.

Reaching across the table, Claude gently took Myrtle's hand. Looking deep into her gray eyes he could see the grief she was burying deep inside herself. As she returned his gaze she felt something odd stir within her. At that moment the realization came to both of them that love was beginning to bloom. "I've tried to get him to slow down. But he won't listen to me." He spoke gently, slowly releasing her hand.

"I know." Myrtle rose from the table and quickly began clearing the breakfast dishes. "He's a very stubborn man, my father."

"I'd best be getting out there. He probably has another acre plowed by now."

Myrtle stared at the closed door for several minutes after Claude quietly closed it behind him.

In the days that followed, Allison was so consumed by his grief he did not notice how familiar Claude and Myrtle had become with each other. He did not see how thoroughly they enjoyed each others company. Nor did he notice how easily, and often, Myrtle laughed these days. There was a sparkle in her eye and a bloom to her cheeks. Claude had eased the ache and filled the emptiness left by her mother's death. Her girlish dreams of love and marriage were alive after all.

Rising as usual before daylight, Myrtle stoked the fires and put the coffee water on to boil. Claude liked it strong so she put in an extra handful of coffee in the heating water. After dumping broken eggshells into the coffee pot to keep it from boiling over, she lifted the large iron skillet out of the oven and set it on the stove. Soon aromatic bacon and eggs were sizzling in the skillet and the coffee was boiling.

Thinking that her father was out in the corn fields alone she was surprised to hear the voices and footsteps of two men coming up the back steps. Filling two plates, she had them on the table when the men came in the door. She was more than a little surprised to see a stranger come in with Claude.

"Myrtle, this is John Oesch. Kate's brother. He's offered to help get in that last five acres of corn." She knew Kate was Grace Brunner's sister-in-law. Myrtle had met her briefly at the restaurant. "John, this is Myrtle, Allison's daughter."

As she politely shook his outstretched hand, Myrtle had a strange feeling of foreboding.

Chapter Two

In the first week, as John worked alongside Claude and Allison, the three men became fast friends. Myrtle could see that her father was beginning to take an interest in life again. She was glad of that. But Claude was spending more time with Allison and John than with her these days and she resented it. She missed the special, quiet conversations with Claude in the evenings after Allison had gone to bed. Now she and Claude were never alone. Her father and John dominated his time. It wasn't that she didn't like John, she just felt that he was intruding.

One evening after supper as Myrtle was clearing the table John announced he had bought a river ferry at Fort Randal and would be leaving the next week to take over the business of ferrying passengers and goods across the Missouri River. "It's a sturdy one. Built by a Mr. Rust. Big enough to hold two wagons with teams of four."

"Ought to make a man a decent living then," Allison said.

"Yes," John continued, "the former owner made enough to raise a family and save enough to buy a farm down in Kansas."

"Sounds like you made a good deal, John. A man's got to be able to support his family, that's for sure," Allison mused.

Myrtle paused with a cup in her hand staring directly at Claude. Avoiding her eyes, Claude rose from the table saying, "Need to get that last acre planted before you leave, John. So I best get the plow fixed tonight." Myrtle was confused as to why Claude seemed to be avoiding her.

"Here, I'll give you a hand." John rose from the table. "Myrtle, that was a grand dinner. You'll make a fine wife one day."

"Thank you," she mumbled, color rising in her cheeks. John's remark caught her off guard. She wasn't sure how to take it.

Without a word Claude quickly turned and went out the door. But not before Myrtle saw the color rising in his face as well. He was jealous. She was sure of it. *Good,* she thought to herself. *Now maybe he will finally ask me to marry him.* She had given him every opportunity during many of their long evening conversations, but he had avoided the subject completely.

Early the next morning Myrtle quickly fed the chickens and gathered the eggs. As she passed the woodshed she called softly to Claude. "Claude, Claude. Breakfast will be ready in a few minutes. You'd best hurry."

Still a little groggy from sleep Claude entered the kitchen surprised to find Myrtle alone. There was no breakfast cooking on the stove. He knew it was earlier than he usually got up but thought when Myrtle woke him Allison must be anxious to get out in the fields.

"Has Allison left already?" he asked.

"No, he's still asleep. I wanted to talk to you alone, Claude. We never have a chance any more. I know you care about me, but I need you to tell me. I need to hear the words." The words poured out like water out of a bucket.

Taken by surprise, he was unable to speak for a moment. He spoke slowly, measuring each word. "Yes, I do care for you, Myrtle. I care very much. But I have nothing to offer you. I can't even support myself. You deserve much more than I can give." Claude knew John's remark about her making a good wife had brought this on and he wasn't sure what to do or say. All he knew for sure was that he loved her too much to bind her to a life of poverty.

"I don't care that you have nothing. Most people start with nothing," she pleaded, imploring him with her eyes.

"I care, Myrtle. I would never put any woman through what my father put my mother through because they had nothing." It was the first time he had ever made any reference to his family. "You deserve a better man," he said quietly.

"I suppose you think John is a better man," Myrtle snapped. He was rejecting her and she was hurt.

"John would be very good to you, Myrtle," he said softly. He slowly turned and quietly walked out the door. He couldn't tell her Allison already had made plans for her to marry John. Allison had even asked him what he thought of John as a suitable husband for Myrtle. Nor could he tell her how painful it was for him to listen as Allison and John made plans for her future.

It was then that Claude realized he could never let his true feelings be known. There was no future for them. He had nothing, he was nothing. He wasn't even a hired hand. He just worked for room and board. He could never ask her to marry him, but he would always love her.

Myrtle stood trembling as she stared at the closed door. Conflicting emotions she had never experienced before surged through her entire being. She wanted to go after him, but stubborn pride would not let her. She stood rooted to the spot. A single tear slid down her cheek.

That evening at supper Myrtle barely looked at or spoke to Claude. Her attention was now directed at John. This pleased her father and encouraged John. She was not aware that she was playing a dangerous game.

"Kate told me they were having a dance over at the Johnson barn this Saturday night. Would you like to go, Myrtle?" John spoke up as he knew she liked to dance. He had just been waiting for an opportunity to ask her.

"Yes, John, I would." Her lips were smiling but her gray eyes were not. Glancing across the table at Claude she added, "It's been a while since I've been to a dance." Claude did not look up from his plate.

Saturday night came too quickly for Myrtle. She was having second thoughts about leading John on the way she had but she was still angry with Claude. *If he really cared about me he would not allow me to be going out with another man*, she reasoned to herself as she slipped into her dress. Her mother would have admonished her for wearing the blue gingham this time of year. "Now Myrtle, that won't be warm enough. You'd best wear the brown wool." Myrtle could almost hear her mother's voice. She was still smiling at the thought when she entered the parlor with her shawl over her arm. Allison and John were seated beside the fire. Both men rose to their feet when she walked in. Her smile faded when she saw Claude was not there. Her efforts to look especially pretty were in vain.

"My, don't you look right pretty." She could not remember her father giving her such a complement before.

"You sure do." John took her shawl from her. "Here, let me help you with that." Her cheeks colored slightly when he lightly touched her shoulders as he draped the shawl around her. She had never had a man touch her person before. Not even Claude. It gave her an odd sensation.

"We might be late, Allison. So please don't wait up," John said as he and Myrtle started out the door.

"You two just have a good time." At this moment seeing his daughter in her gingham, Allison missed Sara terribly. They had never missed a barn dance. Entire families went. Everyone brought more food than could be eaten during the course of the night. When the hour grew late the children were bedded down in the corners and the dancing continued until dawn. Allison remembered coming home with Sara just as the sun was peeking over the horizon. He felt the familiar dull pain in his chest as he watched Myrtle and John drive away in the buggy. Tears filled his black eyes. He knew he would miss Sara terribly until the day he died. "Yes, John will make her a good husband." He threw another log on the fire and settled back into his rocker.

Chapter Three

"Myrtle. Myrtle." Her mother's voice grew sharper. "Myrtle! Come along now! It's time to go. Papa is already in the wagon." She reached out for her mother's hand but could not grasp it. The hand kept withdrawing just out of her reach. Myrtle clutched her love worn rag doll that her mother had made for her from an old wool sock. She didn't want to leave this place. She didn't want to go to that strange place. It was too scary. She could hear her mother's voice again calling her to hurry.

Myrtle woke with a start, her heart pounding. Grief washed over her as reality hit her. It was only a dream....the same dream she'd had ever since her mother had died. It had only been three months, but it seemed like an eternity. To Myrtle it was as though her own life had come to an end. And in a way it had; her life as she had always known it was over.

The rose scented breeze gently blew the white lace curtains out and away from the open window. The morning sun flooded the room with its warmth. Fear and dread shot through her as she realized that today was her wedding day. For the first time in her life she had slept late. She wanted to sleep forever. She didn't want to face this day. From her narrow iron bed Myrtle stared blankly at the billowing curtains. She felt her soul was dying. "I will never forgive Papa for this. My body may go on living, but my soul will not." Tears began to well up, threatening to choke her.

Slowly she rolled onto her back, dread and fear ripping through her body. Fighting the tears that stung her eyes, she clenched her fists and gritted her teeth. "No!" She quickly sat upright throwing off the quilt. "I will not cry. I will never cry again. Nothing or no one will ever make me cry again!"

Her heartache slowly turned to anger; a deep, seething, smoldering anger. "I will make them both pay for this...pay dearly...if it takes the rest of my life." Taking several deep breaths, she got out of bed with a deliberate determination. A plan began forming in her mind...a long term plan, but a plan nonetheless. Sitting at her small vanity table she picked up Sara's picture. After gazing at it for a moment she turned it to the wall. Her mother had also abandoned her when she needed her the most. Then her father and Claude had sold her to the highest bidder. Now she would have to survive alone. Well, she would show them. In spite of them both, she would survive.

Picking up her tortoise shell brush, Myrtle began vigorously brushing her long brown hair. Quickly twisting it into two braids, she pinned them in a flat crown on top of her head. There would be no ribbons today. Going to the washstand she poured cold water from the pitcher into the washbowl and carefully washed her tear-swollen eyes and face. She dressed slowly in a simple brown wool dress with no collar. It had long sleeves and the hemline barely brushed the floor. It was a plain dress, very plain. The last thing Myrtle intended to do today was to look pretty.

Entering the kitchen she saw the fire was already blazing in the cookstove and the coffee was boiling. As she tied on her apron, Claude came in the door with an armful of wood. Their eyes met and she saw, for an instant, a flicker of pain in Claude's soft brown eyes. Seeing his pain gave her heart a twist. He quickly looked away and dumped the wood in the wood box. Once more Myrtle steeled her heart. *No! No! No!* She screamed inside herself as she turned back to the stove. She would not give in to her feelings. She would learn not to have feelings of any kind for the rest of her life.

"Thank you for putting on the coffee," Myrtle said coolly. She took the large black skillet out of the oven and dropped it on the stove top with a bang, poured bacon drippings in it and thumped the grease can down on the sideboard. She and Claude had hardly spoken since Allison had announced Myrtle would soon marry John. Claude seemed to avoid her as much as possible now.

"Myrtle, I...," he faltered. How he desperately wished things could be different.

Cutting him off, she interrupted sharply, "Breakfast will be ready in ten minutes." Claude nodded his head, turned and slowly walked out the door. Myrtle dropped the eggs into the sizzling pan, breaking the yolks. At the same time she slammed the door to her heart.

"It wasn't supposed to come to this. It wasn't supposed to go so far," she muttered. All she had wanted to do was make Claude propose. When she had tried to extricate herself from this planned marriage her father would not allow it. In a moment of flirtation she had given her word. Allison would see to it she kept it.

John was a handsome man. His sky blue eyes set off a round ruddy face framed with auburn hair. His five foot ten inch stocky frame towered over Myrtle. "He's a nice person," Myrtle muttered, "But I don't really know him. And I certainly do not want to marry him!" She suspected her father had arranged this somehow and she had inadvertently fallen into his plan.

Speaking to the empty kitchen, Myrtle lamented, "If Claude had really cared about me he would have stood up like a man, courted me, and asked me to marry him a long time ago." Taking a deep breath she said with finality, "Well, it is too late now. It does not matter any more. I am not going to care anymore."

Myrtle turned back to the stove when she heard her father scraping the mud off his boots on the porch just outside the kitchen door. When he entered the room, she refused to turn and greet him as she normally did. He set the milk bucket on the dry sink and stood with his back to her. Tension was thick in the room.

"Myrtle, John is a good man and he will take care of you, so it will do you no good to take on like this. And I will no longer tolerate this attitude. I want to see a smile on that face when John gets here." Allison spoke with authority. When Allison Tenbrook Little had his mind set there was no changing it.

When she had tried to tell her father she did not want to get married, he would not even hear her out. It was partly her fault for accepting John's proposal so quickly. She only did so because she was mad at Claude and hoped to force him to commit to her. "What a mess. Now I'm trapped and there is no way out," she whispered under her breath. All her hopes and dreams would end today.

Myrtle did not acknowledge her father's presence in the room as she set a large platter of steaming ham and eggs on the table. The table was covered with a red- and white-checked oil cloth and set, as usual, with her mother's Blue Willow china. The dishes were hers now.

"Daughter. You *will* make John a good wife." It was an order, not a statement. "He's a good man." Allison let the door slam as he went out on the porch to wash up. Claude was standing at the weathered wash board table drying his face with a towel. Allison quickly splashed cold water on his face and ran the comb through his hair. When the two men entered the kitchen, Myrtle retreated to her room without a word. The two men ate breakfast in silence on this balmy spring morning.

Putting the last of her things in a small valise, Myrtle stood and looked around her tiny room. She wanted to remember it exactly as it was. The white narrow iron bed with the patchwork quilt she had made with Sara the day George drowned, and the small painted wash stand with the blue and white floral pitcher and bowl. Sara had brought these with her from Missouri.

The white-washed walls at the head of her bed displayed two small paintings of fields filled with wildflowers. There was the wooden dressing table skirted with calico her father had made for her when she was twelve. She remembered her mother insisting he make it, as "All young ladies need a dressing table," she had told him. A tortoise shell hairbrush, comb and hand mirror lay neatly beside a small wooden box. Claude had carved the box for her last birthday to hold her hair ribbons and pins. The sides were plain with a single rose intricately carved in the lid.

Myrtle's girlish dreams died a painful death as she glanced around the room at the memories and the hopes these things had held for her. She picked up only the tortoise shell set and placed it in the valise, leaving the little wooden box on the table. She straightened her spine, closed the valise with a snap and walked out the door.

The ride to Butte was long and dusty. Kate and Bill Brunner had insisted they drive the bride and groom in their new buggy with a matched team of Bays in the hitch. John sat on the front seat beside Bill. Myrtle was cordial but her tone remained cool as she sat beside Kate in the back. Allison rode his Dunn gelding close behind the buggy watching her every move, and Myrtle was sure he was listening to her every word.

The wedding ceremony was brief and simple. As the Minister spoke the words, other thoughts were racing through Myrtle's mind. She had never expected a large wedding but now she didn't want a wedding at all. Not this wedding. It was all she could do not to turn and run out the door. She knew John was a good and honorable man but she did not love him. She barely knew him. She felt betrayed by her father, by Claude, and even her mother for dying and leaving her alone. *This is so medieval,* she thought. *Somehow Papa arranged all this and like a fool I fell for it.* And yet, Myrtle knew deep in her heart it was her own pride and stubbornness that had trapped her.

During the entire ceremony Myrtle remained stiff and unemotional. Her gray eyes were as cold and dead as pewter. She barely heard what the minister was saying and never heard the words her father uttered when he gave her away.

"You may now kiss your bride," the minister was saying. Myrtle turned her face away slightly as John leaned down to kiss her. Pausing just for an instant, he kissed her on the cheek. During the round of congratulations by all, Myrtle's empty, lusterless eyes belied the thin smile she fought to maintain.

After the wedding picture was made with the date, May 28, 1902, stamped on the back, the small group headed back to Gross. Sitting stiffly beside her new husband, Myrtle barely heard the conversation, speaking only when spoken to. As the horses trotted steadily along John and Bill chatted animatedly about how the country was changing. "There are just too many people here now," Bill commented. John nodded in agreement.

"Over-population will ruin the country one day," Bill continued. "There are already five hundred or so people in Gross."

John's thoughts were focused more on Myrtle than the conversation with his brother-in-law. *I'm a lucky man,* He said to himself. *Myrtle is so tiny and pretty. She must be scared to death. I will have to be patient and gentle with her."*

During their short courtship he knew Myrtle enjoyed his company. They always had a good time at the dances, even when she hadn't danced many dances with him. However, her attitude toward him seemed to change soon after she accepted his proposal. He attributed this new attitude to the wedding jitters some brides seem to go through. He smiled slightly as he remembered how nervous his sister Kate had been just before she married Bill. But now there seemed to be a sharp edge to Myrtle's nature - a hard edge he had not seen before.

As they neared Gross, Myrtle's stomach began to knot up. To her dismay her father had insisted they spend the night with him and go on to Fort Randall the following morning. Myrtle was incensed but had not said a word. She would suppress all emotion but anger. There was no pain in anger.

Grace was standing on the front porch of her restaurant drying her hands on her apron when the wedding party arrived. Myrtle had to endure more congratulations as Grace quickly ushered then inside. All Myrtle wanted to do was go home to her old room and lock the door behind her. Grace had the table covered with Kate's prized Battenburg lace table cloth and set with her own fine china. A Bavarian lead crystal vase sat in the center of the table filled with fragrant wildflowers in hues of purple, lavender and gold.

While the wedding party was eating, they heard shouts coming from the street. "Fire! Fire!"

Grace jumped up and ran to the window. "Oh, dear Lord!" she exclaimed. "The hardware store is on fire!"

The three men jumped up and ran outside and joined the already forming bucket brigade. Men and women were working furiously dumping water on the blaze. But it was useless. The entire north side of the street was in flames and they could not stop it. Grace, Kate, and Myrtle stood helplessly, watching the buildings across the street collapse in the inferno. Retreating back into the restaurant the women slowly began to clear the remains of the wedding feast of pot roast from the table.

"Myrtle, you go on home. Kate and I can finish this," Grace told her. "I know you must be tired. It's been quite a day." Myrtle politely thanked them both and slipped out the back door. At least the men wouldn't be there yet and Myrtle needed time alone. She wanted a lot of time alone. She hoped Claude would not be there. It had been arranged between her father and John that the newlyweds would take her mother and father's room for the night. Her father would sleep in her bed. She wanted to sleep in her own bed alone. It seemed to Myrtle that suddenly her whole life had been arranged for her without her permission.

She had a general idea about the Wedding Night but she was not exactly sure of the details. Her mother had never gotten around to explaining anything to her. Whenever she would ask about the "birds and bees" all Sara would say was, "Later dear, when you are older." What Myrtle did know was that she could get with child after her marriage and that idea scared her to death. But she wasn't sure what caused this condition, and she was afraid to ask anyone. All she did know for certain was how you knew you were with child. Her mother had told her that much. Myrtle could hear her mother saying, "You will miss your monthly curse and you will be sick every morning, sometimes for months." She pondered this as she slowly undressed, donned a flannel night gown, and crawled into bed pulling the quilt tightly around her.

Much later when John entered the room, Myrtle pretended to be asleep. She scarcely breathed as she clung to her side of the bed. She wore her heaviest flannel night gown and had tried to tuck the quilt around and under her. John lit the lamp, keeping the wick turned low. Glancing at the tiny lump in the bed, he smiled and murmured to himself, "Poor little thing, she's terrified. Well, we have all the time in the world. And it has been a long day." Stripping to his long johns he slipped under the quilt. It barely reached across him and then he realized that Myrtle had two thirds of the coverlet tucked under her. Smiling to himself, he lay on his back uncovered, tucked his arms under his head and fell asleep beside his bride. Tomorrow they would be in their new home.

Chapter Four

Snow glistened on the roof of the tiny cabin nestled in a small grove of Aspen trees. Tendrils of smoke curled from a stone chimney into the clear, deep-blue winter air. A snowbird called for its mate in the silence. It had been six months since the newlyweds first arrived at the two room cabin on the Missouri not far from John's ferry.

The cabin was small but snug and clean. The furniture consisted of a small table with two chairs in the center of the room, and a small cast-iron cookstove by a tiny window. A sideboard was against one wall with shelves beside it that held Myrtle's Blue Willow dishes. There was a window beside the front door and a second window in the bedroom above the bed. The bedroom was dominated by a double iron bed with one small table beside it that held a cobalt blue coal-oil lamp. A tall narrow chest of drawers stood against the wall at the foot of the bed. There were hooks on the wall to hang their clothes.

Myrtle had made plain muslin curtains for the windows and a new dark blue wool quilt for the bed. She planted a large vegetable garden and fragrant colorful flowers beside the cabin door. She was a good wife to John; good in every way except one. The marriage had yet to be consummated.

As the weeks passed into months it became increasingly difficult for John to continue to be patient with her. He began to worry if she would ever really try to be a wife to him - a wife in every sense of the word. They both worked hard. He spent long hours on the ferry. However, it seemed to John that Myrtle was obsessed with work. Their conversations were polite as they ate together. But Myrtle never went to bed when John did. She always made some excuse of some chore or mending to do and stayed up long after he retired for the night. She would wait until she could hear him snoring softly before she quietly climbed into bed herself.

There had been no confidante Myrtle could talk to before she married. She had needed a woman she could talk to. But the only women she knew were Grace and Kate and she was too embarrassed to mention such a personal subject. Myrtle was terrified of becoming pregnant. All her mother had told her was that intimacy between a man and wife brought about the children and childbirth was both the worst time and the best time in a woman's entire life. She did not understand what her mother meant and had been afraid to ask Sara to explain it. She had looked up the word 'intimate' in the dictionary so she knew it meant 'to be on familiar, affectionate, or personal terms'. What Myrtle did know was the fact that sometimes women died in childbirth, so she wasn't taking any chances herself.

Disaster struck the night John and Myrtle attended the annual dance at the local school house. John had talked long and hard to convince Myrtle to go. He knew she liked to dance and he knew it would do them both good to have some fun for a change. Everyone came from miles around and keeping with tradition, entire families attended this affair. When the hour grew late the children were bedded down and the adults danced until the sun came up.

John asked a friend to tend the ferry for him as it would run later than usual bringing families from across the river to the dance. It was early March and the Missouri river was swollen with the latest downpour. A large tree, uprooted by the rising water, was carried by the swift current and slammed into John's ferry. The passengers aboard managed to reach safety just before the ferry sank to the bottom of the river.

Several days had passed after the disaster, and with each passing day John was getting more and more anxious about what he would do to support the two of them. If he were alone, he could pick up and move on. But now he had a wife. For the first time in their married life, Myrtle felt a degree of compassion for him. And for the first time after supper they went to bed together. They talked in the dim lamplight, but Myrtle kept to her side of the bed.

"We have a little money left, maybe we could buy a farm somewhere or try homesteading," John suggested.

"Yes, homesteading would not take much money and the land would be ours," Myrtle agreed.

John was pleasantly surprised that the idea appealed to her. They had never been this companionable and comfortable with each other. "I need you, Myrtle," John murmured as he wrapped his arms around her. And before Myrtle realized what was happening, her marriage was finally consummated. Myrtle lay awake long after John had drifted off into a peaceful contented sleep. She felt defiled and betrayed.

As the morning sun filled the cabin, John woke to the smell of ham frying and coffee boiling. He hadn't slept so well in a long time. The ferry was destroyed but he knew together, he and Myrtle would make out somehow. When he came out of the bedroom, Myrtle was putting breakfast on the table. "Good morning," he said cheerfully kissing her on the cheek. He felt so good this morning he didn't notice her stiffen as he kissed her. He sat at the table and hungrily began to eat. "The rent's due in a few days. I think the best thing for now is go back to your father's place until we can decide what we are going to do."

"I could go back to work for Grace so we could rent a place." The last thing Myrtle wanted to do was to move back in with her father and Claude. They had visited there often and that had been awkward enough.

"No, there's no need for you to do that. You know Allison will put us up for awhile." John did not want his wife working to support him. He would make their living. "We will load the wagon today and leave first thing in the morning." Myrtle knew she had no choice but to go along with his plan.

During the entire trip back to Gross, John did not notice that Myrtle hardly said a word as he talked animatedly about their future. When John pulled his team to a stop beside Allison's small house, Kate came rushing out of Grace's restaurant drying her hands on her apron. "John! Myrtle! Grace told me she saw you pull up. What on earth happened?"

Without a word to either of the women, Myrtle climbed down and began to take small items off the wagon into the house. She was grateful that Claude and her father were still out in the fields far from the house.

"My ferry sunk. I'm out of business," John said dejectedly as he climbed down and began to help Myrtle unload.

"Oh, John. I'm so sorry." Turning to Myrtle she said, "Here let me help you." Kate took a bundle of quilts off the wagon and followed Myrtle into the house.

John had finished unloading the remainder of their meager belongings and was stacking them in the barn when Allison and Claude returned. Claude jumped down from the wagon as Allison pulled the team to a halt. "John, what happened?" Claude asked anxiously. As the men tended to the horses, John told them about the accident.

While Myrtle was cleaning up after supper, Claude quietly removed his things to the woodshed and Allison moved into Myrtle's old room.

As they lingered around the table that evening, Myrtle busied herself with some mending while the men smoked their pipes. John casually suggested the possibility of homesteading in Canada.

"My family emigrated from Switzerland to Huron County, Ontario. I was born there, but I don't know much about Canada. They moved to Milford, Nebraska, when I was about six weeks old." He puffed on his pipe. "I remember my mother telling me how difficult it was traveling in the wagon such a distance with a baby. Of course she only spoke German... never learned English. I didn't learn to speak English myself until I was nine years old." John smiled as he remembered his mother and her 'old country' ways.

"Are your folks still in Milford, John?" Allison asked.

"No, they're both gone now. But I remember the stories they would tell about Canada. A wild, hard country to live in. It was too uncivilized for my mother. But my father loved it. He said it was the most beautiful country he had ever seen. I think he missed Canada until the day he died," John mused tapping the ashes out of his pipe into the hearth.

"I hear they have land up there just for the taking. You can homestead six hundred and forty acres," Allison said. "A man needs his own land to work." The men nodded in agreement.

"I would like having my own land." Claude spoke softly, almost to himself.

"By Jove, then we need to find out how to get some land up there. What do you think, John?" The adventurous side of Allison was coming out and he was getting excited.

"It would be good to own our own land. What do you think, Myrtle?" John asked. She had been listening intently to the conversation and was feeling a little adventuresome herself. Not looking up from her sewing, she answered, "A woman needs her own land too." She would endure what she had to in order to have land of her own, even Claude's presence on the long journey.

When the evening ended the decision had been made. They would all go to Canada where they could homestead more land than in the States. John would ask Bill and Kate to go with them. He and Kate had always been close and he hoped she would agree to go. He knew Bill would be eager to go, but Kate had a baby now. Ruby was not quite three months old. He was not sure his sister would agree to such a difficult move.

The next few weeks were spent in preparation for the long journey. Once the decision had been made it hadn't taken John long to find out all they needed to know about homesteading in Canada. "We can get a whole section of land by just paying $10.00 and prove up on it. That means we have to live on the land at least six months out of each year and make improvements on it," John informed them.

As soon as John had mentioned migrating to Canada to homestead, Bill and Kate readily agreed to go with them. While the men prepared the wagons and their teams of horses,

Kate and Myrtle readied more quilts with thick wool batting, heavy wool coats, and warm clothes for baby Ruby. John had been told the winters were bitter cold in the Northwest Territories. He was also told that the mosquitoes were so big they ate the oxen and used their horns for tooth picks. They all laughed at this wild tale. John felt they were doing the right thing by going to Canada. It was open territory where a man could stretch out...where a man could breathe...where a man could raise a family.

When the wagons were ready Myrtle had everything packed to load. She felt a tug at her heart as she looked at the four small crates stacked beside the door. It was all she could take with her. The furniture, except for her iron bed, would have to be left behind. Quickly extinguishing an emotion of loss that began to well up inside her, she picked up her valise, sat it on the table, and began to fill it with a change of clothes for herself and one for John.

Picking up the family Bible, she started to tuck it in with the clothing but paused, looking at it thoughtfully. Slowly she began to leaf through the beginning pages. At the top of the first page elaborate Old English lettering spelled out 'Marriages, Births and Deaths'. Quietly and unemotionally Myrtle read down the page, "Allison Tenbrook Little and Sara Athen Murphy, married May 12, 1882, Tarkio, Missouri, Children Born: Myrtle Grace Little, December 1, 1884, George Allison Little, March 20, 1887. Deaths: George Allison Little, August 12, 1899. Sara Athen Murphy Little, February 1, 1902." Turning the page her own marriage was recorded in her father's hand, "John Oesch and Myrtle Grace Little, married May 28, 1902, Butte, Nebraska." When she came to the line, 'Children Born', she quickly shut the book and stuffed it in the valise. Picking up her shawl and the valise she did not look back as she walked out of the small house for the last time.

Dew glistened on the grass with the first rays of the rising sun as the two heavily burdened covered wagons pulled away from Gross forever. Steam shot from the horses nostrils as they leaned into their collars. The wagons creaked and groaned in protest under their heavy loads. Pulling her shawl tightly around her, Myrtle sat stiffly beside John on the hard wagon seat. Allison and Claude rode on horseback alongside the Brunner wagon. Myrtle barely spoke to her father these days and she and Claude had become polite strangers.

In her own wagon, Kate sat beside Bill smiling radiantly at him. She believed they were doing the right thing. Ruby, wrapped tightly in a bright multicolored quilt, slept soundly in her mother's arms. Kate knew she would be looking at the back of John and Myrtle's wagon for several weeks and to her it was a pleasant and hopeful thought. Taking a deep breath of cool, damp air, she made a mental note of the date, July 8, 1903.

By the time they reached Fort Randall, the sun was hot and directly overhead. It took most of the remainder of the day to cross the Missouri River. There was only one small ferry running now that John's large ferry was gone. It was barely big enough to hold one wagon with the team unhitched. After reaching the South Dakota side of the Missouri they traveled until the sun touched the horizon. It had been a long day. Myrtle's back ached and her bottom felt bruised from sitting so long on the hard wagon seat.

While the men unhitched the teams, Kate and Myrtle started preparing supper. Holding the fussing baby on one hip, Kate helped Myrtle open the tail gate of the wagon behind which John had built shallow shelves for storing food and cooking utensils.

"You go ahead and feed Ruby. I'll get the fire going," Myrtle told Kate.

"I won't be long. I'll make the biscuits as soon as she's through eating." Climbing into the wagon, Kate settled herself on a box near the back and began to nurse the baby.

Gathering wood for the fire, Myrtle tried not to think of her own condition. But she couldn't shake the icy dread she felt in her soul. She had been sick every morning for the last two weeks. She was still furious with John for what she called, "taking advantage of her".

"If I had known that was part of marriage I would have never, ever married anyone. Even if Papa had beat me senseless." She muttered, angrily throwing sticks on the fire. Her anger was also directed at her mother for not answering her questions.

Lifting down the heavy cast-iron pot of beans she had hung on the side of the wagon that morning to soak, Myrtle carried it to the fire setting it over the flames on two large stones she had placed in the center. With Ruby now fed and sleeping soundly, Kate joined Myrtle in preparing supper. In no time the coffee was boiling and the biscuits were baking in the Dutch oven. The beans with chunks of bacon were simmering in the pot.

After their meager meal, Allison and Claude spread their bedrolls next to the fire. Myrtle and Kate had spread tarpaulins on the ground under their respective wagons to keep the dampness from seeping into the wool quilts they placed on top. It had been a long grueling day and Myrtle was exhausted. She didn't know how she could be so tired from just sitting. *Tomorrow*, she thought to herself, *I'll walk*. At dusk the weary travelers crawled into their respective bedrolls still fully dressed. Myrtle finally dozed off long after John started snoring softly beside her.

36

Chapter Five

It took four long, hot days to reach Platte, South Dakota. Camping a few miles out of town beside a small river, Claude caught trout for supper while the other men tended to the horses and the women built a cook fire. He cleaned the fish at the river before taking them to Myrtle to fry. Muttering a quick "thank you" as Claude handed her the trout, Myrtle quickly began placing the fish in the bacon fat already sizzling in the large Dutch oven that hung over the fire.

From the back of her wagon Kate watched Claude look sadly at Myrtle as she bent over the fire then slowly walk away. Myrtle was always so aloof with him. Kate felt there was something between them but couldn't quite put her finger on it. Myrtle was so straight laced, and Claude was such a nice young man, Kate knew it was nothing improper. Dismissing her musings she turned her attention back to Ruby who was making soft suckling noises as she nursed.

The next morning the first gray streaks of dawn barely lit the Eastern sky when waves of nausea hit Myrtle, jolting her fully awake. Scrambling out from under the wagon, quickly grabbing her apron, she ran into the trees. She barely made it out of sight of the camp before she became violently ill. She was thankful that the only things she removed to sleep at night were her high top shoes. Taking deep breaths, she pressed her forehead against her forearm as she leaned against a tree. The faint rose glow of dawn began to creep over the horizon.

Myrtle breathed deeply of the cool damp air. She began to feel a little better and did not hear Kate come up behind her.

"Myrtle, are you all right?"

Nearly jumping out of her skin, Myrtle quickly wiped her face with her apron. "The fish must not have agreed with me last night."

"It isn't the fish, is it?" Kate suggested softly. Myrtle sadly shook her head.

"Oh, Myrtle. I think this is wonderful. John must be so pleased. And he never even let on," Kate beamed.

"John doesn't know," Myrtle said in barely a whisper.

"What?"

"He doesn't know!" Myrtle hissed sitting down on a log.

"Then you must tell him right away. He'll be so happy!"

Kate's excitement rankled Myrtle. "No!" Myrtle snapped.

"For heaven sakes, why not?" Kate was stunned.

"I don't want anyone to know." Kate had never seen Myrtle in such a state. She had always been so distant and indifferent. Now she seemed frightened, frail and vulnerable. Kate's heart went out to her.

"Oh, my dear Myrtle." Kate took Myrtle's hand as a mother would her child's. "This is a wonderful time in a woman's life. To be giving life."

"I don't think it's so wonderful." Her voice quivered but there was not a sign of a tear.

"Oh, but it is. You'll see." Kate rose pulling Myrtle up off the log. Placing her arm around Myrtle's waist she guided her back toward the camp. "Now, John needs to know that he has a child on the way," Kate said gently.

"Good morning, Claude. Would you mind getting us some fresh water?" Kate poured the water out of the bucket and handed it to him.

"Ah, well, sure." He had just filled it, but if she wanted fresher water, he'd get it. He liked Kate. She was always smiling and had such a cheerful, positive attitude about everything.

"Oh, and Claude, would you tell John that Myrtle wants to see him?" Kate instructed as he walked away. Myrtle shot her a hard, cold look. Kate smiled and ignored her as she began preparing breakfast.

Leaving Allison and Claude to finish watering the horses, John hurried back to the wagons with a feeling of dread creeping over him. His brow was furrowed with worry lines. His mind was racing. Maybe Myrtle had changed her mind about Canada and wanted to go back. How would he convince her they must go on. There was no turning back now. Not wanting to stir her quick temper he approached her guardedly.

"Something wrong, Myrtle?" His heart was thumping against his ribs, afraid of her answer. Focusing on the ground, Myrtle quickly tied on her apron. She could feel the heat as her face began to redden. She opened her mouth to speak but no sound came out. John had never seen her so unstrung. She was always so controlled and unemotional. He was now sure something was terribly wrong.

Stepping in front of her, he gripped her by the upper arms trying to control his fear. "What is it?"

"I'm in the family way!" She spat out the words. He was so unprepared for her answer he wasn't sure he heard her correctly.

"What...what did you say?"

"I'm in the family way." Her voice grew hard and cutting as she tried to pull from his tight grasp.

Relief and joy washed over John as the meaning of her words hit him. He stepped back holding her at arm's length. "Myrtle, that's wonderful! A baby...a baby!" Grabbing her to him he hugged her hard, smiling from ear to ear. A child! He was going to be a father!

She stiffened. "Let me go. I have to help Kate." Her tone was as cold as her pewter eyes as she twisted from his embrace.

Puzzled by her strange reaction, John watched as Myrtle stomped angrily to the wagon where Kate was rolling out biscuit dough on the tailgate. Kate looked at her brother, smiled, and nodded her head slightly. *Everything will be all right. Kate will take care of everything. Must be one of those woman things*, he thought to himself. Smiling and humming as he returned to the river, John could hardly wait to share the wonderful news with the others.

The rest of the morning was a nightmare for Myrtle. She wanted to scream as Kate and John went on and on about her condition. She didn't even want to think about it. Allison had told her at breakfast how pleased he was that she was giving him a grandchild. He told her the same thing Kate had, "Once the sickness is over you will feel much better". Well, Myrtle knew she would not. She knew the worst was yet to come.

While the men hitched the horses to the wagons, Myrtle was silent. She helped Kate scour the pans and tin plates with sand, rinsed and dried them before repacking them in the wagon. Before the sun had risen too high in the clear azure sky, the small pioneer party continued their slow migration northward.

Days and miles passed slowly. South Dakota seemed to be an endless rolling prairie. The hot dry wind in the tall grass made it appear to be moving in gentle rolling waves. The relentless sun beat down from a cloudless sky. Myrtle's long dark skirt and muslin blouse were covered with a fine coating of dust. Dark wet stains showed under her arms and fine beads of perspiration glistened on her upper lip. She envied John his wide brimmed hat. Her bonnet seemed to do little to keep the sun from baking her head.

Myrtle was mesmerized as she watched the bending grass interlaced here and there with wildflowers. Her mind wandered back through the country they had passed through seeing it all again in her mind's eye. They had camped by Red Lake, passed by Chamberlin and on to Gannvalley. Not wanting to trespass the men agreed it would be best to go around the Cow Creek Indian Reservation. "It will take less time to go around than to get permission to cross," John had told them as he consulted his map.

Moving onward toward the direction of Peno, the tiny wagon train forded a small river and pushed on to Highmore. They had been on the trail 19 days. They needed to replenish some of their supplies and make some repairs. John had been told Highmore was a clean little town with a good livery stable and blacksmith. The men decided it would be a good place to spend a couple of days to make the necessary repairs on the wagons and mend the harnesses. They had little money between them, but John and Bill agreed to rent a room for Myrtle, Kate and the baby. The men could sleep in the livery stable with the horses, without extra cost.

Stopping the wagons in front of the livery stable, John asked Allison, "Will you and Claude tend to the teams while Bill and I get the women folk settled at the hotel?"

"You and Bill go on and get the women folk settled. It's been a long day. Claude and I can take care of things here."

"Is there a hotel in town?" John asked the blacksmith.

"There's only Mrs. Schmidt's boarding house down the street," the big man told him.

John and Bill helped their wives get what they needed from the wagons and the four of them started off down the dusty street with Ruby nestled in the crook of her father's arm.

"There it is," Kate pointed, spotting the black and white sign that read, 'Boarding House'. It was a small white washed two-story frame house with flowers lining the stone walkway to the narrow porch. Mrs. Schmidt stood at the front door to greet them. She was short and rather plump with gray hair twisted into a knot on the top of her head. She had sky-blue eyes that sparkled, a wide smile and a stream of constant chatter.

"Saw you coming down the street. Don't get too many strangers here anymore. Come on in. Come on in." Holding the screen door open wide for them she rattled on, "That's what I would like to see more often, a man carrying his own baby." She patted Bill approvingly on the arm as he entered the house. He was a big man and Ruby looked tiny in the crook of his arm. Bill turned a little pink as he smiled down at the woman. Not stopping to take a breath Mrs. Schmidt continued, "So, you'll be needin' two rooms then."

"No. Just one for the women folk." John told her. "We'll be staying down at the livery stable with our stock."

After showing them the room at the top of the narrow stairs, she told Kate and Myrtle their men would be welcome to take supper at her table for a little extra cost. When they told her there were two other men she said non-pulsed with barely a pause. "Bring them on over. There's always plenty. Now I'll leave you to get settled in. Have a cake in the oven," she said, scurrying down the stairs.

John set down Myrtle's valise and turned toward the door to leave. The baby started to fuss. As Kate took her from Bill he kissed his wife on the cheek and followed John down the stairs. Myrtle opened the window and started unpacking. Kate settled into a rocking chair in the corner of the room by the window. It was hot and the room smelled musty. The cool breeze coming in the window smelled of roses.

"How I miss my own rocking chair," Kate sighed, leaning her head against the back as the baby began to nurse. "I'll be glad when we're settled and Bill can make me another one." Rocking gently with eyes closed she wished that John and Myrtle could be as happy as she and Bill were. She hoped the baby would change things.

John and his brother-in-law walked back to the livery stable in companionable silence, each man lost in his own thoughts. Claude and Allison had the wagons pulled in back of the building; the horses were unhitched and munching hay in the corral. Claude was sitting on a sawhorse just inside the stable mending a harness. Allison had talked the blacksmith into letting the men work off the board for the teams as well as themselves. They agreed to pay for any repairs to the wagons. Both John and Bill agreed that it was a good arrangement as they picked up a pitchfork and began to clean out the stalls.

The two days in Highmore passed quickly. Supplies were purchased, harness mended, minor repairs to the wagons completed, and one of the horses shod. They all enjoyed Mrs. Schmidt's copious dinners. She had not exaggerated when she had said there was plenty of food for everyone. The woman loved to cook and loved seeing people eat even more. Enjoying their company, she was sorry to see them go but wished them a safe journey when they departed.

It was three long hot dusty days when they passed by Roy and another three days to Gettysberg. In the five days from Gettysberg to Mobridge they crossed two rivers, one creek, and three sets of train tracks. Allison had made several comments about civilization choking the country. He really hated what progress was doing to the country.

It was nearly dark by the time they stopped for the night just outside Mobridge and were up on their way before sunrise the next morning. Kate loved the intense colors of the sunrise. To her it was the best part of the day, the air still fresh, damp and fragrant. Everything was renewed. It was a promise of good things to come. Myrtle was often annoyed by Kate's enthusiasm over such things. Sunrise to Myrtle meant you should be up and get your work started for the day. Kate thought it was sad that Myrtle missed so much and seemed to have no joy for living.

When the wagon seat became too hard to sit any longer, Kate would climb off and walk, leaving Ruby in her little box behind her father. Kate smiled to herself as she listened to the one-sided conversation Bill carried on with his tiny daughter. Ruby would wave her fists and kick her feet and make funny little sounds which convinced her father that she knew exactly what he was saying. Myrtle walked with Kate when she wasn't driving her own wagon. She wanted to learn how to do everything for herself. It pleased John to teach her, but he did not understand why she pursued everything with such a vengeance. She had a determination about her that was almost obsessive. To him she seemed more like a competitive male comrade than his wife.

The horses plodded on, mile after dusty mile. The wheels were squeaking with every turn, dust billowing beneath them. Dust was everywhere, on everything, in everything, in their clothes and hair, even in their teeth. Both women agreed that walking felt better than riding in the wagon. Their backs were stiff and their backsides bruised. Myrtle had asked to ride one of the horses but John absolutely forbade it. "Not in your condition," he told her firmly. She did not say a word when everyone agreed with him, but she was furious. Having seen her quick temper many times they all steered clear of her for a while.

When they passed Pollock, they knew they were finally in North Dakota. Wanting to cover as many miles as possible before dark they pushed on past Campbell and Gale. The stars were blinking in a black velvet sky when they finally stopped to set up camp. Too tired to make a fire the women put out the beans that were left over from the noon meal while the men tended to the horses. Myrtle had hung the bean pot on the side of the wagon so the beans were still warm from the hot sun. With a sliver of a moon giving a faint light to eat by, they all sat together between the two wagons eating a quick supper.

"What did you do to these beans, Myrtle?" Allison asked as he chewed a mouthful. "They taste even better now than they did at mid-day. Did you put peppercorns in them?"

45

"They are good, but I had better not eat any more. They may not agree with the baby," Kate said laying her plate aside.

"I didn't do anything to them," Myrtle protested.

"Maybe they just seasoned themselves hanging on the wagon," John teased her gently.

Claude laughed, "Well, I like my beans a little spicy."

They were all tired but in good spirits as they finished their meal in the dim moonlight. While the men checked on the horses, Kate and Myrtle prepared for bed.

Dawn seemed to come just as they closed their eyes and it was time to be up and on their way again. The horses stood in their traces switching flies with their tails while the last of breakfast was cleaned up. Myrtle hung the bean pot back on the wagon so they could finish them their next meal.

It was late afternoon when they stopped beside a small stream for the day. Myrtle put the beans on the fire to heat, and Kate made biscuits. When supper was cooking the women gathered up dust encrusted clothes to wash in the stream. Myrtle was scrubbing a pair of John's trousers with a large bar of lye soap. Kate knelt beside her and began washing the baby's things. "I swear I'll never get these clean again," Kate commented as she dunked a small white dress in the cold water.

With their spare clothes washed and hanging on bushes to dry, Myrtle called the men to eat. Allison was the first to bring his plate to the fire for Myrtle to fill. When she plopped a large spoonful of beans on his plate, she saw them. Ants. Big red ants. Their cooked bodies were commingled with the beans.

"Oh, no!" she exclaimed, dropping the spoon back into the pot. Allison had a look of such incredible disbelief on his face that Myrtle began to laugh. Then her father started laughing with her. Dropping the pot in the dust, she laughed so hard the tears ran down her cheeks. Holding her sides she sank to the ground beside the bean pot. Soon everyone joined in; laughing at the realization that they had all eaten red ants along with the beans thinking the spicy, crunchy taste was peppercorns.

The next day, much to John's disappointment, Myrtle had returned to her somber, serious self.

The August sun was intense and they were grateful for the cool nights. The prairie was level now and the wind blew constantly. They were drenched twice by thunderstorms. As she gazed out over the gentle rolling prairie of North Dakota, Myrtle remembered her father telling her about the miles and miles of buffalo he saw during his drover days. But all the buffalo were gone now.

"Herds were so large," he had told her, "they reached from where a man stood clear to the horizon." Along with the disappearing buffalo, most of the deer, elk, and antelope had vanished as well as their predators the bear and wolf. "It doesn't take man long to annihilate whatever his greed dictates," Allison had said.

It was another six long, hard, hot days to Naughton. Continuing to skirt most of the towns like Hampton and Glencoe, they gave Bismark a wide berth as they didn't want to get too close to any large cities. They spent four days in Naughton but this time they stayed just outside of town with the wagons. This was their way of life now; heat, wind, cold, dirt, and living in the open. Myrtle didn't even miss her iron bed anymore and Kate was doing well without her rocking chair. Ruby was thriving and Myrtle was beginning to grow a

47

little round with her unborn. Both were strong women, each in their own way.

Moving steadily north, John marked Wilton and Darling off his map. By now they had crossed six small rivers with thick timber growing along them. Most of the time, they camped in these wooded areas, fishing or killing small game for supper, washing clothes, and bathing in the cold rivers. Skirting Minot, the trail weary party plodded steadily on to Portal.

After nearly two months of hard travel, they crossed the border into North Portal, Canada. Canada encouraged immigration so the little party of Nebraskans had no trouble crossing the border. "Well, we're half way home. We can camp by that stream over there," John said as he urged the team forward with the second wagon following his lead. He did not expect a reply from Myrtle as he was accustomed to her silence whenever they shared the wagon seat. During much of the trip whenever John drove the wagon, Myrtle would walk. Sometimes she walked with Kate and sometimes alone. When she drove the wagon, John rode with Allison and Claude.

Home. The word sounded almost foreign to Myrtle. Since her mother had died she felt she had no home. It was a stranger's house she had moved into. A stranger whose child she was now carrying. But soon she would have a home of her own. A real home. "Whoa," John said, pulling the horses to a stop under a large poplar tree. The sound of his voice brought Myrtle out of her deep thoughts. "The Mountie at the border told me we should be able to book passage on the train for the rest of the trip. I'm afraid the wagons and the horses will not make it the rest of the way."

"The money is nearly gone so you best find out what the fare is first," Myrtle chided him.

As soon as camp was set up, the four men went into North Portal to see about their passage to Prince Albert, Saskatchewan. It was a long rugged trip and the men agreed that neither the wagons nor the horses would make it that far. And winter had already begun. After the men left, Kate and Myrtle set about preparing their meager meal for the day.

The sun was setting as the men rode excitedly back into camp. "Must be good news," Kate said to Bill as he stepped down from his horse.

"It is. The Canadian government has granted special rates on the railroad for immigrants. We can go all the way for one cent a mile including all the livestock and the wagons we can get in one box car as well as one of us to look after the stock," Bill told her excitedly.

"Yes, and we have jobs to pay for our passage," John added. "Seems that the railroad needs men with horses to grade the road beds. The foreman suggested you and Myrtle could do laundry and mending for the crew."

"We will be loading the wagons and stock tomorrow," Allison said.

Encouraged by the good news, conversation was lively around the campfire that night with everyone making plans for the homesteads that would soon be theirs. Too excited to sleep, they stayed up much later than usual. But as the sun broke over the horizon the next morning the travel worn settlers were busy loading their wagons and horses onto the boxcar assigned to them.

Progress was much slower on the train. Myrtle's tiny body was swollen with child and she was grateful for a soft seat to sit on. She was also glad to be away from the constant billowing, blowing dust and the unmerciful heat of the sun and the cold damp nights. During the days the two women sat in their train car on a siding waiting as men built the next section of track. They washed stacks of laundry and did piles of mending that the crew brought to them. Neither one of the women minded the work. It helped pass the time and each made a few extra dollars they needed for baby clothes.

Chapter Six

As they washed, mended and waited in the passenger car on the narrow siding, Kate and Myrtle were fascinated by the stories told to them by men who had been part of the crew that had built the Canadian Pacific Railroad. The men told how William Cornelius Van Horn had completed the last five hundred miles of track in four years. The crewmen recalled how men called 'navies' worked in temperatures ranging from 100 degrees Fahrenheit to forty degrees below zero, seven days a week, ten to fourteen hours a day. The laboring men were also tormented by black flies in summer and arctic cold in winter. Those who had the misfortune of becoming sick or getting themselves injured were fired. They claimed they were fed food not fit for swine.

"Working on this rail is as easy as pie. Laying track is a lot faster here. In some places on the Canadian Pacific we could only lay down six feet a day. That is if nothing went wrong. But I'm here to tell you, Missus, it was a proud day when we drove the last spike at Craigellachie, British Columbia," One man told them.

As they slowly progressed northward, Kate and Myrtle enjoyed listening to the different parts of the same story as told by each of the men bringing mending and laundry for the women to do. Many long days were spent on the siding waiting for the next section of track to be completed. Kate and Myrtle shared a passenger car with three other women whose men were also part of the work crew. At night they folded the narrow double seats down to sleep. It was early September and the nights were cold so a fire was kept burning in the small stove at one end of the car. The women also cooked their meals on this stove.

The dining car was not a place designed for ladies. It had two long wide planks along both sides that served as tables. The men would crowd in, wolf down their food with loud coarse conversation, then go directly to the bunk car to smoke before turning in for the night. The four Nebraska men slept in the box car with their own wagons and stock.

When they reached Saskatoon, Myrtle knew they were finally in the Province called Saskatchewan. From here the train would continue on to Prince Albert without the long delays. It was early October, the sun had lost its warmth and the nights chilled one to the bone. Even though they kept a fire burning in the stove it was impossible to keep the drafty car warm.

Kate and Myrtle were packed and ready to step off the train as soon as it stopped at Prince Albert. It was late afternoon and already starting to get dark. They were so far north Myrtle noted how short the daylight hours had become. As she and Kate, with Ruby in tow, made their way into the train station the first thing that caught Myrtle's eye was a large calendar that read, October 8, 1903. *If I had a watch,* she thought to herself, *I'd mark the exact time.*

It seemed like no time at all before the wagons had been unloaded from the boxcar, the horses were hitched and Myrtle was sitting beside John on the wagon seat. She had not looked forward to such intimacy with him again. She had enjoyed the time in the train car away from him as well as her father and Claude. In fact she had enjoyed the entire journey, but now that it was coming to an end she was beginning to feel a little afraid as the reality of it all washed over her.

Quickly dismissing her fear, she focused on the passing scenery. Prince Albert was a bustling little prairie city. Kate had told her nearly three thousand people lived in Prince Albert as it was a center for farmers, traders, and travelers in Saskatchewan. Seeing several groups of dark skinned people she commented to John, "I didn't know there were so many Negroes here."

"They aren't Negroes, Myrtle, they are Cree Indians," John informed her.

"Well, they look like Negroes to me," she said curtly. Then quickly changing the subject, "I hope we can find a place to stay before it gets much darker."

"The crew foreman told us there was a rooming house at the edge of town with a large barn for the wagons and horses. He said it looked like it could snow tonight so we had better stay here for a couple of days before going on to Shellbrook."

Myrtle hoped that there would be a nice cozy house they could rent when they got to Shellbrook. Perched on the hard wagon seat she could feel the bitter cold begin to seep through her thick wool coat. The skin on her face was stiff with cold.

The rooming house they located was small and had only two rooms left to rent. It was cheaper than the Prince Albert Hotel so the men agreed to share one room and let the women have the other. For the next three days the men made all the necessary repairs to the wagons, had the horses shod, bought supplies and mended harness. Kate and Myrtle bought a few necessities including some flannel to make gowns and diapers for the new baby. Myrtle had grown quite round by now and needed to let out both of her skirts a little more. Soon she would have to put gussets in them. There was no heat in their rooms so Myrtle and Kate passed the time sitting by the fire in the parlor of the small rooming house sewing tiny gowns and a baby quilt of wool scraps Kate had dug out of her trunk.

On the third day the weary travelers headed northwest out of Prince Albert. A light snow was falling adding to the three inches already on the ground. The two wagons began slowly making their way toward Shellbrook. Keeping a steady pace the horses blew steam from their nostrils as they leaned into their collars. It had taken nearly the last of their money to buy a warm steer hide lap robe. Myrtle had been irritated with John for being so extravagant. "We will need every dollar we have when we reach Shellbrook," she admonished him.

But after she had ridden several miles with the snow continuing to blanket everything, she was glad to have it over her lap to keep out the cold. And she was thankful for the heated stones they rested their feet on. However, her stubborn nature would not allow her to let John know how much she appreciated these comforts. Every now and then she would have a twinge of compassion for Claude and her father who were still riding on horseback. She knew that they must be half frozen.

It was a long cold three days from Prince Albert to Shellbrook. Camping in the open, they slept close to the fire, keeping it burning throughout the night. Late afternoon on the third day the weary travelers pulled their wagons to a halt in front of a two story log building. It was the Shellbrook post office and general store. The storekeeper came down the wide porch steps to greet them.

After a warm welcome, the portly man ushered the half frozen group inside. He introduced them to his wife who had six steaming cups of strong tea setting on a small round table beside a pot bellied stove to warm them. The man and his wife were delighted to hear that the newcomers would be homesteading.

"We built this building ourselves," the storekeeper proudly informed them. "Our living quarters are on the second floor."

"Is there a place we could rent until we get on our homesteads?" John asked.

"If you don't mind being a bit crowded I have a two room cabin about a mile west of here with a small barn and corral I'd be glad to rent to you," the storekeeper said.

Bill and John agreed that it sounded fine and said that they had better be going as it would soon be dark.

"Now when your time comes, you come get Granny McTaggert. She's the local mid-wife," the storekeeper's wife told Myrtle.

Following the directions given to them by the storekeeper, the homesteaders halted their wagons beside the rental cabin. Kate and Myrtle went directly inside while the men went to inspect the barn. There were two fair sized rooms and with a sturdy wood floor. After Kate and Myrtle cleaned the dust off the top of the large cookstove and had a blazing fire going, they set about bringing in the cooking pots and the food.

While Myrtle dumped a few jars of canned meat and vegetables in the pot for some quick stew, Kate began to tidy up the place. In no time the cabin grew cozy and warm, and the smell of simmering stew and biscuits baking in the oven made it almost feel like home. Soon the wagons were unloaded and their sparse furnishings were in place. Allison and Claude made themselves sleeping pallets on the floor in the corner by the stove. Kate and Myrtle went in the second room to make up their prized iron beds their husbands had set up. The women both had agreed that whatever else they had to leave behind it would not be their beds.

Both women were pleased when they saw a blanket hanging between the two beds, dividing the room. John came in behind them with a bundle of quilts. "We thought you women would like some privacy," he said quietly to Myrtle.

She opened her mouth to thank him but stubbornness and pride stopped her. "Just put them there," she said as if he hadn't spoken to her. John hid the disappointment he felt.

"This will do just fine," Kate said reassuringly, spreading a quilt out on her bed. She gave John a sad but knowing smile. She knew how hard her brother tried to please Myrtle. At times it was hard for her to keep still when Myrtle treated him with such indifference.

The next morning after breakfast the four men each saddled a horse and rode out to look over the area. They were hoping to find good homestead sites and file on them as soon a possible. They decided the Shellbrook area had good possibilities as it was near supply stations and was not too populated yet.

Chapter Seven

It was beautiful country, fairly flat with thick stands of timber. Frost had gilded the trees a shimmering silver set against a deep-blue sky. The frozen landscape reminded John of something out of a fairy tale. After searching the surrounding area on horseback for several days, John, Allison, and Claude had carefully selected their sections. Now it was time to go to Prince Albert to file on their respective homesteads. While John and Bill were busy loading the wagon with enough supplies to last them the week, Claude and Allison hitched up the team. Bill had not found the section he wanted but would continue his search and file on one later.

As soon as they reached Prince Albert they immediately found the land office and filed for their homesteads. John filed for the Northwest Territory Township 50, SE quarter of Section 12, Range 4 West of the 4th Meridian, exactly seven and one half miles west of Shellbrook. Allison filed on Northwest Territory Township 50 range 3 NW 1/4 of section 6 W of the 3rd Meridian. His northwest corner met John's southeast corner. Claude filed his homestead in Township 49.

On the trip back to Shellbrook Claude excitedly told his comrades, "I'm going to put up a shack on my homestead right away." His dream was coming true. He was now a land owner and soon he would have his own home. But one dark cloud hung over his happiness...Myrtle would not be sharing it with him.

Failing to dissuade him to wait until spring, they insisted on giving him a few supplies and a tarp for a tent. Wanting to go it alone, Claude bought two of Bill's horses, packed up his meager belongings and headed for his homestead. He did promise Kate he would be back for Thanksgiving dinner the following week.

Claude kept his promise to Kate despite the fact that on Thanksgiving Day the snow began to fall in huge fluffy flakes quickly covering the landscape with a soft white blanket. Not even a breeze disturbed the silent decent of the snow. Inside the cozy cabin the large table that Bill had made was laden with platters of grouse, fish and rabbits along with bowls of canned vegetables that Kate had saved for this day. The thankful group feasted on canned sweet potatoes, Irish potatoes, pickled beets, green beans, pickled eggs and pie from the pumpkin that Kate had canned the year before. Not even a scrap was left over.

For several days after Thanksgiving the wind screamed and howled, blowing the falling snow in huge drifts. There seemed no end to the bitter cold and the blowing snow. A rope was tied from the house to the small barn so they could feel their way to the horses in the blinding blizzard. Another rope led to the outhouse. As they waited out the storm, John and Bill mended harness and planned cabins that would be built in the spring. John made a tiny cradle for the newcomer that was expected any day now. Kate and Myrtle sewed, cooked, and watched after Ruby.

Having become accustomed to the howling wind, the total silence brought Myrtle fully awake. It took her a few moments to realize that the wind had stopped. The storm must be over she thought with relief. As she started to get up to put more wood on the fire a pain hit her so hard and sudden that she nearly cried out. Gripping the edge of the bed until it passed, she slowly got to her feet. A cold sweat caused her to shiver as she wrapped her long wool robe around her. Quietly she made her way out of the bedroom to the stove. After taking several deep breaths, satisfied that the pain had passed, she lit a lamp and began to feed the glowing red coals with small pieces of dry wood. When the fire was blazing she put the tea kettle on. Without looking at the clock she knew it would soon be daylight.

Bracing herself on the edge of the table she eased herself into a chair hoping the pain would not return. Picking up the mending she had left on the table the night before, she gasped as another pain tore through her back and abdomen gripping her like a vise and sucking the breath out of her. Suddenly Myrtle was terrified. She knew she was going to die.

A low animal-like moan woke Kate from a deep sleep. Rising quickly she wrapped her thick wool robe around her and pulled on her knitted wool slippers. Pushing back the blanket that served as a bedroom door, she saw Myrtle hunched over at the table, her face ashen. "I'm going to die," Myrtle gasped.

"No. No. You're not going to die, Myrtle. It's going to be all right. Everything's going to be all right," Kate said soothingly. "The baby's coming. We've got to get you back to bed. Here, hang on to me." Myrtle's water broke leaving a wet trail across the floor as they made their way slowly back into the bedroom.

"John! John! Get up! The baby's coming!" Kate shouted excitedly. Myrtle leaned heavily on Kate for support as another pain bore into her.

John was up in an instant and jumping into his pants. "I'll go get Granny MacTaggart," he said throwing on his shirt and pulling on his boots. Bill was awake and up nearly as fast as John.

"See to your wife, John. I'll saddle a horse," Bill said as he shrugged into his coat. The commotion had roused Allison out of a sound sleep. Without a word he quickly pulled on his clothes and followed Bill out the door. Seeing the concern on John's face Kate ushered him out of the bedroom. "She'll be fine, John. You just go on," She said softly.

"I thank God that you're here, Kate. She's so small....and...," his voice trailed off.

"Everything will be fine." Linking an arm through his, she walked him to the door. "She may be small, but she's tough. Now you'd better hurry or we will have to deliver that baby ourselves." With those words he was out the door. Bill and Allison stood outside the cabin with two saddled horses.

"You think I need a spare?" John teased. He did not want Allison or Bill to see how worried he really was.

"I'm going with you," Allison said as he climbed on one of the horses. "Don't want you getting lost or anything. Besides, I figure this would be a good way to get out of the chores this morning."

"Come on you two," Bill interrupted. "Quit the chatter. It's a good five miles to Granny's place and I don't think Myrtle will wait any longer than she has to." With that the two men kicked their horses into a lope, ploughing through the snow drifts.

The men brought the aging mid-wife back in plenty of time. After seventeen hours of hard labor, Myrtle gave birth to a beautiful baby girl. Allison and John named her Leta Elizabeth. Allison was extremely proud to be a grandfather.

60

John was in awe of this tiny human being that had so quickly wrapped herself around his heart. The event was duly recorded in the Family Bible. John smiled as he wrote his first entry: "Born to John Oesch and Myrtle Grace Little Oesch, a girl, Leta Elizabeth Oesch, December 4, 1903."

Before she left, Granny Mac Taggart carefully went over the list of instructions as how to care for Myrtle and the child with Kate. Kate listened respectfully even though she already had a child of her own and knew what to do. Satisfied that her instructions would be followed to the letter, Granny climbed onto her pony, kicking him into a lope, churning up the powdery snow.

As Myrtle drifted of to sleep, John and Bill quietly moved their things out of the bedroom, letting the women and babies occupy it.

Bill and Kate knew it was time to find a place of their own and it wasn't long before Bill found a cabin to rent near the homestead he had filed on. Allison and John helped him make the necessary repairs before he and Kate could move in. When the Brunner's moved into their own place, Myrtle took it as a matter of course. Kate knew she would miss Myrtle much more than Myrtle would miss her. As they sat beside their own fire the first night in their new home, Kate said to Bill, "How sad that Myrtle cannot let herself enjoy the life around her. I hope in time baby Leta will soften her a little."

"Maybe. Maybe it will." Bill was doubtful anything would soften Myrtle.

Chapter Eight

The two families seldom saw each other after the birth of Leta. They were all too busy making improvements on their respective homesteads and building their new lives.

Christmas of 1903 came and went in the Oesch household without any mention of celebration. When Kate had tried to invite them to her house, John just shook his head, closing the subject. "Myrtle does not believe in such 'frivolity' as she calls it," he sadly told his sister.

Before the Christmas holiday, Allison had also moved into his own cabin. The Brunner's were settled in their new home, and Claude was struggling with his homestead, still refusing the offers of help. "I need to be on my own land," Allison told John. So the day after Leta was born, Allison and John had started construction on the cabin.

Early in January the Oesch family moved out onto the Belfry place to be closer to their homestead. They had six horses, one wagon and two dollars to their name. They could no longer afford the rent for the small cabin Leta was born in. John erected two borrowed tents, one against the other to make two rooms. Each room had a small stove but even with the fires kept burning constantly, it was impossible to keep warm. The snow that piled up around the tent helped to keep out some of the drafts. John made a 'convenience' in one corner of the sleeping tent. Most mornings the thunder mug was frozen solid when Myrtle tried to empty it. She did not believe she would ever get used to the long dark, frigid winter nights.

Many days it was impossible to go outside to work as the temperatures dipped to nearly sixty below zero. The relentless wind piled the snow higher and higher around the tent. John mended harness, sharpened his saws, and worked on a horsehair bridle for his baby daughter. Allison was an expert at making braided leather bridles and hackamore head stalls and bosals with reins to match. He made them all with a eight string square braid. Each string was one-eighth inch wide. In her tent, Myrtle worked on wool quilts and caught up on her mending and melted snow for washing. Damp clothes and diapers hung constantly close to the stove to dry. Her hands were red, chapped, and raw.

When weather permitted, John and Allison worked together from dawn to dark clearing the land of its thick timber. The logs would be used to build John and Myrtle a cabin and a barn for the stock. On clear days Myrtle would bundle up Leta, wade through the snow drifts to the Belfry place and spend the day sewing and chatting with Mrs. Belfry. She missed female companionship but could not openly admit it. Myrtle knew she would never get used to the heavy clothes she had to wear in this North Country to keep warm. By the time she struggled through the snow carrying Leta and her sewing bag she was exhausted.

Allison ate his meals with John and Myrtle but slept in his own cabin each night. He and John had constructed the small building in just two days. It had a sod roof and a dirt floor. The snow would blow in through the cracks between the rough hewn logs making it colder than their tents. Allison told John he would worry about chinking them later. "It's more important to get your cabin livable so Myrtle and the baby can move in as soon as possible," he told John. But he missed the long evenings playing with his granddaughter. As he told her of some of his adventures she watched him intently with big round blue eyes. He knew she understood every word.

Myrtle never played with or talked to Leta. The only time Myrtle picked the baby up was when she needed to be fed or changed. Without maternal warmth herself, Myrtle never seemed to notice the tender moments between Allison and his granddaughter. And she failed to see the way John's face would light up and his look of awe when he held his daughter and she would wrap five soft tiny fingers around his big rough calloused one.

It was a calm, clear, bitter cold day when John and Myrtle finally moved their few meager belongings into their new homestead cabin. The one small room smelled of newly cut wood and was cozy and snug. The log walls were chinked with mud and straw, along with a mixture of wood ash and moss to keep out the bitter cold wind and snow. Myrtle was so pleased with the split log floor that she forgot for a moment her resolve to be cold and indifferent toward John. When she placed her two small braided rag rugs on the floor she blurted out, "Oh, John, I'm so thankful to have such a fine wood floor in my house."

Myrtle had come with the men on many occasions to help construct this cabin. She worked alongside her father and John with Leta, content and wrapped in a warm wool quilt, asleep in the wagon. There were only two small windows, one at the east end of the cabin and one beside the door. Glass was hard to come by so the window panes were made of split oiled skins to let in some light. John had built a cupboard by the east window to hold the Blue Willow dishes. This cupboard had a small sideboard attached that fit directly under the window.

The roof was shingled, not made of sod like so many of the cabins. After a hard rain a sod roof would leak for two or three days and it harbored fleas.

John and Allison set up the small ornate iron cook stove, brought in the crude table and four chairs they had made, as well as the iron bed and the crate of dishes. At long last Myrtle could enjoy her mother's Blue Willow china. With the baby tucked in her cradle, John set her out of harms way in a corner. Myrtle helped the men haul everything in and immediately began to unpack. She was a hard worker, and John admired her industry.

In no time, it seemed, the family had a cabin, corral, and shed that would later be finished into a barn. A small chicken house was ready to be inhabited. An outhouse sat 25 feet behind the cabin. At long last it was home.

It was March and it seemed to Myrtle like the winter would last forever. On the days the sun sparkled on the snow a bitter cold wind blew across the newly cleared flat land. Each morning they rose at dawn to clear the thick timber of pine, poplar, tamarack, and spruce. Trees were felled and branches trimmed and the logs, pulled by the horses, were stacked to be used for buildings and fences. Myrtle would drag the smaller branches and brush into a pile that would later be burned. The larger branches were cut up for firewood. The stumps would be removed when the ground thawed.

While her parents labored, Leta slept snug and warm in her wool quilt cocoon tucked into a wooden box with runners on it. John had made the tiny sled so Myrtle could easily pull the baby out to the field with her. Around mid-afternoon they halted their labor to eat the stew or beans Myrtle had thawed near the edge of a pile of brush she was burning. When the food was heated through, the two pioneers huddled near the fire's warmth and ate their fill and then resumed their laborious task until dusk.

Late June of that year finally brought the thaw. It was time to dig a well and start clearing the stumps out of the fields so they could begin planting. But with the warmer weather came the mosquitoes and black flies in swarms. No one had warned them about these pesky insects and they hadn't believed the stories they heard. To gain some protection, they covered their faces and Leta's box with cloth netting. Smudge pails were tied to the wagon tongues to help keep the pests away and smudge fires were built around the house and the barn.

Another problem also confronted them. Now sixty years old, Allison's health began to fail him. He tired easily and had spells of choking nearly every time he ate. Allison kept insisting he was feeling fine, but John worried about his father-in-law who was also his friend. John had insisted he stay with them most of the winter.

Despite Allison's failing health, he did not give up. It took the two men a week to dig the well as the ground was still half frozen. It was a fine well, three feet square increased to four feet square just above the water level. Filled cream and milk cans would later be lowered onto this ledge to keep them cool. It was only early July and yet ice began would form near the bottom of the well before they had finished digging.

With the laborious work of digging the well behind them, they began the task of clearing stumps from the fields. At first they tried pulling the stumps with the team, but as soon as the horses met resistance they would stop. A neighbor told John that oxen were much better for this task, so he traded a few hours of labor for two unbroken oxen. In short order they had them trained to pull and these beasts were much better at pulling out the large stumps than the horses. The oxen would keep pulling until the stump was out. Sometimes the stump roots were so deep that the only way to dislodge them was to dig them out by hand.

The oxen were also easier to care for than the horses. They didn't tire as quickly, would forage for themselves and, unlike a horse, would not wander far. But what the neighbor neglected to tell John was that oxen were dumb and single-minded. Whenever the flies and mosquitoes got too bad, the oxen, chains dragging from their yokes, would begin running for the nearest water, usually a slough. They would stand belly deep in the cool water and mud to relieve themselves of the biting pests. There was no stopping them, and, what was worse, there was no budging these determined beasts until they were ready to get out.

To clear the land, some farmers would burn an area, chop down the large snags, hitch a horse to each end of a log about twenty feet long, and pull it over the burned area. All the brush and smaller snags would be scraped into a pile and the area would be burned again. But neither John nor Myrtle approved of waste and would not burn trees that could be used for building. Only snags that couldn't be used for firewood, buildings, or fences would be burned in the field.

The back breaking work of these homesteading pioneers was slow and tedious. They could only break about an acre and a half a day. John wanted to plow at least thirty acres to put to seed before the short summer growing season was over. But many days the temperature would rise to around 100 degrees. Neither man nor beast could tolerate a long day in the fields in this kind heat and their nemesis, the files and mosquitoes, made it all the worse. Add to that the stench of smoldering oily rags in the air from the smudge fires and it was truly miserable work.

Finally, the Oeschs had their first crop planted which they did by hand broadcasting the seed. John and Allison had been able to clear nearly forty acres to plant wheat. Being this far north, the summer days were longer and afforded more time for them to work. The night sun hovered close to the horizon and they could put in twelve to fourteen hours a day in the fields.

After the wheat was planted, John hitched a horse to the walking plough and tilled up a large area near the cabin for a vegetable garden. With Allison's help he had built a tamarack split rail fence around this plot to keep the range horses out. Several wild herds roamed the area and every now and then the two men would round up a few of these horses to break and sell. Myrtle helped to break them as well, and she also knew how to break the wild oxen. A green broke horse or oxen could be sold or traded easily. To begin to build their stock, John traded some of these ponies for a flock of chickens, three cows, and four weaned piglets. A neighbor brought his bull over to the Oesch homestead to begin to build the herd. He and John agreed to build a herd on shares, splitting the bovine offspring.

Just as the farms were beginning to flourish, Allison suddenly became seriously ill. He could no longer swallow solid food. Myrtle kept thin soup and broth simmering on the stove for him. Most days he wasn't able to help John with the work. Myrtle took her father's place then, helping to build the barn and corral and put up the split rail fences. She plowed the fields, hand broadcasting the seed for their crops, and worked on clearing more land as well as tending the large vegetable garden she had planted. On these days Allison remained in the cabin and tended to Leta. He loved these precious moments with her. He carved her little wooden toys that she could grasp easily, and made her a tiny braided leather doll.

As soon as Myrtle and John left the cabin each morning Allison would begin another adventurous story for his granddaughter. He spoke softly while he whittled and Leta seemed to hang on to his every word, chewing on the tiny leather doll, drool dripping from her chubby chin.

"Did I tell you about my drover days, driving cattle from Stockton, California, to Kansas City, Kansas?" Allison said to Leta who looked at him with serious eyes. "Went through Yellowstone, Wyoming, each time. And those Teton Mountains were a sight to behold. Never saw mountains so pointy. Looked sharp as knife points." He paused, thoughtful. "Well, those were the days a man could roam free as the wind. I quit herding cattle in eighteen an' eighty-two. Progress had choked out the old way of life.... That's when I met Sara, your grandmother. What a fine lady she was. Loved her more than anything...in fact, still do."

A tear formed in the corner of his eye as he remembered the love of his life. "But I already told you that story," he whispered. Leta had fallen fast asleep so he leaned down and covered her with her small quilt. Resting his head against the high back of his chair, Allison closed his eyes, and, as warm memories of Sara filled, his head he fell asleep.

In the next few days Allison seemed to recover and resumed his daily work with John. The July sun was barely breaking over the horizon when John and Allison herded six ponies out of the corral heading toward Shellbrook. It was seven and one-half miles away and they wanted to be back home before dusk. Dust from the horses hooves drifted across the field in the light morning breeze as they trotted down the road. The horses were blowing steam from their nostrils in the crisp air.

Allison buttoned up his coat to ward off the cool morning air. He was glad to be working again. The horses would be sold or traded for badly needed supplies and farming tools. Myrtle looked up from the wash tub as they trotted away. Pausing with a soapy shirt on the rub board, it struck her unexpectedly what a handsome man John was. How straight and tall he sat in the saddle. She liked his sky blue eyes set in a strong ruddy face, framed with his tousled auburn hair. Feeling a sudden odd twinge in her heart, she quickly turned back to her wash. The snowy white bed sheets that hung on the line made flapping sounds in the breeze as she scrubbed the shirt hard against the rub board, scraping her knuckles. Keeping her body occupied with hard work kept her mind from wandering.

At mid-morning the July day was beginning to turn hot. Flies and mosquitoes were already thick in the air. Stopping at the Shell River to water the horses and light the smudge pails they each had hanging from their saddles, John dismounted from his horse as it drank from the river.

His voice was angry. "Why didn't you say something before this?" he remonstrated the older man.

Allison stood beside his horse, holding the reins loosely in one hand as it drank. In a tired, resigned voice he responded, "Didn't see the need. Wouldn't change anything."

John blurted, "You've known since Nebraska." It was not a question.

Allison nodded his head." Yes," he muttered. His horse began pulling at the grass beside the river as he put his hand on the saddle horn ready to mount. Looking directly at John he said quietly, "I don't want you to say anything to Myrtle until after."

John gave him a short nod of agreement, mounted his horse and started the ponies moving again.

In Shellbrook it had not taken long to sell three of the ponies and trade the rest for goods. As the two came out of the General Store, Allison noticed a little dapple gray mare tied to the hitching post.

"Now there's a horse for Leta." Allison said to John. He went directly to the mare and began running a hand over her withers, down her legs, also examining her feet. He was checking her teeth when the owner appeared. "You like her, Allison?" the big burley man asked.

"She's a fine one, that's for certain," John said as he joined Allison and walked around her.

"Aye, that she is," Angus said as he leaned against the post hooking his thumbs around the straps on his bib overalls. "And she's for sale."

"What'll you take for her, Angus?" Allison stepped back to eye the mare.

Angus McPhearson nodded to John. "T'would make a fine pony for the Missus. Her bein' such a wee mite and all."

"She sure would, but we're selling today, not buying," John said to Angus, thinking that a horse for pleasure would be the last thing Myrtle would want.

"She would make Leta a fine pony, John," Allison said quietly.

John was surprised by his father-in-law's unexpected statement. "Don't you think Leta's a little young yet?"

"By the time she's big enough to ride she should have a good horse." Allison's jaw was set. John knew there was no use to argue with Leta's grandfather.

Angus smiled as he watched the exchange between the two men. "Ah, 'tis for the wee granddaughter. Well, Allison, why didn't ya tell me." He stepped off the porch and untied the little mare's lead rope. Handing it to Allison he said, "I'll take fifty dollars and two of yere fine braided hackamores." Angus believed the sun rose and set in Leta's little face. He had stopped by the homestead several times with a string of ponies he had rounded up. John always insisted that Angus stay for a bite to eat. Even Myrtle seemed to enjoy his colorful presence.

"Done!" The two men shook hands and the deal was sealed. John had bought a new plow and hand cultivator for the garden but would have to come back for them later with the wagon. Taking the rope from Angus, Allison mounted his horse with a big smile on his face. "Angus, you are such a pushover for a pretty face." The men laughed as John and Allison headed for home with Allison leading his prize.

"She's a fine little mare, but if she turns out to be too much horse for Leta, I want you to sell her, John, and get a gentler one." John nodded agreement as he nudged his horse a little faster. He wanted to get home. Maybe he could get a little more land cleared before dark.

The hot sun beat down on Myrtle's back as she chopped at the weeds around a squash plant with her hoe. She had planted beets, carrots, cabbage, potatoes, cucumbers, turnips, parsnips, radishes, onions, and three different kinds of squash. All would be ready to harvest in a few weeks. Then the chore of canning would begin.

Stopping to stretch her back, Myrtle looked through the netting that covered her hat and face. Seeing the dust cloud first she saw the two men and three horses coming toward her. "Must not have been able to sell them all," she muttered, bending back to her task.

Myrtle looked up from her hoeing again as the two men stopped in front of the barn. Seeing the strange mare, she frowned as she lifted the netting from her face to get a better view.

"Myrtle!" her father called. "Come see what I have for Leta." Myrtle tensed up. Her hands became fists as she stomped toward them.

As she approached, the men were admiring the mare's perfect conformation and color with pleased grins on their faces. Myrtle was incensed.

"For Leta? What do you mean for Leta? She won't be able to ride for years!" Not stopping for a breath she spit out the words through clenched teeth. "How could you waste money like that!"

"Now, Myrtle," John said quietly.

She was undaunted. "There are a lot of things we need around here and a fancy riding horse is not one of them!" she continued, her voice rising. "That money should have been used..."

"That's enough!" John cut her off sharply.

Stunned by his reproach, Myrtle stood with her mouth open, the sentence unfinished. John had never been sharp with her before. Without another word she clamped her mouth shut, turned and stomped back to the garden. She was seething. John would pay for this.

During the several days after Allison had brought the mare home, Myrtle had not spoken a word to either of the men. She went about her work with a vengeance. There was not a weed left in the garden. She whitewashed the inside of the cabin and scrubbed the planks on the floor to almost a shine. She nearly rubbed holes in their clothes on the washboard, and she made enough lye soap to last them two years. It seemed that Myrtle was always getting in a huff, but she had usually gotten over it quicker. This time she was savoring her anger. Even Leta could sense the tense atmosphere her mother had created around the family. John and Allison knew to leave her be. She would come around eventually. She always did.

Chapter Nine

As soon as John heard the familiar sound, he was awake instantly. Allison's choking spells had become more frequent. John had tried to get him to stay out of the fields but he wouldn't hear of it. Allison insisted on going out every day and would not quit until dusk when John quit.

"Myrtle," John said quietly as he quickly pulled his trousers on without stopping to light the lamp. The full moon shining through the small window illuminated the room. As soon as John spoke she was awake. She sensed something was wrong. Her long flannel gown brushed the tops of her bare feet as she quickly followed John to her father's cot across the cold planks of the floor.

"Quick, get him up. He's choking on something. Pound on his back. I'll get him some water." Forgetting her vow of silence the words tumbled out of Myrtle like an avalanche. John quickly helped Allison to sit up and swing his legs over the edge of the cot. Bending forward Allison seemed to catch his breath and the choking ceased. Myrtle handed him a glass of water. He sipped it slowly, barely able to swallow.

"You all right?" Myrtle asked him, a hint of concern in her voice.

"Must...must be my tonsils swelling up on me again," Allison croaked. Myrtle did not notice the knowing glance he and John exchanged.

It surprised John when Myrtle agreed to work with him in the fields that day so Allison could recuperate from him 'tonsillitis'. But the two worked in less than companionable silence. When they were finished in the fields they both worked in the garden. Myrtle was a hard worker and she was tough. John was proud of her, and of how she could work as hard as any man.

Each morning before leaving for the fields, Myrtle put Leta in the small pen John had made for her on the porch. She had lined it with a thick quilt and covered it with cotton netting to keep the mosquitoes and files from the baby. Allison placed his chair close beside the tiny pen and Grandfather and Granddaughter spent their days enjoying each other's company in the cool shade of the porch. Allison worked on the promised hackamores while Leta chewed on her tiny leather doll and listened intently to his stories. The pungent odor of oil soaked wool rags smoldering in the smudge pails at each corner of the cabin filled the air.

"Did I tell you about riding with the Pony Express?" Allison began his narrative, laying the hackamore aside and started carving a small toy horse. "Well, it was eighteen and sixty one. I was about sixteen years old at the time and thought that working in my father's gristmill was too tame for me. Worked before and after school. My mother, your Great Grandmother, wanted me to be a teacher. About broke her heart when I quit school and joined the Pony Express. We lived in Stockton, California then, we moved there around eighteen and fifty two from Illinois. Don't remember much about Illinois though."

Allison continued to pass along the family history to her young ears. He spoke softly and slowly. "Your Great Grandmother immigrated from Holland and your Great Grandfather from England. They met and married in the state of Illinois. She always laughed when she would tell me that she had to come all the way to America to meet my father." Allison smiled as he remembered his mother. "She would have loved you, Leta...Anyway, back to my story. When I saw the poster advertising for tough, daring, adventurous young men of small stature, I knew I fit the bill. Barely standing five foot six inches in my shoes, back then I maybe weighed one hundred twenty pounds. I disappointed my father and broke my mother's heart, but I joined up anyway."

He paused, lost in his own thoughts for a moment. "But the Pony Express didn't last long. Only about eighteen months. From April 3, 1860, to October 24, 1861. The mail was carried from Sacramento, California, to St. Joseph, Missouri, by more than four hundred horses and eighty riders. Imagine that. It was something all right. But when the telegraph reached from coast to coast we were out of business. The men who started the Express, Russell, Majors, and Wadell, they were called the principal backers, went broke. And eighty riders, hundreds of station keepers, and all the assistants were out of a job. Best job I ever had though. Made $100.00 a month. Some made $150.00. But it was also the most dangerous job a man could have. I guess that's why I liked it so much. I always liked the danger part. Only had two minutes to jump from one pony to a fresh one, grab the mail pouch from the station keeper, and be off again at a dead run.

"How those ponies could run! They were a special breed that could outrun the fastest Indian ponies. Sometimes we made twenty five miles at just under an hour. Once a pony delivered the mail alone. Indians must have got the rider."

Smoothing the rough spots off his carving, Allison continued. "I met one of the riders who had helped set the record. He raced from Fort Klarney, Nebraska, to Fort Churchill, Nevada, in just six days. Abraham Lincoln was elected president that year and this same rider had carried the election news with his dispatch."

Allison put the finished horse in Leta's outstretched hands and she promptly stuck the head in her mouth. Allison closed his pocket knife and slipped it back into his pocket. Leaning back in the chair he gazed out across the wheat growing in the fields he and John had cleared. "Postage was too expensive. Too expensive for ordinary folk anyway. Started out at five dollars an ounce then later reduced to one dollar an ounce." He looked down at Leta who had fallen fast asleep. "Well, I think both of us could use a nap," he said resting his head against the high back of the rocking chair he had made himself. Thoughts of his wandering days filled his head as he dozed off with a smile on his face.

The sun was setting as John walked slowly toward the cabin. It had taken him longer than usual to unhitch the team, feed and water them and give them a quick rub down. It had been a long hot day and every muscle in his body ached. With head down his shoulders drooped with fatigue. Hearing a strangled choking sound he looked up and saw Allison sprawled on the porch. Leta was still asleep in her pen, clutching the tiny wooden horse.

"Myrtle! Myrtle!" John yelled as he started to run. "Come quick!"

Myrtle had worked non-stop in the garden all day. She had kept a steady pace, with back bent, chopping the stubborn weeds row after row. She felt a spasm in her back as she straightened up. Quickly dismissing the pain she pulled the netting from her face that hung from her hat, and saw John running toward the cabin. Her heart froze. "The baby! Something's happened to the baby!" she breathed. Dropping the hoe, she hiked her skirt up to her knees and started racing to the cabin. When Myrtle reached the steps John had Allison sitting on the edge of the porch gasping for air.

Myrtle realized then she had been so absorbed in herself she had not noticed how fast Allison's health had declined in the last few days. How thin and frail he had become. His skin was now a pasty gray. For the first time since her mother died she was scared. It suddenly hit her. She was losing her father.

John carried Allison inside and gently laid him on his cot. Reaching under the pillow John took the bottle of laudanum Allison had hidden there and gave it to him. He took some straight from the bottle having difficulty swallowing it. He was soon asleep.

After seeing that Allison was going to be all right for awhile, John went out on the porch where Myrtle sat in her father's rocking chair holding Leta, staring out across the newly plowed field, slowly rocking back and forth.

"It's a cancer, Myrtle," John said quietly. "He didn't want to worry you with it. He told me the day he bought the mare for Leta. That's why he bought it. He knew he wouldn't be here to buy her one when she was old enough to ride."

Myrtle did not respond. She stared out across the open field and kept rocking. Her face remained expressionless. Her eyes were dry.

A few days later on July 24, 1904, they buried Allison in the small cemetery in Shellbrook. John made the marker for his grave carving the inscription, 'A strong man, an honest man,

Allison Tenbrook Little, 1844-1904'. John loved his father-in-law and would miss him terribly. Neighbors from all around the Province came for the service. When the minister concluded his part of the service, John read Ecclesiastes 3:1-8 from Allison's old worn Bible. "To everything there is a season, and a time to every purpose under the heaven: A time to be born, and a time to die; a time to plant, and a time to pluck up that which is planted; A time to kill, and a time to heal; a time to break down, and a time to build up; A time to weep, and a time to laugh; a time to mourn, and a time to dance; A time to cast away stones, and a time to gather stones together; a time to embrace, and a time to refrain from embracing; A time to get, and a time to lose; a time to keep, and a time to cast away; A time to rend, and a time to sew; a time to keep silence, and a time to speak; A time to love, and a time to hate; a time of war, and a time of peace." Slowly closing the book, he brushed a tear from his eye. Myrtle stood beside him silent and dry eyed. A single tear slid down John's cheek. Bill handed Kate his handkerchief. She wiped the tears from her eyes and softly blew her nose.

Claude stood near the foot of the grave twisting his hat, the tears rolling down his cheeks as John and Bill lowered the hastily built coffin into the ground. He had loved Allison like a father. He had once been so close to Myrtle, he had loved her, but no longer knew the woman she had become. His heart gave a twist as he realized at that moment he had lost them both forever. First he had lost Myrtle, and now he had lost Allison. He mourned for the loss of the two people who had meant so much to him.

Bill and John began shoveling dirt back into the grave. Myrtle watched expressionless as Claude mounted his horse and slowly rode away without a word to anyone. He never looked back. There was a strange tug at her heart as Myrtle realized she would never see him again.

Chapter Ten

By mid-August the wheat was waist high, golden heads waving in the soft summer breezes. In less than two weeks it would be ready for harvest. Even in the short growing season, crops matured rapidly in the rich, heavy loam. While the wheat ripened on the first thirty acres, John and Myrtle cleared another section. Having learned how to handle the stubborn oxen they could now accomplish more each day. Myrtle had inherited Allison's homestead and they needed to get enough land cleared to plant winter wheat.

Before she went out to work with John in the fields, Myrtle would lay a thick wool quilt on the floor, set Leta on it, and anchor her long dress tail under a table leg. She had outgrown her small play pen and was crawling and climbing over everything. This was the safest place for her. When John and Myrtle came back to the cabin for their noon meal, they would find Leta fast asleep under the table, with a pink thumb stuck in her mouth, and the tiny wooden horse next to her.

By the end of August, John had dug a root cellar and was building another room onto the cabin. Just before harvest time, a dance and pot luck dinner was being held at the newest building in the district - a one room school house - and every family in the district would be there. Everyone looked forward to this occasion with great anticipation. For the occasion, Myrtle had made herself a new off-white muslin blouse with long sleeves and high neck, as well as a long black wool skirt with fabric she had frugally held back to use when her other clothes wore out.

The big day finally arrived. Dressed in his new flannel shirt and clean, faded dungarees, John loaded the food and extra quilts in the wagon. He waited with an eager Leta in his arms as Myrtle climbed up and settled herself on the wagon seat.

"You look right handsome, Myrtle," He noted a faint smile playing on her lips as he settled himself next to her. Myrtle's cheeks colored slightly at his complement. Pulling off the brake, he clucked to the team and the wagon pulled away from the small cabin with the ever present smoking smudge pail swinging from the single tree.

As the sun dipped toward the horizon, the air cooled and the sky exploded into a magnificent sunset. Bright pink faded to deep rose. Reds and magentas became streaked with oranges and golds. The two and one-half mile ride to the school house was a pleasant drive for them both. Myrtle was in a rare light mood and John was savoring every minute of it.

When they reached the festooned school house there were several wagons with unhitched teams tied to the wheels. The strong odor of wool smoldering in smudge pails hung in the air to discourage the unwelcome flies and mosquitoes.

"Looks like Kate and Bill got here just ahead of us". John waved to Bill who was unhitching his team. Kate, with little Ruby in tow, was walking the short distance to the school house carrying a large basket filled to the brim with good things to eat. Seeing John and Myrtle pull up, Kate set the basket on the ground, and waited for Myrtle. Watching the two women ascend the stairs and disappear into the building with baskets and babies, John wished Myrtle could be just a little like his sister. Quickly pushing the thought aside he busied himself unhitching his team.

The band comprised of a fiddle, guitar, banjo and a concertina, was boisterously warming up inside. Even though it would stay light outdoors for several hours yet, lamps glowed from the school house windows. Long planks atop saw horses, covered with white sheets, served as a table to hold the abundance of food. The delicious aroma of the food competed with the smell of freshly hewn wood in the room. A bell rang and a short stout woman called, "Come and get it before we throw it to the hogs." Everyone laughed and rushed into the school.

After nearly every morsel had been consumed, what little that was left over was covered, dishes scraped, stacked in their individual baskets and set aside. Toddlers and infants were put to bed on quilt pallets in one corner of the room. A few older girls volunteered to watch over them. A few older boys stood close by to keep watch on the older girls.

The small band began to play a loud and lively tune. Husbands and wives sashayed around the room, young girls were dancing with each other, and smaller girls stood atop their father's shoes while they moved slowly to the music. Occasionally a brave young man would ask a shy young lady for the pleasure of the next dance with her. The laughter and joy was exciting and continued into the wee hours of the morning.

The dancing continued until the sun started peeking over the horizon the next morning. It had been so long since any of them had had recreation of any kind, they didn't want to give up and go home. But everyone had chores that had to be done. The men hitched up their respective wagons while the women packed up their baskets and bundled up their children. Tired and happy, each family said their good-byes, vowed they would get together again soon, and then pointed their teams of horses toward home.

The warmth of the sun had dried the dew on the grass by the time John and Myrtle arrived at the cabin. Spirits renewed, they did not notice the rising temperature or the pesky insects that buzzed around them.

Before she tackled her own chores, Myrtle fed and changed Leta and then anchored the toddler on a pallet under the table. John had made a Dutch door for the cabin. Myrtle could leave the top part open so aired out the cabin and kept the varmints out at the same time. She hung some cotton netting from the top of the door jamb to keep flies and mosquitoes out of the house.

Coming in only for a quick noon meal, John went back to work splitting tamarack logs for the pasture fence. Leaving Leta asleep on her pallet, Myrtle returned to hoeing in the garden. At dusk when she returned to the cabin she found Leta sitting on her pallet with her thumb in her mouth, soaked to the skin. Myrtle quickly changed her, stood her in her bed and gave her a piece of bread to chew on. Before starting the fire in the stove, she emptied the ashes out of it with a small shovel. She carefully poured them into a bucket used just for this purpose so they would cool. The cold ashes were saved in a tight wooden box and kept inside to keep them dry. As Myrtle filled the bucket she made a mental note to take some ashes and sprinkle a ring around the cabbage plants to discourage the cut worms. She also needed to dump ashes down the privy. It helped to keep down the flies as well as deodorize it.

Stove ash was used for many things and was never wasted. Myrtle would sprinkle some in a bucket of water, let it settle to the bottom, then pour off the water into another bucket to be used to bleach out the wash. A stronger solution mixed with animal fat was used to make soap. John also mixed the ash with moss to make a thick paste to chink the cracks between the logs in the cabin. Myrtle reminded herself she also needed to dump a pile of ash in the chicken yard. Fowl liked to dust themselves with it. An ash bath would rid the chickens of vermin.

After trimming all the lamp wicks, Myrtle quickly cut up some vegetables and dumped a jar of canned venison into the stock pot. The stew was simmering on the stove and biscuits baking in the oven when John came in, hot, dusty, and tired. Hanging his hat on the peg beside the door, he picked up the water bucket. "Smells good." He hoped she was still in good spirits.

"It will be ready soon as you are washed up."

Outside he stripped off his shirt, and poured water into the wash basin that sat on the small washstand he had built on the porch. The cold water felt good. Sometimes John wished he had the time to enjoy a long lazy swim. How he wished Myrtle could enjoy pleasures like that too. He was sure she would if she would just let herself relax like she did at the dance. Smiling to himself, he thought of her dancing and laughing. She looked so pretty. She was a different person when she would let herself forget, for a time, to hold that door deep down inside her so tightly closed and let it open just a crack. Maybe, just maybe, after last night her heart would remain open so she would, once again, be the cheerful person she had been back when he courted her.

Tossing his wash water out into the yard, John shook some of the dust off his shirt and put it back on before going into the cabin. Myrtle would not tolerate a man coming to the table without his shirt on. The meager meal was on the table when he re-entered the cabin. He never ceased to marvel at her organization, industry, and unlimited energy. She would work alongside him in the fields then tend to her household chores, till the garden, complete her other outside chores and take care of Leta's needs. However, John wished she could learn to bend a little, to relax, to enjoy life...to love.

In the short week after the dance, summer rapidly turned to fall. Trees were beginning to show brilliant golds, yellows, oranges and reds. John liked autumn. To him it was the most beautiful season of the year. He loved the cool, crisp mornings and the warm afternoons.

Heavy frost covered the ground, crunching under John's feet as he approached the barn. The horses in the corral stomped and snorted steam in anticipation of their morning meal. They snickered in anticipation as he pitched a forkful of hay down to them from the hayloft. Having secured Leta on her pallet under the table for the morning, Myrtle was already in the barn herding a cow into her stall. After filling the manger with hay, she locked the cow into the stanchion, settled herself on a three legged stool at the cow's flank and began to squirt warm foamy milk into the bucket. The muscles in her small forearms bulged with every pull on the teats. Myrtle had two cows to milk now and they each produced over two gallons every day. There was ample cream and butter for their use with some left over to sell. Soon her chickens would be laying enough for her to sell eggs as well. Both John and Myrtle had to get their chores done quickly this morning. The thrasher and crew would be here soon.

Chapter Eleven

Leta sat quietly in her high chair chewing on a biscuit, watching her mother strain milk into a five gallon milk can. Dropping the white strainer cloth into a pan of boiling water on the stove, Myrtle gave the huge pot of simmering stew a stir. She punched down the bread for the second time, quickly rolled it into loaves, dropped them into greased loaf pans and slid them into the hot oven. Soon the fragrant aroma of baking bread filled the cabin. She was in such a hurry to get it in the oven she had almost forgotten to put the left over mashed potatoes in the dough. It increased fermentation and the bread would not crumble when sliced.

Even with eight loaves there wasn't much chance of any bread being left over to store in the stone jar today. No threshing crew ever left a crumb. Quickly grinding a handful of coffee beans, she made a huge pot of coffee. She learned early in her marriage that store bought ground coffee usually contained half ground peas or other fillers in it. When she bought coffee, she sorted through every bean.

Setting a small bowl of cooled mush in front of Leta, Myrtle grabbed the heaping basket of wet clothes on her way out the door. Ignoring the spoon, Leta began shoving mush into her mouth with both hands.

Stepping off the porch, Myrtle could see the huge thresher slowly approaching in the distance, pulled by eight horses abreast. Two large wagons, filled with men, followed close behind. The wagons and the threshing machine stopped at the far edge of the field.

Scanning the clear blue sky, Myrtle muttered to herself, "At least we're not the last farm on the list this year for the threshing crew and it looks like the weather is going to hold." Hanging the last diaper on the line with a straight clothes pin she remembered John telling her, "One day I will have my own thresher."

With the advancing sun the morning frost made a hasty retreat. The day grew warm as the crew labored in the wheat field. One team of men cut the grain with hand scythes, tied it into bundles, and stacked them in shocks. Another team loaded the shocks onto the wagons that hauled the grain to the stationary threshing machine. The noisy gasoline motor was hooked to the thresher by a thirty foot long pulley belt which made the huge machine work. The straw was blown into a pile on one side of the thresher. On the other side the grain was poured into wagons to be hauled to the granaries.

At twilight the threshing crew had finished the field, packed up and were headed for the next farm to get an early start the next morning. Myrtle had worked in the garden most of the day filling boxes and baskets with produce. Barely glancing up from her task, she saw John pulling the wagon up to the barn. Horses and man alike were streaked with sweat and dust. Picking up a large basket overflowing with carrots, Myrtle carried it to the cabin and sat it on the porch. She would fix supper while John bathed in the barn.

When John entered the cabin Myrtle was frying eggs and potatoes in bacon fat. "The boxes in the garden are full. We need to get them in the root cellar tonight," she said without turning around.

"I'll take the basket of carrots down now." He was bone tired and would have liked nothing better than go straight to bed.

During supper that night John held Leta on his knee, feeding her from his plate. Every night, no matter how tired he was, John would tell Leta a story about one of the small animals or a bird he had seen in the field that day. "And there was a big fat fuzzy squirrel stuffing as much of the grain he could get into his cheeks to store in his own cupboard for the winter." Leta listened intently, alternately chewing on the tiny leather doll her grandfather had made and the food her father fed her.

"You are just spoiling her, John. You need to let her feed herself. She will never learn with you feeding her all the time."

"Now, Myrtle, you know what a smart little thing she is and she will be doing everything on her own soon enough," John patiently told her.

After a quick supper, the remaining boxes of vegetables were carried into the root cellar. These vegetables would be buried in dry sand to keep them fresh during the long frigid winter. Any vegetables left over in the spring would be canned.

Each day the sun was measurably losing more and more of its warmth. Frost lingered in the shadows all day. Myrtle didn't mind winter so much as all the layers of heavy clothing she had to put on before going outdoors.

As winter set in, a fire was kept burning continually in the small cookstove. Myrtle would get up several times during the night to stoke the fire. But even with the fire burning low during the night, ice would form on the inside of the windows in their small bedroom.

The eight-by-ten foot addition to the cabin barely held their double iron bed, a small chest of drawers, and a small table beside the bed for the coal-oil lamp. The crib Allison had made for Leta was at the foot of the bed. Like the other windows in the cabin, the small window above the bed was also made of split oiled skin.

A workbench now took up the corner where Allison's cot had been. Here John mended his harnesses using wax-end thread coated with bees wax. He sharpened his saws and scythes, made skis, and bow and arrows for hunting. Myrtle appreciated the larger table he had made, but could never bring herself to tell him. She didn't have quilting frames but the table was large enough so she could lay her quilts over it to work on them. And it gave her an ample surface for cooking and canning.

Many winter evenings were spent with John at his workbench and Myrtle leaning over the table meticulously sewing small quilt pieces together by hand with tiny, perfectly even stitches. During these long evenings few words were exchanged between husband and wife. Both worked in silence each lost in their own thoughts.

One early morning in November, Myrtle rose quietly, pulled on her heavy wool robe, glanced in Leta's crib as she passed on her way to stoke the fire. Leta was sound asleep, buried deep in a wool quilt, with just her fist and the tip of her nose showing, a tiny thumb stuck in her mouth. Even with the fire burning low all night it was still cold inside the cabin. When the fire was blazing in the cookstove Myrtle slipped her stocking-covered feet into low rubbers.

Opening the door to go out to the privy, she shouted, "John! Get up! The house is buried in snow!" He was up and on his feet in an instant. Not stopping to pull on his trousers, he ran from the bedroom in his gray wool union suit. Myrtle stood with the door open. A wall of snow filled the doorway with barely a two foot space at the top. John started to laugh but when he saw the despairing look on Myrtle's face he thought better of it.

"Get the wash tub down," he said as he grabbed the water bucket, scooped out a bucketful of snow, and dumped it into the tub. "The shovel should be just outside the door." By the time he located the shovel, the cabin was freezing inside. It was then that he remembered to put on his pants! After getting dressed, John made quick work of clearing a path. While the snow was deep, it was soft and easy to shovel.

Quickly finishing his chores that morning, John packed up his fishing gear with anticipation. Sturgen Lake had frozen over and it was time to go ice fishing. Myrtle filled a small lard bucket with bannock biscuits and tucked them in John's knapsack.

"I'll be gone three days at the most," John told her as he shrugged into his heavy wool coat. "The ice house will be full of fish and game this year. Next year we should have enough pigs and chickens to butcher. Bill is meeting me at the cross road. Don't want to be late." Ruffling Leta's hair in a swift tender farewell, he picked up the knapsack, went out on the porch and began strapping on his skis. John had been looking forward to this cross country ski trip for months. He pulled his wool cap low over his eyes, slung the knapsack on his back, picked up his ski poles, and without any further good-byes, glided across the yard and disappeared into the woods.

For the next three days Myrtle busied herself with her mending and the outside chores. As she gathered the eggs each morning, she checked the coal-oil in the lantern hanging in the chicken house. She did not want it to go out and have her hens freeze to death. She had wrapped the roost with rags so their feet would not freeze to it. As soon as the eggs were gathered,

Myrtle quickly took them into the cabin. If left outside they would freeze in no time.

After breaking the thick ice in the double water trough, Myrtle turned the pigs out into their pen and the horses and cows into the corral. John had built the water trough between the fence of the corral and the hog pen so it would be easier to fill. She often marveled at how ingenious John was but never let him know what she thought.

"If it turns much colder," she said to the pregnant sow who was grunting nosily as she gobbled her feed, "you will be staying in the barn with the rest of the stock."

It was nearly mid-day and it was beginning to snow when Myrtle finished the chores. She was thankful the wind was not blowing. She hated the cold wind. Stepping up on the porch of the cabin she kicked the powder-dry snow off her low rubbers before entering. Leta was asleep on her pallet under the table. The fire was still burning in the stove and the cabin was snug and warm. Myrtle believed that hers was the only cabin that did not have so much as a draft. Not even on the floor. She had John to thank for that too, but she would never tell him.

Myrtle relished this time alone. She did not mind the extra work. In all her years she had never been completely alone before and found she liked it. While she sewed by lamplight, Leta played quietly on the floor. She was such a good baby, so undemanding, that Myrtle would almost forget to feed and change her.

All the laundry had to be done indoors now. When Myrtle hung it out on clear days it would freeze solid in minutes and her fingers would be nearly frost bitten. She learned the hard way to be careful taking it off the line after it had frozen. She had snapped off one of the legs of John's union suit and a couple of sleeves off his shirts.

John had been gone three full days when Myrtle stepped out on the porch to re-fill the wood box beside the stove. Looking off in the distance, she could see him coming out of the timber at the edge of the grain field. It was a clear, calm day with not a single cloud in the deep azure sky. Even from this distance she could see he was bent over from the heavy burden on his back. Filling her arms with wood, she went back inside to heat up the thick vegetable soup for him. Smiling to herself, she was glad they would have plenty of meat for awhile. She was tired of vegetable soup and beans.

Leaving the knapsack - with the fish he'd caught and the small game he'd trapped - on the porch, John came inside to eat and warm up. His face was stiff with cold. There were ice granules in his short red beard. "It was a rough trip back. We got so much we were not sure we could carry it all so far," he told Myrtle as he stomped the dry snow from his rubbers. "But it was sure worth it. We should have meat for several weeks." He was admittedly weary of vegetable soup too. After eating his fill, he went out to take his frozen catch to the ice house.

Stacking John's dirty dishes on the sideboard, Myrtle sat Leta on her pallet under the table, fastened her dress tail securely under the table leg, and went to help John. The fish had been cleaned but there was still plucking and skinning to do. They could not do this inside as they didn't want the game to thaw.

Working quickly with half-frozen fingers at the small butchering table he had built beside the ice house, John moved to the side a little to give Myrtle room to work. "Bill and I saw plenty of deer, elk, and moose by the lake. We'll be going back to shoot us a couple in a few days. That should do us for the winter," he said to Myrtle as she picked up a skinning knife and began skinning a rabbit.

"I can use these skins and the feathers," she returned. Myrtle would clean the feathers and tan the hides later. She would make new pillows, stuff them with the feathers, and piece the hides together for mittens and jacket liners.

After the game was cleaned it was hung in the ice house along with the fish. Without stopping to warm his hands, John went to tend to the stock. Myrtle went in to check on the stove and see about Leta. This time Leta was soaked through and needed a complete change. Perfunctorily performing the task, Myrtle sat Leta in her high chair with a crust of bread to chew on.

A bushel basket sat in the corner overflowing with cabbage. "Now, I've got to get that sauerkraut made," Myrtle said to herself as she dumped several heads in a wooden barrel used for this purpose only. Picking up the short spade she began chopping up the cabbage heads in the bottom of the barrel. When she had chopped it up fine, she sprinkled in a measure of salt. Then she picked up the stomper John had made out of a post and stomped it all together. She would repeat this process until the barrel was full. Every now and then she would stop and taste her mixture to make sure it had enough salt.

By the time John came in from his chores the sauerkraut barrel was full and setting by the stove to ferment. When it was ready it would be set out on the porch to freeze. A small hatchet was kept on the lid to chop some out whenever Myrtle wanted some for their supper.

"Looks like you made plenty of kraut this time, Myrtle."

"If there is any left come spring, I can always put up a few quarts," she said with a slight edge to her voice. John turned away wondering why she always took his comments as criticism.

Chapter Twelve

Dusk was settling in around the Oesch homestead when John finished the last of his chores. The milk white sky had threatened to spill snow all day and now it was making good on its threat. Small scattered flakes began floating slowly to the ground. As John stepped up on the cabin porch snow was already falling thick and steady. Stomping dry snow off his feet he saw three red coated Mounties riding toward the cabin. Having read everything he could find on the Northwest Mounted Police, John was anxious to meet them.

From the information John had gleaned from several publications, he learned that the Northwest Mounted Police were established in 1873. Men between the ages of 18 and 40 were recruited, selecting only those of the highest integrity. Other qualifications were: they had to be of sound body, a good rider, and able to speak French as well as English.

The Northwest Mounted Police followed Sir Robert Peel's ideas in the Metropolitan Police Act, introduced in 1829, focusing on crime prevention rather than punishment. A solitary Mountie, patrolling a vast area, could keep law and order without hardly a mishap. Diplomacy skills were legend in the law enforcement field. Mounties were highly respected. As well as keeping law and order in the Northwest Territories, they carried the mail, were postmasters, customs collectors, census takers, Indian agents, recorders of vital statistics as well as many other public services...all for a mere seventy-five cents a day.

"Evening." John stepped off the porch in greeting as the three Mounties pulled their horses to a halt in front of the cabin.

"Evening, Sir," The Sergeant replied, snow quickly blanketing the horses and their riders. "Looks like we're in for a good one. Thought you might put us up for the night."

"Be glad to." John was thankful the barn was finished so there would be plenty of room for the extra horses. On these frigid winter nights all the stock was kept in the barn and the breath of so many animals created a frost that filled in the cracks helping to keep out the wind and snow, keeping the barn cozy. After the horses were tended to, the four men trudged through the deepening snow to the warmth of the cabin.

"We've got company for supper, Myrtle," John said as they entered the cabin.

Thinking it was a neighbor, Myrtle turned from the stove and was surprised to see the Mounties. "Company's always welcome. It's not often we get visitors out here. Looks like you could use some hot coffee." Her face suddenly radiant, she quickly poured three large steaming mugs. The men removed their coats and hats, hanging them on the pegs beside the door. "John, I'll need some fish and potatoes," Myrtle told him. She lifted the large cast iron skillet out of the oven, placed it on the stove and dropped a large spoon of bacon grease in it to heat. There was a large kettle of soup simmering on the back of the stove but she would offer more than just soup to the Mounties.

"Hi there little lady," One of the Mounties said to Leta. Leta didn't see many strangers and wasn't sure what to make of these men but it wasn't long before she was enjoying all the attention.

During desert, before Myrtle could stop him, the Sergeant had Leta on his lap and was feeding her blueberry cobbler from his plate. The men chuckled as the toddler grabbed cobbler in both hands getting more on her face than in her mouth. John could see that Myrtle disapproved but he knew she would not voice her disapproval to the Mountie. But he knew he would hear about it later.

"We could use you, Mr. Oesch," the Sergeant was saying. "The Crown furnishes all the supplies and will pay you to haul freight to the Cree up in the Green Lake District. Men like you with teams and sleighs are desperately needed. Since yours is the last place North I thought you might be interested. Of course it would mean leaving the Missus and your young one here alone for a couple of weeks at a time." Taking the last bite of cobbler he turned to Myrtle, "This is the best cobbler I've ever tasted, Mrs. Oesch. Don't get cooking like this very often."

"We'll be fine John, and we could use the money." Myrtle rose and began stacking the dishes on the sideboard. After exchanging a brief knowing glance with his wife he knew he had no choice but to accept the job. John held out his hand to the Mountie, "You've got a deal, Sergeant." With a firm handshake the deal was closed.

In less than two weeks after the Mounties visit, John was busy preparing for his first trip to the Green Lake District. The icy wind whipped the snow around the corner of the barn as John finished hitching the team to the lead sleigh. Having removed his mittens for this task, every now and then he would hold his hands up to the lantern to warm his nearly frozen fingers. The thick wool socks Myrtle had knit kept the bitter cold from creeping into his low rubbers and freezing his feet. Steam from the horses nostrils made small white clouds in the pre-dawn darkness and frozen snow crunched under hooves protesting the cold.

After checking his provisions - the small wooden box was filled with soup, bacon, beans, and bannock biscuits - John climbed on the lead sleigh, gently tapped the rumps of the team with the reins, and was on his way. It was thirty miles to Prince Albert and he hoped to cover the distance in two and one-half days, but he wouldn't push his team in this sub-zero weather.

With the temperature still well below zero John arrived in Prince Albert on the third day, driving directly to the supply depot. Men were bundled up against the arctic cold, busy loading their own sleighs with freight that would be taken to other northern locations.

Soon both John's sleighs were loaded with flour, salt, sugar, bacon, wool blankets, and tea. After covering his load with tarps and tying it down, he climbed on the lead sleigh and urged his team toward Shellbrook. He rested his feet on the large stone he had heated on the big potbellied stove in the depot. John had not wrapped the brown paper and wool cloth around it as well as Myrtle had before he left home, but it would keep his feet warm. As the horses plodded down the busy street, he tucked the steer hide lap robe tighter around his legs. He would spend one night at home before continuing on to Green Lake.

It had taken a little over two weeks for his first freighting trip to the Green Lake District. Spending one night in the Cree camp, John had enjoyed the company of the Cree people tremendously. He found them intelligent, proud, gracious, and hospitable. *How sad*, he thought, *that people are so quick to form preconceived ideas about things they know very little about.* He had been warned about the 'savages' up North. "More likely we are the savages," he said aloud, adding more wood to his campfire. He spread out his bedroll on the tarp under the small makeshift lean-to beside the fire. Melting snow in a small bucket to water the horses, he set the small crock of soup and a few bannock biscuits on a stone beside the fire to thaw while he tended to the horses.

It was the first clear night since he started this trip and the stars looked close enough to touch. The Mounties had told him where the trappers' cabins were located along the trail, but since there were none along this stretch, he enjoyed sleeping out in the open. When John signed on for this job he had no idea how much he was going to enjoy it, even with the extreme dangers. And the dangers were too numerous to count.

The arctic cold coupled with the bitter wind made the temperature drop to nearly seventy degrees below zero. A blizzard was in full bloom. The frigid cold woke John as it crept through his bedroll, penetrating his thick wool clothing and into his bones. Crawling out of his bedroll, John stirred the glowing embers of the fire, feeding it pine boughs that had been his bed. The horses stood huddled together with their backs to the wind. They looked more like white phantoms than Bays. Quickly giving each a ration of oats he threw more boughs onto the fire. "Thank God I left their feed bags on all night," he thought. "If they had breathed this air their lungs would have frozen in a minute."

When the flames were blazing John brought the frozen harnesses closer to the fire to thaw. Sitting cross legged in the lean-to he worked the leather until it was soft enough for him to harness the teams.

With the dawn the howling wind died down but the snow was falling thicker and faster. John knew he must leave now or he would not find the trail. Working as quickly as he could, he hitched the teams to the sleighs, and made sure their noses were covered with wool cloth. Taking the lead team by the halter he led his small train south toward Shellbrook.

As he crossed a frozen lake, he cautiously looked for air pockets in the ice. Walking slowly he poked the ice in front of him with a long stick as he lead his teams. He remembered the stories of freighters that had stood by helplessly watching their entire rig sink into the lake. Not only did he have to probe for air pockets, he had to be careful the horses did not sweat. If they did, they would soon freeze to death.

On this first trip he had felt that his bones would snap from the cold. But it was out here in this vast wilderness of quiet and solitude that John felt an overwhelming peace deep in his soul.

When John arrived back home and before he could sit down to supper, Myrtle's only greeting was, "The first week you were gone a blizzard hit. For three days the wind blew, drifting snow around the cabin and nearly covered both the pig pen and the chicken house. By the time Bill made it over here he thought he would find Leta and I froze in our beds. It took all morning to clear paths to all the out buildings. The lantern in the chicken house had not went out but was almost out of coal oil. I'll have to have a bigger lantern." Somehow she had made it sound like John was to blame for the storm.

"I'll see to it you get a bigger lantern, Myrtle." Without further comment, John finished his supper in silence.

Chapter Thirteen

Three weeks after John's return, Leta began walking around the cabin without having to hang onto everything and anything she could reach. In the evenings he would try to get her to repeat words after him. Whenever he attempted to get Myrtle involved with the game, she snapped, "I have no time for such foolishness. If you just leave her be, she will be talking soon enough. You are just spoiling her."

December 4, 1904, dawned clear and cold. It was Leta's first birthday and Myrtle had not remembered. John knew she refused to recognize her own birthday, but he thought she would at least remember Leta's. Despite Myrtle's objections, John proudly presented the little doll he had brought back from the Cree village to Leta. "She's a child, Myrtle. She needs toys," John said gently. Without another word, Myrtle set her mouth in a firm line and began attacking her chores with a vengeance. *Sometimes I am not sure who I feel sorriest for, my little Leta or Myrtle*, John thought to himself as he bundled up to go out to begin his own chores.

A few weeks later John entered the cabin noisily stomping powdery snow off his feet. He had just returned from a short hunting trip with Bill. "Kate has asked us over for Christmas," he said, hanging up his heavy coat on the peg beside the door.

"Christmas is just another day and no sense in wasting time fussing over it," Myrtle said matter-of-factly, taking the biscuits out of the oven.

John's shoulders drooped a little in disappointment. "We haven't visited them in quite a while and they are family, Myrtle."

"There is too much to do around here to go off lollygagging," Myrtle said firmly.

Taking a deep breath, John said evenly, "I thought you would enjoy the day with Kate. You could take your handwork or that quilt you've been wantin' to finish. I know she would love to help you with it." For the life of him he did not figure Myrtle out. He had thought she would jump at the chance for some female company.

"You know I like Kate and Bill and enjoy their company, but I still think it is a day wasted," she returned stubbornly.

"Well then, if that is the way you feel I will take Leta and go myself. Kate was hurt when we did not come for Christmas last year and I will not disappoint her again." Myrtle knew John's mind was set and the issue was settled. They would all go.

On Christmas day the Oesch sleigh pulled up to the Brunner cabin. Kate ran out to meet them with a red knitted shawl wrapped around her shoulders. "I'm so glad you came," she said to Myrtle, taking Leta from John. The two women went inside as Bill and John led the team to the barn.

The two families sat down to a table overflowing with steaming food. Kate had roast goose with apple stuffing. Dinner included sweet yams, turnips, candied carrots, a large bowl of stewed cranberries with apple, and blueberry pies for dessert. Myrtle had brought fresh bread and rolls with a crock of fresh butter. She had put it in stone jars wrapped in wool cloth to keep it warm until they reached the Bruuner's.

Kate knew Myrtle was not happy about 'wasting the day', as she had put it, but hoped she would relax and enjoy herself. However, Myrtle just fussed about the chores at home. Work seemed more important to her than family. Bill, John, and Kate enjoyed their camaraderie and carefully skirted around Myrtle's prickly words. Kate knew Myrtle was an expert on tongue lashings and hoped John wouldn't get an earful when he got home.

John admired the way Kate always made her home warm and inviting. It wasn't just the blazing fire in the stone fireplace, or the gaily decorated tree that stood against the wall by the tiny window, or the many feminine touches sprinkled around the small cozy room. John knew it was Kate herself. She was, by nature, a warm and cheerful person. Puffing on his pipe, John smiled as he watched Leta and Ruby playing contentedly on the braided rug at their feet as he and Bill sat beside the fire in quiet companionship.

"I think it is time we started for home, John," Myrtle said hanging the dish towel on the back of a chair to dry. "We still have chores to do." Reluctant to leave their warm spot by the fire, the men went out to hitch up the cutter. John had bought it the week after he returned from his last trip to Green Lake. Even though it had needed a few repairs he felt it was a bargain. He had soon discovered it was impossible to get around in snow with a wagon and the large sleighs he used for freight were not built for passengers.

Myrtle wrapped the sleeping Leta in a thick quilt. Donning her own heavy wool coat, mittens, and low rubbers over heavy wool socks, she said a quick good-bye to Kate as John entered the cabin. "The team's hitched. Guess we best be on our way. Thanks again, Kate."

"You know you are all welcome anytime, John." Kate handed him the leftovers she had packed. "Come back soon."

Kate stood at the door, the red shawl wrapped tightly around her, watching John and Myrtle get settled in the cutter. John covered their laps with the steer hide then pointed the team toward their own homestead. Myrtle had warmed the stone for their feet on the stove. In the gathering twilight the snow illuminated the landscape in a phosphorescent glow. The wind was picking up and sleet stung their faces.

Man and wife rode along in silence, each submerged in private thoughts. John was basking in the warmth of family. Myrtle was bristling that John should have stayed so long with chores waiting to be done.

Chapter Fourteen

As his sole heir, Myrtle had inherited her father's homestead. As allowed by law, she could prove up on it herself. She would have to plant a crop and live on it six months out of the year. To make Allison's cabin livable for his family during the required six months, John shingled the roof, caulked and chinked all the cracks, and replaced the small air-tight heater with a cook stove. John and Myrtle agreed they would live on the Little Homestead from January to June each year. The remainder of the year would be spent on the Oesch Homestead.

A week after the sumptuous dinner at Bill and Kate's, Myrtle packed everything they would need in wooden crates for the move to the Little Homestead. Hitching the team to the stoneboat, John disassembled most of the flooring in their cabin, stacked it on the stoneboat along with the crates to transport all it to their home for the next six months. The flooring would be reassembled in Allison's old cabin. Within a day they were settled in the smaller cabin.

March came in like a lion. The cabin creaked and groaned against the relentless wind. Myrtle sat at the table mending one of John's shirts, her face pale and expressionless in the lamplight. She was terrified of the wind when it blew like this but she would never let on. John sat at the opposite end of the table repairing a harness. Watching Myrtle out of the corner of his eye, he knew she was afraid and wanted to assure her there was nothing to fear. But he knew better than to let her know he knew so he kept still. Setting the harness aside John picked up the small skis he was making for Leta.

"Why do you waste time on those when she's barely walking?" Myrtle said, not looking up from her sewing.

"She will be running all over the place by the time I get these done," John said, glancing up, waiting for a stinging reply. But there was only silence from his wife. The remainder of the evening was spent in strained silence.

The next morning, Myrtle woke with a start. Light flooded the small room. "John! Get up! I overslept!" Leaping out of bed, she threw on her robe and pulled on thick wool slippers.

John was up in an instant pulling on his overalls. "The wind has stopped," he said, listening. "I had better go check the stock first thing."

Before Myrtle had the fire blazing in the stove he was out the door. Opening the door to a blinding sunlight, Myrtle called after him, "I'll be over as soon as I get Leta ready."

"No, you'd best stay here with her. No telling what I'll find." John feared he would find nothing but frozen stock. For the last three days he could not even make it out the door let alone make the distance to his homestead. Praying the stock had survived, he trudged through the powdery glistening snow. The clear deep blue sky contrasted vividly against the sparkling thick white blanket that covered everything.

Coming out of the thick stand of timber that lay between the two homesteads, all John could see were huge mounds of snow. He knew the buildings lay beneath them. When he reached the barn he was relieved to find the snow only covered three sides. Quickly making his way inside his relief was doubled when one of the horses nickered a welcome, the pigs grunted and snorted, and the oxen stood switching their tails. The animals were thirsty, but otherwise had weathered the storm well. After breaking the ice in the outside trough with an ax and filling each water trough inside the barn, John forked hay to the horses, cows, and oxen as well giving each a ration of grain. *The pigs would have to make do with some grain also*, John thought to himself. *Myrtle could cook up some sour mash and peelings for them later.*

Making his way from the barn to the chicken house, John found it completely buried in snow. Digging a path to the door he hoped against hope that he would find the chickens still alive. When he pulled the door open, his heart fell. He saw that none of the chickens had survived. "Myrtle will not take this well," he muttered to himself as he began to haul the frozen poultry outside. "I will have to see if the Cabnaughs or the Schmitz' might have a few hens I can trade for."

Within a few days, John had most of the snow cleared from around all the buildings. Myrtle traded milk and potatoes for a few laying hens and a rooster. Fortunately, the remainder of their first winter in Allison's small cabin passed with no more big storms.

Winter slowly melted into spring. It was late May before the plowing and planting could begin. Their days were long and laborious. Myrtle tilled the garden with the hand cultivator keeping every row straight as an arrow. John plowed the fields with his team hitched to the heavy plow. As John hand broadcasted the seed grain in the newly plowed field, Myrtle planted vegetables in her large garden. At each end of her garden, Myrtle planted a variety of fragrant flowers to add color.

After two weeks of hard labor, the garden was planted and seeds were sown in the field. Supplies were low and it was time to make one of their rare trips into Shellbrook. The Cabnaughs would be going with them today so Myrtle packed a large picnic lunch for all of them. Mr. Cabnaugh had mentioned to John a few days earlier that his supplies were low also, so the two families had decided to make it a day. John knew that this would be the last leisurely day they would have until after the harvest in the fall.

The seven and one-half miles to Shellbrook seemed, to Myrtle, to take forever. *Oxen never walk*, she thought to herself, *they just plod*. But she understood with the extra weight of all the supplies and equipment that would be loaded into the wagon, it was these beasts of burden that were needed today.

As soon as they reached Shellbrook, the women went directly to the General Store to make their purchases. The men began selecting the necessary equipment and supplies. After everything had been purchased and packed into the wagon, John pointed the oxen toward home. About half way from Shellbrook they decided it was time to eat the lunch Myrtle had prepared. John turned the oxen off the road and down a steep hill to the river. Myrtle suddenly demanded, "Let me off! I'm not riding down there!"

"Now, Myrtle...," John began.

"Stop those stupid beasts and let me off!" she snapped.

Afraid she would start a row in front of the Cabnaughs, John stopped the oxen and Myrtle scrambled off the wagon.

"I think I will stretch my legs too," Mrs. Cabnaugh said handing Leta down to Myrtle. Giving her husband a quick smile and a wink, she climbed off the wagon.

"Here, I'll carry her down," Mrs. Cabnaugh said to Myrtle, taking Leta from her.

Tapping the oxen with a switch, John urged the oxen to continue down the short hill. It was steeper than it looked. John rode the brake trying to keep the wagon from rolling over the oxen, but it inched closer and closer to their hind quarters. Suddenly the two beasts bolted straight down the hill and didn't stop until they were at the rivers edge. All John and Mr. Cabnaugh could do was hang on as best they could.

"Stupid beasts!" John muttered as he climbed from the wagon.

"Well, that certainly was some ride," Mr. Cabnaugh said shakily, grinning as he shook his head in amazement. "Good thing the womenfolk got out. We would have never heard the end of it."

Chuckling, John said, "We probably won't hear the end of it anyway."

Watching the spectacle from the top of the hill both women sighed in relief when the oxen finally stopped and the wagon had not turned over. Mrs. Cabnaugh was grateful her husband was alright. Myrtle was grateful the supplies had not been thrown out and destroyed. As they descended the hill, Mrs. Cabnaugh asked Myrtle, "When are you due, my Dear?"

"How did you know?" Myrtle asked, surprised. She was still mad at John for, as she put it, "taking advantage" of her during the winter storms. It was no different than the first time.

"A woman knows when another woman is expecting."

"Before Christmas sometime, I think. I would appreciate it if you did not mention it around the men," Myrtle uttered. Mrs. Cabnaugh was puzzled but agreed to her request.

They all sat in the middle of a field blanketed with fragrant wildflowers, eating the picnic lunch Myrtle had packed in companionable silence. With chores waiting to be done, they were packed up and headed toward home in less than an hour.

As June turned to July, John and Myrtle had cleared another fifty acres. They would have more than one hundred acres in wheat this year. Again John used the oxen to pull the stumps and marveled at how strong they were. But beasts were often contrary and Myrtle would have to help him with them. The felled trees were stripped of their branches then hauled to the barn to use for buildings and fences. With a horse hitched to each end of a fifteen foot log, they pulled it horizontally over a cleared area, scraping the brush into a huge pile to burn.

When Myrtle wasn't helping John handle the oxen, she would drag and stack the larger branches in a pile to be cut up for firewood later. John offered to help her but she stubbornly refused. He did not know she was expecting their second child but he knew something was wrong. For the last few months she had been extremely irritable with him.

The glaring sun was dipping toward the horizon as John swung the team around to scrape another swath of brush. He looked up and saw three Mounties galloping across the field toward him.

"Whoa, whoa there." Pulling up the team, John took off his hat and wiped his brow on his sleeve as he watched the men in red coats approach. Myrtle had also seen them coming but did not pause in her work. She continued to drag a large branch toward the growing brush pile. Pushing it up on the top of the pile she dusted her gloved hands on her long dark skirt and walked over to where John stood greeting the Mounties.

"Good afternoon, Missus." the sergeant said, removing his hat as Myrtle approached.

"We've been over to that Russian settlement and thought we would stop by and see how you folks were doing. But we don't want to interrupt your work," the sergeant told them.

"It's time to quit for the day anyway. Be obliged if you would stay and have supper with us," John invited.

"Yes, please do," Myrtle agreed as she pulled off her gloves. "I believe there is some blueberry cobbler that needs to be eaten too," she said, smiling up at the Sergeant.

"Well now, it certainly would be a crime to let that go to waste," the Sergeant said dismounting. "Let us help you with that team, John."

Glancing in her direction as Myrtle made her way across the newly cleared field, it still amazed John how she would treat a stranger better than her own family.

Supper consisted of stew, biscuits, and blueberry cobbler. After they had all eaten their fill, Myrtle began stacking the dishes on the sideboard while Leta played contentedly in her crib.

"That was an excellent meal, Missus. Can't eat another bite," The Sergeant said as he pushed himself from the table. Lighting his pipe, he continued, "Those Dukabors are a strange lot indeed. They try to make us believe that it's their religion and all, but when we saw all those women and young girls hooked up to heavy plows like oxen, we let them know in short order that sort of thing will not be tolerated in Canada."

John looked stunned. "Women being used like oxen?"

The Sergeant went on. "The women were pulling those plows with thick sticks tied to the towlines that cut into their stomachs. You could see each one of them struggling against the towlines with sunburned hands, trying to lessen their pain. A man was guiding them into perfectly straight furrows. Well, needless to say we took care of it!" he finished angrily.

"You mean those women are no more than slaves?" Myrtle was shocked.

"They sure are. But I don't think they will be abusing their womenfolk in that way again," the Sergeant concluded.

"That group did seem a bit odd, but I had no idea they practiced such brutality," John commented. "I remember my brother-in-law, Bill, tried to buy a rooster from them one time. They had a yard full of them but refused to sell him one."

"They actually worship their animals." The youngest Mountie joined in. "All the horses were in the barn. Put up like Royalty. Never saw such fancy stalls. Anyway, we made them unhitch the women and hitch all their men folk to that plow. By the time they had finished the field, they didn't think it was such a good idea for the women to be pulling the plow anymore."

"Dukabors! We let them know that we would be checking on them on a regular basis to make sure of that," the third Mountie volunteered.

"Did some checking on them before we went out to their homestead," The Sergeant went on. "Seems they came from

Russia around 1899. They are fanatics. They were called an Anti-Christian religious sect exiled to the remote Caucasus Mountains in Russia. This was around 1843. They were always in trouble with the local authorities."

"So, they thought they would come to Canada to practice their religion," John said, shaking his head in amazement.

"I think they are learning the hard way that they will have to abide by our laws here," The Sergeant said tapping out his pipe.

Working quietly on some mending while the men talked, Myrtle looked up, "I think those men got off too easy. They all should have been horsewhipped," she snapped.

"Believe me, Missus, if we catch them doing that again they will be." The Sergeant stood. "We thank you for the excellent meal, but we must be going. There is still a lot of territory to cover before night sets in."

A few days after the Mounties visited, John plowed more garden for Myrtle before going out to plow the fields he and Myrtle had cleared earlier. She was already starting to set the seeds before he was done with the last furrow.

The black flies and mosquitoes were so thick again and they had to wear the cotton netting over their hats, tucking the ends into their collars. The annoying insects swarmed the oxen and twice they tried to get away from John but he stopped them before they broke away. He would have preferred using the horses to these ornery beasts, but oxen did not tire as easily as the horses. Plus there was a lot to be plowed, planted, and not much time to get it done.

Chapter Fifteen

All too soon, it was time to move back to the larger Oesch cabin. Taking up the floor, and packing the pots and pans, the bedding and their few clothes, John stacked it all on the stoneboat and hauled it to their cabin. Now that there was a good cookstove in each cabin, it was easier moving back and forth.

John and Myrtle had several head of cattle now. Shelters were built for the stock that would not be kept in the barn during the winter. John built a log frame then stacked bundles of straw on and around them. This would give the cattle shelter as well as something to eat. A large water tank was built in the pasture for the cattle. A cylinder-shaped water-tight heater, with a draft at the top so water wouldn't leak in, was put in the center of the water tank to keep it from freezing.

The chicken house had been enlarged to hold the forty laying hens. Myrtle had traded milk, eggs and vegetables to a neighbor for the needed chickens. She re-wrapped the roosts with clean rags and John built a heater to go under the dirt floor of the coop. When the dirt turned to mud in the winter, it would stay warm. The opening for the heater was outside the coop so it was easier for Myrtle to keep the fire going. One of the neighbors told Myrtle to cook peelings and feed it to the chickens. The warm food would help keep them from freezing and it would keep them laying all winter. She made sure there was always plenty of coal oil in the lantern hanging in the coop. She was determined not to lose any more chickens.

Also, an addition was built onto the ice house. Now there would be more room to put up the meat that would be butchered after the first hard freeze. Another corral was built and the pig pen divided so the boar and sow could be separated before the sow had her piglets.

As with all homesteading farmers, John and Myrtle each worked from dawn to dark every day. The time it took to go back and forth between two homesteads made their days even longer. And, in order to work on Sundays, they had to prove it was necessary or they would be fined. If a check was written on Sunday it was void. Even though John and Myrtle seldom attended the church services held in the one-room school house, the Sabbath in Canada was strictly observed. Myrtle made certain she could always prove it was necessary to continue their work on Sunday.

During the warmer months, smudge fires were kept burning constantly. Once a fire was burning, John piled green wood, leafy branches, and dry cow chips to keep it smoldering and smoking. The cattle stood in this smoke much of the time to relieve themselves of the biting insects. John would cut pea vine that grew in abundance at the edge of the brush and throw it out for the cattle to feed on. Myrtle had several buckets filled with oil soaked strips of wool she burned for smudge. These small smudge pots were placed around the garden and the cabin they now occupied.

It continued to amaze Myrtle how hot it could get in the short summer then turn so bitter cold during the long winter. The temperature ranged from sixty degrees below zero in the winter to occasionally one hundred and ten degrees above in the summer. The heat coupled with flies, mosquitoes and other insects, was at times, unbearable. On these hot days John and Myrtle were unable to toil in the fields a full day.

The chickens were laying nearly four dozen eggs a day now. Myrtle sold the extra eggs in Shellbrook for five cents a dozen. To preserve the eggs she kept them in a water glass. She mixed powdered gelatin with water to make a thick clear substance, placed the eggs in jars then poured the mixture over them. These eggs were used for baking only as they were not very tasty otherwise.

After working in the fields most of the day, John continued working long into the night mending harness, sharpening saws, and repairing the farm implements. When Myrtle finished her outside work for the day, she mended their clothes and cleaned and carded the wool that would later be made into quilts or twisted it into yarn to be knitted into socks, scarves, caps and mittens. Even though it was only the end of July, winter would be coming soon and there was still so much to be done.

July was blending into August and on this day Myrtle planned to go berry picking. Completing her morning chores as the sun was peeking over the wheat field, she was looking forward to this day and some female companionship. She would take the wagon and pick up Kate, Mrs. Bersinger, Mrs. Barkway, and Mrs. Cabnaugh. Myrtle had not seen these women in several weeks.

The team and wagon stood ready beside the cabin. After loading everything she would need into it, Myrtle sat Leta on the wagon seat beside the lunch basket, then settled herself beside them. She took up the reins and urged the horses to a brisk walk. Glancing down at her thickening waist she hoped the women would not notice her condition. Thus far she had kept it hidden from John. The long full apron she always wore concealed her figure but she was afraid Mrs. Bersinger would know. She always seemed to know when a woman was expecting, sometimes even before the woman herself knew. Mrs. Cabnaugh knew but she was sworn to secrecy. "Well, I will cross that bridge when I come to it," she muttered. "Everyone will know soon enough anyway."

As Myrtle drove out of the yard into the rising sun she felt a mixture of anxiety and anticipation. Leta's tiny face glowed with excitement. She loved riding in the wagon. And she loved the horses. Myrtle pulled the wide brim of her hat low on her brow in a futile attempt to shade her eyes from the rising sun.

A week after Myrtle and the other women had picked a wagon-full of berries, Myrtle finished putting up the last quart of blueberries. After covering the warm jars with a cloth, she put a bucket of water on the stove to heat for a bath. When the water was boiling, she poured it into the round galvanized tub beside the stove. After adding cold water to cool it she quickly bathed Leta and readied her for bed. John never came in until late evening, so she would have time for a bath herself before the water cooled too much.

Myrtle was standing nude in the tub pouring a pitcher of water over her body to rinse off the soap. Her heart froze and she stood still as a statue when the door opened and John stepped in the room. Seeing her extended belly and swollen breasts, John suddenly felt betrayed. Why had she not told him? Voice raised and brow furrowed he stepped closer to her, "Just how long did you think you would keep this hidden from me?" he said, more hurt than angry.

Grabbing a towel and quickly covering herself, Myrtle mumbled, her face crimson, "You are not supposed to be here yet." She had never exposed herself to her husband and most certainly had never planned to.

"Well?" In two strides he was beside the tub looking down at her. John kept his hands clenched at his sides as he didn't dare touch her. At this moment he feared for the baby more than for her. "You could have harmed the baby as well as yourself the way you've been working!"

"The work has to be done!" she said belligerently. Quickly recovering from her shock and embarrassment, "I wasn't trying to hide anything," she lied. "You see me every day. And how dare you come sneaking in on me like this!"

"You should have told me! This is my child too." Stepping back he muttered, "But then, babies aren't important to you are they."

"Well, it doesn't matter if they are or not, does it? I get them whether I want them or not!" Her tone and words cut through him like a knife. Angrily yanking her robe off the back of the chair she flung it around her as she stepped out of the tub, water pooling around her feet. "And don't you ever walk in on me like this again!"

Somehow, she had again succeeded in blaming him for everything. Without a word he picked up Leta, grabbed a quilt off the bed and stormed out the door. Despite the love he continually offered her, he swore Myrtle didn't have a heart at all. He did not know how anyone who looked so vulnerable and alluring could be so hard...so cold.

When John slammed the door Myrtle exploded. He could still hear her screaming when he reached the barn. He was sure that he heard something smashing against the door. He had never been this upset with Myrtle before. Silently Leta clung to her father, her eyes round as saucers. Her mother's angry outbursts always frightened her.

The plow had broken and John needed to go into Shellbrook to get it fixed and had planned to ask Myrtle to go along. Now he just wanted to get away from her. He was hurt, angry, and bewildered. Wrapping the quilt around Leta, face grim, he climbed on the wagon, released the brake, and tapped the rumps of the horses with the end of the reins. They started off at a brisk trot toward Shellbrook, the smoldering smudge pail swinging from the wagon tongue.

As Myrtle watched the wagon disappear down the lane she was nearly turning inside out with rage. "How dare he just walk out on me like that! With all this work to be done he goes off and leaves it all to me!" Turning from the window her face nearly purple with rage, her eyes narrowed as she stormed, "You will pay for this John Oesch! You will pay!" Chaotically throwing on her clothes she stormed out the door.

Working the remainder of the evening in the garden, Myrtle hacked and chopped weeds with a vengeance. She ignored the flies and heat as the sweat poured off her. But as twilight turned to night she began to wear out physically and her anger finally began to dissipate. Every now and then she would look up to see if the wagon was coming. She began to get anxious. She could not work this land alone. She wished she did not need a man for anything. This was her land and she would not give it up. But in order to keep it, she needed John.

Looking out over the horizon, Myrtle leaned on her hoe, "Surely John would not leave me in this condition. He will be back...surely he will be back." She muttered as she walked slowly toward the barn.

She fed the chickens and pigs, milked both cows and turned them out to pasture. Her body ached with fatigue. Her anxiety increased with each passing hour. Without pausing in her labors, she began preparing supper. "He will be back. He has to come back," pushing the fear down that was nearly choking her.

The evening star twinkled in a navy blue sky. A sliver of moon balanced on the tops of the timber that fringed the horizon. Myrtle heard the wagon approaching the cabin and quickly stirred up the biscuit dough. Just as John carried sleeping, dirty-faced, Leta into the cabin, Myrtle shoved the biscuits in the oven. Laying Leta upon her tiny bed, John turned to Myrtle and looked into her cold, unforgiving, gray eyes.

"I'm sorry about this afternoon, Myrtle," John spoke softly. He had made up his mind to make peace. "This is a hard country and I know it is not easy for you. You are right, I should have noticed about the baby."

His apology surprised her. "Supper is almost ready." Her tone remained cold. She was unable to let him know how relieved she was he was back.

"I'll just put up the team." He did not know if she accepted his apology or not. His heart was heavy as he tended the horses and stoked the smudge fires in the pasture and around the barn. Rubbing the back of his aching neck, he walked slowly toward the cabin. Lamplight glowing from the windows, the tiny cabin looked warm and inviting from the outside. But on the inside John knew it was as cold as a winter day. It was hard enough to survive in this wild country and of all the hard days of his life, he thought this was the worst. "Myrtle and I do not need to be at odds with one another," he muttered. His shoulders sagged as he knew the burden of keeping the peace would fall on him. If only he could figure out how to keep the peace.

Chapter Sixteen

The root cellar overflowed with the fall harvest of produce from the garden. Jars of canned gooseberries, blueberries, cranberries, choke cherries, and pin cherries were stored along with the potatoes, beets, turnips, cabbage, carrots, and the sauerkraut Myrtle had canned in the spring. The threshing crew had come and gone. They'd had a fine crop this year. The cattle were already beginning to eat their way around the huge mound of straw that had been blown out into the pasture by the threshing machine. By this time Myrtle was heavy with child.

The Oeschs attended the fall dance at the school house again this year, but this time Myrtle did not dance. With her baby due in a few weeks, Myrtle knew it was not proper in her condition. Tapping her foot as she sat, she sewed with the other women who were also expecting, watching couples swinging and swaying around the dance floor. John sat out all the dances along with the older men.

When the sun began to rise over the timber, all the families packed up and went to their respective homesteads.

John did not plan to go on his winter freighting trip to Green Lake until after Thanksgiving. He hoped the baby would be born before then. The ground was frozen solid now and it was time to go hunting. He hoped to get both elk and moose this year. The chickens as well as the pig John and Myrtle had butchered were frozen in the ice house but he wanted it filled with meat before spring.

Both John and Bill were successful on their hunting trip. Each had killed an elk and a moose. After cutting up the meat, John and Myrtle spread it out in the snow to freeze solid, then they packed it in a box, covered it with fresh snow, and stacked it in the ice house. The hides were nailed to the side of the barn and stretched out to dry for tanning later. The hair would be scraped off and the tanned hide would be made into leather.

Winter was nearly as busy as summer for the Oeschs. The fires in the heaters under the chicken house and in the watering trough for the cattle had to be filled with wood twice each day. As the cattle ate around the straw pile in the pasture, it began to look like a gigantic mushroom. They would keep circling it to stay out of the bitter wind as they ate. The wood shed and porch as well as the lean-to on the barn were stacked full of fire-wood. John had built a corral and small shed on the Little homestead that would serve as a barn. It had not been easy, but they were ready for another long, cold winter.

The snow was falling softly from a black sky. As the flakes piled silently upon the roof, Myrtle uttered through clenched teeth, "John! John!" This time Myrtle knew what to expect and had had plenty of warning. She had been in labor most of the night, but now the pains were getting harder and closer together. He woke with a start. She was at the table half bent over with the pain. In an instant he was up, had his pants on and was guiding her to the bed.

"I'll get Granny McTaggart. You just hang on." He was afraid she would have the baby before he could get back.

"Take Leta." The pain eased as she lay back on the bed.

Quickly bundling up himself and his sleeping daughter, he was out the door. Taking no time to hitch the cutter, he threw a bridle on one of the horses. Clutching Leta in one arm he rode off bareback at a gallop with clods of snow flying from the horse's hooves.

John stopped just long enough at Kate's to tell her the baby was coming and leave Leta with her. Kate called after him as he thundered out of the yard. "Hurry, John. Bill will watch the children. I will go be with Myrtle."

Several hours later a second healthy girl was born to the Oeschs. She was round, red as a beet, and squalling her lungs out. John documented the event in the family Bible, "Born to John Oesch and Myrtle Grace Little Oesch, a girl, Leila Evelyn Oesch, November 16, 1905."

After nursing the newborn a few minutes, Myrtle slept while Kate rocked the baby to quiet her. Kate was still rocking the sleeping baby when Bill came in with the children. The commotion woke the baby and she started to cry. "I'll go out and help John with his chores," Bill said to Kate as he helped Ruby and Leta off with their coats. Leta, now almost two years old, did not quite know what to make of this noisy little creature as she cautiously approached Aunt Kate and the squirming bundle she held in her arms.

Two days after Thanksgiving, John left for Green Lake. There had been no Thanksgiving celebration at the Oesch house. John would have enjoyed keeping the American tradition, but Myrtle still would not celebrate Thanksgiving or Christmas.

It took three days to travel to Prince Albert for the supplies. The weather turned brutal. It was another three days back home. Spending one night at home John started out for Green Lake well before dawn. Even though these trips were hazardous, he preferred them to working with the Prince Albert Lumber Company where many men labored during the winter to supplement their incomes. He would be gone a little over two weeks and had asked Bill to tend to his stock again. John appreciated the fact that Kate would be going with Bill this time to help Myrtle with the two girls.

A few days after Christmas a group of Mounties stopped for the night at the Oesch cabin. It had become a regular stop now for them on their way North. Saskatchewan had become a Province earlier in the year. With a population increase of 440% in just ten years, the Mounties were kept very busy. It never ceased to amaze John what a gracious hostess Myrtle could be to visitors. She was so stern and cranky with him and Leta but never in front of company. When the Mounties stopped over, she was always polite, a little cool at times, but polite nonetheless.

After their callers finished the huge meal Myrtle had prepared for them she retired to the bedroom with the girls leaving the main room to the men. She had made certain that none of the Mounties fed Leta this time so she wouldn't overeat and aggravate her dropsy. "I will see to the fire, Myrtle," John told her as she readied the children for bed. He knew she would not, 'parade' as she called it, in her nightclothes in front of strangers to stoke the fire during the night. When the men settled down for the night the room was wall to wall bedrolls.

On a clear cold day in January the Oeschs moved back to the Little homestead. Before bringing Myrtle and the girls over, John lit a fire in the stove to warm the small cabin. Bringing Leta's small crib for Leila, he placed it against the wall next to the stove. Allison's old cot was set up for Leta. The double iron bed was pushed against the opposite wall. It was crowded but they would manage fine. "At least this cabin is snug and not so drafty as most," John mused.

Within a few hours the Oeschs were settled in the smaller cabin. Myrtle had stew cooking on the small stove and biscuits baking in the oven. Tomorrow was wash day and she hoped the weather stayed clear enough to hang it out.

The next morning icicles clung to the edge of the cabin roof making a solid translucent wall of ice from the eves to the ground. Myrtle did not take notice of the snow sculptures the bitter cold wind had formed, nor how the brilliant sun made the snow sparkle like millions of tiny diamonds as she built a fire in the yard for the wash boiler. She hung the boiler on the iron frame John had made, suspending it above the flames. Quickly filling the boiler with snow, she sat the wash tub on a block of wood next to the fire. She poured boiling water from the boiler into the tub and refilled the boiler with snow.

As Myrtle labored over the washboard she could hear Leila squalling loudly through the cabin wall. This could be the last clear day they would have for the rest of the winter and Myrtle was not going to waste any of it trying to quiet a fussy baby.

During the long winter days John and Myrtle tended to their chores making the daily trip between the two homesteads. On the days that John needed Myrtle to help him, Leta was still left anchored to the table leg by her dress tail and Leila was left in her crib. John was thankful that he had the corral and shed built on the Little homestead. Instead of plowing through the snow on foot each day, John would now hitch up the sled and cover the distance between the two homesteads in no time.

It was nearly mid-June when the snow began making a slow retreat, and the ground began softening enough to start the spring plowing. John planned to clear more acreage on both sections to plant wheat, barley, and rye this year. While John labored in the fields, Myrtle canned the vegetables that were left over in the root cellar as well as the meat in the ice house before it thawed.

She was proud of her canned venison and it secretly pleased her that John always complemented her on it. She cut the venison into small pieces, seared it in a little lard, packed it in jars then poured the broth over it. Carefully placing the venison packed jars in the wash boiler and covering them with the lid, they were left to boil for three hours. Packed in its own juice the meat was tender and very tasty.

Chapter Seventeen

John loaded the last gunny sack of seed potatoes on the wagon glancing up at the overcast sky. "Sure hope the rain holds off."

"It's going to take all day to get these planted as it is." Myrtle climbed on the back of the wagon with Leila, wrapped tightly in a small quilt, in one arm. Leta ran to her father, the little bell tied on her back jangling loudly. She had soon discovered her freedom when outdoors and would wander off. To keep track of her, Myrtle tied a small bell around her neck. But that proved to be useless. Leta learned quickly to hold the clapper so the bell wouldn't ring. After searching for her for hours one afternoon, Myrtle had given her daughter a sound spanking and tied the bell on her back out of her reach.

Reaching down, John scooped her up and gently sat her on the wagon seat handing her one rein. "There you go Little One. Now you hold the horses for Papa," he said, giving her a wink. Leta looked so tiny and serious perched on the high wagon seat holding tightly to the rein, John smiled as he climbed up beside her. "You want to help drive the team?" he asked as he sat her on his knee. Her face beamed. A tiny smile played on her lips.

"She can set on the seat. You don't need to be coddling her. You will spoil her yet," Myrtle snapped in irritation.

"You know Myrtle, a little spoiling will not hurt her," he said quietly, pulling the brake off and snapping the reins lightly on the horse's rumps. Leta clung to the end of her rein, the smile gone from her face, replaced with a serious look of concentration. Man and wife rode the distance to the potato field in silence.

The sky began to clear. The wind came up blowing dust devils across the plowed field. Starting at opposite ends of the field, John and Myrtle began planting the seed potatoes. Leta played quietly at the edge of the field. Leila slept on a sack of seed potatoes beside the wagon where Myrtle had laid her. The tinkling of Leta's bell let her parents know where she was without looking up from their labor. Finishing the second row, Myrtle went to the wagon for another sack of seed potatoes. As she approached the wagon her heart froze. Leila and the sack of seed potatoes she was sleeping on were gone. Leta was picking tiny wildflowers several feet away.

"John! The baby is gone!" Myrtle screamed. Dropping his sack of seed potatoes, John ran across the field toward Myrtle.

"Did you see anything? Hear anything?" he asked, his heart pounding.

Myrtle shook her head. "She was on the sack and it's gone too." The cold fear she felt in her heart was not reflected in her face.

John went over to Leta. "Did you see anything around the baby, Little One?" he asked gently, not wanting to frighten her.

"What good is it asking her! She can't talk." Myrtle was almost screeching. "Whatever it was has probably eaten Leila by now!"

"She would talk if you gave her a chance, Myrtle." He picked Leta up and put her on his shoulders. "Come on. We'll find the baby."

Staying several feet apart, they started searching, both afraid they would only find animal-torn remains. They had heard stories of wolves or coyotes carrying babies off and eating them. John did not believe them but Myrtle did. Finding nothing in the tall grass around the field, they started toward the cabin. Still walking slowly, Myrtle went around the back of the cabin while John continued on to the barn. As Myrtle came around the chicken house she heard John yell.

"Over here, Myrtle. Here she is!" She ran to the barn, her heart racing. Rounding the corner of the barn, Myrtle stopped dead in her tracks. The old sow was snuffling in the dirt a few feet from the sack of seed potatoes. Leila was still sleeping peacefully on it. Neither potatoes nor child had been harmed.

"Looks like the old girl was trying to drag it all the way to her pen," John chuckled. Picking up a stick he thumped the pig on the back. "Go on! Get! Get!"

Picking up Leila, Myrtle snapped, "You need to keep that sow in her pen!"

"You stay with your mother." Setting Leta on the ground, he slung the full sack over his shoulder and herded the sow toward her pen. Relieved, Myrtle went back to the field to finish planting her row of potatoes, Leta following closely behind. Laying the baby at the edge of the field, still tightly wrapped in her quilt, Myrtle gave Leta strict orders to stay with her sister. As Myrtle walked away Leta looked after her mother with large solemn eyes. She sat quietly on the grass beside the little bundle gently patting her sister.

When the potato patch was planted it was time to move back to the Oesch homestead. Here John would let Leta follow him to the barn so she could help do the chores. He would sit her on the big Belgian horse while he brushed it down after a long day. When he was finished, he would hand her the brush so she could do the wide back of the huge horse. Holding the brush with both hands she scrubbed more than brushed the broad back, but the gentle giant did not mind. He seemed to relish the extra attention. When John lifted her from the horse he always told her, "Fine job, Leta, fine job, indeed." Her father always made her feel special.

It had turned out the little gray mare that Allison had bought for Leta had been too spirited. When he was offered $300.00 for the mare, John sold her and bought the Belgian team. Now he had some horses he could really work with. With the remainder of the money he bought Leta a gentle older mare they called Old Nell.

Summer quickly turned to fall. The fields were harvested and vegetables from the garden were picked and stored in the root cellar. Berries were made into jams and jellies. And with the first hard freeze pigs and chickens were butchered, frozen, and stored in the ice house. Dirt and sand was banked up around the house. They were ready for whatever winter would bring.

Myrtle had soon learned that many foods were scarce in this Northern wilderness and had to be substituted for. The women in the area gladly shared their creative secrets with each other. Myrtle was surprised at some and was sure they would taste terrible, but was even more surprised when she could hardly tell the genuine from the imitation.

Crushed crackers in vinegar stood in for stewed apples, sour milk replaced sweet, parched rye or corn replaced coffee, and wild grapes were dried for raisins. Myrtle soaked potatoes in vinegar to make a tasty mock apple pie filling. She used sour green tomatoes or pumpkin in vinegar to make mincemeat pie. Many of the homesteaders used egg-white - they called this whey - in their coffee or tea when they had no milk. Women also learned to brew an imitation butter from the broth of caribou horns. The horns would be boiled for two nights then dunked in the snow to congeal the fat.

John and Myrtle knew in order to survive in this harsh, unforgiving land, food preservation was vital. Information was shared freely among the pioneers as to what method was best. Everything was used, nothing was ever wasted, not even the smallest piece of string. Vinegar, burlap sacks, and ashes had many uses. Salt and pepper warded off flies from wrapped meat for several days. Sometimes Myrtle wrapped meat in a piece of cloth, and laid it in a charcoal bin, then covered it with a shovel of coal. Or she would dip a cloth in vinegar and wrap it tightly around the meat which would keep it fresh for several days. Hams were tightly sewn up in coarse cloth or stiff brown paper and packed in cold ashes.

This year, winter settled in so quickly Myrtle barely had time to get the last of the produce out of the garden before it was covered with several inches of snow. John had been gone for three weeks, much longer than his normal freighting trips and Myrtle was getting anxious. Her thoughts ran wild as she scrubbed the floor. *What if he has frozen to death...what if he has fallen into an icy lake...if something happens to John, I will lose everything.*

A knock at the door startled her out of her morbid thoughts. Quickly getting to her feet and drying her hands on her apron she opened the door and was surprised to see Angus McPhearson standing there alone. His hat was in his hands.

Inviting him in, Myrtle poured him a steaming mug of coffee. "Everything alright at your place, Angus," she asked haltingly.

"The loss of our wee one has left the house a bit empty." Angus slowly turned his steaming cup on the table. "And the Missus was wondering, well, we were wondering if you might spare your Leta to come spend some time with us. It sure would help fill the empty place in our hearts left there by the passing of our firstborn. We wouldn't keep her long mind you, just until the spring. The wee one would sure help ease our loss. I know tis' askin' a lot..."

"Of course she can go with you, Angus. I will pack her things now." Myrtle knew John would not agree with her decision, but John was not here, Myrtle reasoned.

As Angus drove off with Leta in his small sleigh, she sat beside the big man wide eyed with excitement and confusion. She loved to ride in the sleigh, but why wasn't her mother coming?

Two days later John came home caked with snow and ice. It had been the most difficult trip he had made to the Green Lake District. He was thankful to be home. When he found Leta gone, he was hurt and disappointed. She was the bright light of his life. But to keep the peace, he said nothing when Myrtle told him Leta would be gone until spring. He knew Myrtle would have her own way regardless of how he felt.

John knew the McPhearsons were good people. Angus thought Leta was the sunshine in spring. And Leta liked them both. John knew she would be all right. He also knew he would miss her very much.

"Then I will be going over every Sunday afternoon to see her," John told Myrtle.

"There is no sense in wasting a day going over there to check on her when you know she is fine," Myrtle snapped defensively. "I explained to Angus about her dropsy and not to let her eat too much at one time. She will be fine."

"Myrtle, I am not worried about the dropsy. I know the McPhearsons will take good care of her. I just do not want her thinking we gave her away like a kitten or a puppy. I want her to know that when the snow melts, I will bring her back home."

It was the longest winter ever for John. He knew he would miss his little Leta, but he never knew how much until she was gone. Leila was constantly fussy and demanding. When Leila was left anchored by her dress tail under the table leg while Myrtle did her outside chores, she didn't begin to fuss until someone came in. Leila learned at an early age that you needed an audience to play to.

With the first sign of spring, John was on his way to Angus McPhearson's. Keeping the team at a brisk walk, he was anxious to bring Leta home. With the warm sun on his face and the cold wind at his back, he leaned back on the seat with a foot propped next to the brake. At times like this, he felt a deep peace and a oneness with the land. He had not felt this good in a long time. It was good to have a day to oneself...especially on a beautiful day like this. He enjoyed the solitude on his trips to Green Lake, but with the bitter cold and constant danger, he had to remain alert. But today he could just relax and dream a little.

In all the weeks that had passed, Myrtle had not once gone with John to see Leta. Every Sunday as he prepared to leave he would ask her if she wanted to go with him, but she always refused and would start harping on all the work that had to be done. Quietly ignoring her sharp tongue he told her the work could wait for one day. He had made a promise to Leta. And John Oesch always kept his word.

Pulling the sleigh to a stop in their yard, John smiled at Mrs. McPhearson waiting on the porch with Angus beside her, holding Leta in one large arm, the other around his wife's shoulders. As they watched John approach, they felt a little tug at their hearts. In the few months Leta had been with them she had certainly wrapped herself around their hearts. They would miss her. As soon as Angus set Leta down, she ran to her father. He scooped her up swinging her high into the air, setting her on his shoulders.

"Come in for a bite and warm yourself, John," Mrs. McPhearson invited. "Angus will take care of your team."

During their meal, Angus chuckled as he told John about Leta asking when they were going to quit having so many lunches and have a meal.

"She talked to you!" John was amazed. "She actually talked to you!"

"Why yes. She has been just a little chatter box." Mrs. McPhearson smiled at Leta. "She has been such a help. In more ways than one."

"Aye. Tis' the wee one that filled our hearts this cold winter. We are missin' her already," Angus said.

"She has never talked at home. We thought that maybe something was wrong." John lifted Leta onto his lap. "Well, how about that." He gave her a big hug as she buried her face in his neck. "Angus, I guess you had better come over and get some of our potatoes so you can have a meal," John chuckled.

Having eaten his fill, John pushed himself away from the table. "I thank you both for taking such good care of her. We had better be on our way."

"Let me wrap up some cookies for you to take along with you," Mrs. McPhearson said, rising from the table.

As John shrugged into his coat Mrs. McPhearson bundled Leta up. Angus brought John's team and sleigh from the barn. "We will miss you, Leta." Mrs. McPhearson said, giving her a hug. "You come back and see us soon."

John promised he would bring Leta back to visit as often as he could. Laying his arm around his wife, Angus confided to John that they now had another wee one on the way. Mrs. McPhearson blushed slightly as she smiled up at her husband. John felt a twinge of envy as he drove away. It was obvious the McPhearsons shared a wonderful loving relationship. "If only Myrtle and I could be that close," he muttered to himself.

On the way home Leta snuggled close to her father. She had missed him very much. Wrapping one arm around her as he drove the team he said, "Did you miss your Papa, Little One?" Not saying a word, she hid her face in his thick coat. Her silence puzzled him. But he wouldn't push her; she would talk to him when she was ready. "Well, how about eating one of those cookies?" Leta smiled up at him, her big blue eyes sparkling as she dug into the cloth bag, pulled out a large oatmeal cookie and handing it to him. Taking the offered cookie, John pulled her cap down farther covering her honey colored hair, giving her a wink. It was growing colder and even though she was bundled up in her long wool coat, he protectively tucked the quilt around her.

John pulled the team to a halt in front of the cabin and lifted the now sleeping Leta off the seat. A lantern hung on the porch glowing dimly in the twilight. When he stepped on the porch, Myrtle opened the door for him to carry Leta on inside. "You should have waited until we moved back to the bigger cabin to bring her home. I'm sure the McPhearsons would not have minded keeping her a bit longer. Now I will have both the girls underfoot all the time," Myrtle complained.

The smell of stew simmering on the stove filled the crowded room. "Now, Myrtle, we have been over that before. She belongs here at home. I made her a promise and I will not break a promise," John said evenly. He gently laid the sleeping Leta on the cot, and without another word turned and went out to put up the team. Irritated, Myrtle removed Leta's clothes and tucked her into bed. Leila squirmed and whimpered in the crib but didn't waken. With both girls asleep Myrtle returned to her mending. John could dish up his own meal when he finished his chores, she thought angrily.

When John came in he washed up, then helped himself to a large portion of stew. As he ate he told Myrtle what Leta had said to the McPhearsons about the potatoes, trying to smooth her ruffled feathers. In spite of herself, Myrtle laughed. "If I didn't know them all so well I would say you were making up this story."

A few days later Leta was in the barn, perched on a pile of straw watching her father replace a shoe on one of the oxen. He didn't realize that he had moved a little too close to one of the horse stalls. When Leta saw the horse start to kick him, she yelled, "John!"

Her voice startled him and he moved quickly out of harm's way, the horse barely missing its mark. "You saved your Papa for sure, Little One," he said smiling at her.

After that episode, she would talk a mile a minute to her father. She was asking questions faster than he could answer them. He would chuckle and tell her to slow down a little so he could catch up. He would patiently answer every question to the best of her understanding. But when she was around her mother, she barely spoke, if at all.

Leta was her father's shadow while he was doing chores close to the house. Where he went, she went. He would set her up on Old Nell in the corral while he fed the other stock. She would hang on to the mane kicking her short legs trying to get the mare to go. He would also let Leta help with the chores he felt she could handle. She had tried to help her mother with the chickens once, but Myrtle was afraid she would just break the eggs and scare the chickens. So Myrtle put an end to that.

Whenever Myrtle would discourage Leta in a task, John would encourage her. But never within sight or hearing of Myrtle. Leta showed a knack and a great desire to learn everything and he did not want her to ever lose that desire.

Chapter Eighteen

The years were passing quickly. The Territory was growing by leaps and bounds. A young man from Scotland was now living on the section to the north of the Oeach's. The property had once belonged to Ann Marguerite Anderson, a Metis widow. She sold it to another widow, Mrs. Renner from whom Scotty purchased the property. At eighteen, Scotty was disinherited by his wealthy family because, it seemed, he was uncontrollable. "A bit more than on the wild side," so the story went. He was given the choice of going to Australia or Canada. Many times in the early days, John was sure Scotty had wished he had chosen Australia. Canada was not a place for the weak or foolhardy. John liked the young man and was thankful to have another place he could find shelter on his long trips to Green Lake.

The New Year had barely begun when John left for Green Lake. Hoping to make it to the Reservation and back while the weather still held, he left a month later than usual. As soon as the supplies were unloaded at the Reservation, John turned his teams toward home.

Progressing slowly, John carefully cleared snow from the ice with a large sleigh stake checking for air pockets. The horses followed so close behind him there was no need to lead them. The temperature was falling rapidly. "It must be sixty degrees below zero or more. If the wind picks up we will have to find shelter," he said to the big mare. Even at this snail's pace, traveling on the lakes was faster than trying to make his way through the thick timber.

Suddenly the lead team balked. The rear team crowded against the sleigh in front. Taking hold of the halter, John spoke with calm and quiet to his horses, "Whoa. Whoa there. Easy now. Easy old girl." John gripped the halter tighter as the horse tried to lunge. "Easy girl." Eyes rolling, ears forward, nostrils flaring, steam billowing through the wool that covered their noses, the frightened horses would balk then try to run. The rear team pushing against the sleigh in front of them frightened the lead team even more. Keeping his grip on the lead horse, afraid they were going to break into a sweat, he prayed that the rear team didn't break loose.

Then he saw them. A pair of wolves circling the sleighs. Fear caught in his throat. "Why didn't I think of bringing the gun?" he said, waving the stake at the wolves as they circled closer. Keeping a tight grip on the mare's halter with one hand and gripping the stake with the other, John knew he could keep the wolves off the lead team, but he could not protect the rear team should the wolves attack them. It wasn't far to Scotty's. If only he could make it. Watching for air pockets and keeping an eye on the circling wolves as well as trying to calm the horses was quickly sapping his strength.

It was nearly dark when John saw the tiny cabin. Scotty was coming toward him, rifle in hand. Suddenly the wolves disappeared into the timber. "Saw ya comin' and that ya were having a bit of trouble," Scotty said, taking hold of the rear team's lead rope.

Scotty helped John unhitch and hobble the teams under the lean-to. The horses wouldn't range far from the cabin with the wolves roaming around. After putting enough hay out to last them the night, the two men headed for the tiny, but cozy cabin. The warmth felt good to John as he shucked his heavy coat. His wool shirt was damp from perspiration. When Scotty shed his coat John noticed Scotty was thin as a rail.

"You been sick, son?" he asked.

"Tis' starvin' I am. Don't know the first thing 'bout cookin' a meal," he admitted, embarrassed. "Tried to make the biscuit, but..."

"Well, I can show you how. We've got to get some meat on your bones or the wolves won't even have you." John patted him on the angular shoulder then went out to bring in some of his provisions. He put the remainder of his beans on the stove to thaw and as he mixed up the biscuits he began explaining to Scotty exactly how it was done. As John spoke, Scotty carefully wrote the instructions down.

"These are called Bachelor's Biscuits. You mix 1 quart of flour, 2 teaspoons tartar, 3/4 tablespoons soda, add some sweet milk to wet up the flour to the consistency of biscuit dough." He patiently continued, "Rub the flour and cream of tartar well together, dissolve soda in milk, wetting up flour with it and bake immediately. If you have no milk use water in its place. Add a spoon of lard for richness. Bake them until the tops are brown," John finished as he slid the pan in the oven. Scotty was so hungry by this time that he was pulling them out of the oven and trying to eat them before they were done.

Early the next morning as John prepared to leave for home he asked Scotty, "Are you sure you can make it, son?"

"Aye. I can make the biscuit now," Scotty replied with a grin. "You best take this along," he said, handing the gun to John.

"I'll bring it back the next time I come up and some of Myrtle's recipes so you can fix yourself some real food." John said waving a good bye as the team headed for home.

It was late afternoon when John pulled his teams to a stop beside the barn. He was weary to the soul and chilled to the bone. All he could think of was a warm hearth and a hot meal. But his horses must be tended to first.

Stomping the powdery snow from his feet and brushing it from his shoulders before entering the house John was surprised to find the neighbor's 12 year old daughter sitting at the kitchen table crying. His own daughters stood trembling in the corner, eyes as round as saucers with fright.

"Papa...," Leta began.

"Leta, hush!" Myrtle snapped.

"What is going on here?" John asked, alarmed.

"Girls, get upstairs." Myrtle ordered. The Oesch family had outgrown the tiny cabin and John had built a small frame house for Myrtle the previous summer with a room over the kitchen for Leta and Leila.

Without uttering a sound the two girls scampered up the stairs to their room. Not quite disobeying their mother they stopped at the top of the stairs to listen. They had never had so much commotion in their house before.

Maintaining outward calm, John took off his coat and hung it on the peg beside the door.

"Tell him what happened, Ione." Myrtle said without emotion.

"He...he tried to...to..." Ione sobbed, tears streaming down her face. "I had to hit him with the iron skillet to get him off me and then he chased me around the table." Struggling for control she continued, "Every time my mother was out at the barn, he would start after me." Looking at Myrtle, tears flooding her eyes again, "I screamed and screamed but my mother didn't hear me." Looking from Myrtle to John, she asked, "Why didn't she hear me?"

"The man is an animal." Myrtle spat. "John, you have to take care of this." It was an order not a request.

"Did he harm you, girl?" The deep sadness in her eyes struck a chord in John's heart. He knew her stepfather was a drinker and had a vile disposition but was shocked at what she was telling them. No man had a right to force himself on a woman let alone a young girl. He wanted to horse whip the man.

Shaking her head, voice quivering, "I will not go back. I will not. Please don't try to make me."

"What can we do, John? We can't let her go back to that."

"We will have to report this to the Mounties. I am sure they will take care of him." John continued quietly, "You will have to tell them everything you told us. Can you do that?" Ione nodded, sniffling.

"We will take care of it first thing in the morning. You can sleep with Leta tonight, girl. But first we best get some hot food into you." John's words seemed to calm her. "You go upstairs and tell Leta and Leila to come down and wash up for supper."

The next morning John took Ione to report the incident to the Mounties. When they returned, Ione's mother was waiting in the house with Myrtle. Both women had the look of determination on their faces, but each for a different reason.

"You have to come home, Ione. You can not stay here. You are needed at home," her mother insisted.

With the Oeschs standing beside her it gave her the courage to tell her mother, "If you make me go back home, the Mounties said I can have him publicly horsewhipped."

Not wanting to risk public humiliation for her husband's actions, Ione's mother said quietly, "There will be no need for that. You can stay with the Oeschs for a time, Ione. But mind you, this is only temporary."

To Myrtle's delight, Ione proved to be a hard worker. At twelve she could cook, sew, make soap, butcher, and clean chickens almost as well as Myrtle. Preferring to work outside herself, Myrtle put Ione in charge of the household chores as well as keeping an eye on Leta and Leila. She had come to the Oesch place with only the clothes on her back and her old dog and pup that had followed her.

Ione had been with the Oesch family two years and as one day flowed into another, Leta had become her shadow. To Leta's delight Ione did not seem to mind a bit. In the evenings when all the chores were done and the girls retired upstairs to their room, Ione taught Leta how to do embroidery with plain thread and how to knit with store string. Leta learned quickly and loved doing what she called her 'fancy work'. However, she had to keep it hidden from her mother as Myrtle felt that anything that did not have a practical purpose was useless and a waste of time.

It was Leta's job to bring in the cows each evening for her mother to milk. On occasion, if her own work was caught up,

Ione would go with Leta. John would saddle two ponies for them and watched from the barn as they trotted into the timber, Old Dog and her pup following behind Ione's pony. Both girls were bundled up in thick wool coats, caps and mittens, resembling small bears perched atop their respective ponies.

As dusk began falling, John became concerned that the girls might not be back before dark. Before he could get his horse saddled to go look for them, he saw them racing out of the timber toward him. There was no sign of the dogs. Pulling their horses to a sliding stop beside him, both girls jumped down and simultaneously began jabbering excitedly.

"We couldn't find the cows and it jumped out and attacked Old Dog and..."

"Whoa there, girls. One at a time."

"It got Old Dog, Papa," Leta said tearfully.

"It was a big coyote. It started after us and Old Dog attacked it," Ione said, trying to catch her breath. "Sorry about the cows. We looked and looked but the coyote..."

"I'll get my gun and go see about Old Dog. You girls take care of your ponies and tell Myrtle I will be back with the cows." As John rode off he could picture the terrified girls maneuvering their horses out of the thick timber as quickly as they could then racing for home as soon as they reached the open. He was concerned the coyote might be rabid.

He found Old Dog limping toward home and no sign of the coyote. Quickly scouting the area, he found the cows unharmed, contentedly munching tall grass in a small meadow. Herding them toward home he made a mental note to watch

Old Dog for signs of rabies. In the weeks that followed everyone was relieved that Old Dog showed no signs of the dreaded disease and seemed to mend well.

John continued making improvements on their homestead. One day, he proudly replaced the oiled skins on the windows with real glass, thinking Myrtle would be pleased to be able to look out these windows and see the land, crops, and her garden. When he had them installed, Myrtle only muttered, "It is about time." When the temperature dropped and the fire burned low in the cookstove, a half inch of ice would form on the inside of the new windows, much to Myrtle's annoyance.

Chapter Nineteen

Seasons came and went. It was 1908. At five years of age, Leta was milking her first cow. She would squirt the milk in a cup and drink it warm, fresh from the cow. She soon learned to squirt some in the direction of the barn cats much to their delight.

John became a naturalized citizen and that automatically made Myrtle a Canadian citizen too. He always kept up on what was happening in his new country. When he had read about the Russell, a 100% Canadian car built in 1906, he was proud that every bit of it was Canadian: materials, labor, and the capital used to finance it. Three models and five types were built. It sported two cylinders with a nine inch ground clearance so the wheels would fit the deep wagon tracks. It was an expensive car at the unheard of price of $1,500.00.

Another year passed. Everything was rapidly growing and changing. Shellbrook now had a general store, a hotel, and a church as well as a school. Outlying communities were growing, homesteads were becoming farms, and tiny cabins spread into houses. Now neighbors visited each other more often.

During the short summer months the garden was planted, fields were plowed and crops sown. Ione was kept as busy as Leta and Leila. "Idle hands are the Devil's workshop," Myrtle would remind them. For a little tyke, Leta worked hard. There was no time for play. Everyday was filled with chores. Myrtle gave each girl two long rows a day to weed in the garden as well as milking the cows, feeding the chickens and gathering the eggs. Leta would finish her rows and most of Leila's as Leila would lie down in the middle of a row and go to sleep when she got tired. Leta did not mind the extra work or watching after her sister. She wanted to please her mother and make her proud of her. But no matter how hard Leta tried, Myrtle only found fault.

As was his custom, Scotty would stop at the Oeschs every month on his way home from Shellbrook with a treat for the girls. Scotty thought Ione was the prettiest little thing he had ever seen next to the Oesch girls and hoped that John would allow him to court her as soon as he could summon the courage to ask. After all, she was nearly sixteen now.

Myrtle and Ione were sitting on the porch shelling peas when Scotty rode up. Leta sat on the step churning butter. "Afternoon, Missus," Scotty greeted Myrtle as he dismounted. "Might have something for the girls here," he teased as he searched his pockets.

"Get Scotty some coffee, Ione," Myrtle directed. Smiling shyly at Scotty, Ione sat down her bowl of peas and went into the cabin. Leta's eyes sparkled with anticipation.

"Aye, here it tis'," he said, pulling a sack of old fashioned chocolates from his pocket and handing it to Myrtle. "And I thank you, Miss," he said to Ione as she handed him the steaming cup of coffee.

"Here, one piece for each of you. The rest will be saved for later." Myrtle said handing Leta and Ione a piece of the rare treat. Each girl thanked him politely. Downing his coffee, Scotty prepared to be on his way.

"I thank ya for the coffee, Missus. Best be gettin' on home. Tell John sorry to have missed him."

As Scotty rode out of the yard, Myrtle went inside and put the sack of candy on a high shelf next to the sideboard, picked up a bucket, and rejoined Ione on the porch. "We need to get the rest of those peas picked before sundown, we can finish shelling tonight," Myrtle said to Ione. Leta waited until her mother and Ione were busy in the garden before going into the house. Having finished her piece of chocolate she was ready for more.

Climbing up on a chair, she retrieved the candy, tiptoed past the sleeping Leila and went into her parent's room to eat every last piece of chocolate in the sack. When Myrtle and Ione came back into the house Leta was no where to be found. Knowing how Leta was prone to wander off, Myrtle was about to send Ione after John when she heard retching sounds coming from her bedroom. She discovered Leta under the bed about to be sick. Grabbing her by the feet, Myrtle angrily drug Leta out from under the bed, quickly getting her outside where the little chocolate thief was promptly very ill.

Later that evening after supper, John went upstairs to check on Leta. Sitting on the edge of her small cot he smoothed her hair back from her face as he explained, "How can you help me with the horses if you are going to be sick, Little One?" Leta sniffed and wiped a tear from her eye as her father continued. "I need you to help me, so promise you won't eat so much at once again." He worried about her dropsy. The doctor had long ago advised them that if she lived to be seven years old she should outgrow this affliction. "Your mother says you will have to stay in bed for a couple of days. Now you go to sleep," he said pulling the quilts up around her.

"Is Momma going to whip me for eating all the chocolate?" Leta asked timidly.

"No. You have punished yourself, I think." Giving her a wink as he started down the stairs, he whispered, "We won't tell Leila about the chocolate."

Leta snuggled down under the quilts with a tiny smile on her lips as she closed her eyes. Her Papa always made her feel so much better.

In a few days Leta was up and out in the barn with her father helping him tend the horses. He would let her brush the Belgians after he had unharnessed them for the day. The huge horses would stand quietly munching on hay while Leta cleaned their legs, walking under their bellies as she brushed. She had no fear of these gentle giants. While she worked studiously, John would patiently answer the many questions that seemed to flow from her like a fountain. If her mother was around, Leta was silent as the falling snow.

May brought more surprises. Myrtle coldly announced to John at supper one night that, come November, there would be another mouth to feed. The girls had no idea what their mother was talking about but they knew without a doubt that she was very angry about it. They also knew that the entire family would feel the sting of her anger.

In the weeks that followed, Myrtle barely spoke to John. So in the evenings after supper, John would read the newspaper aloud. No matter that it was several months old. "Old news is better that no news," he told the girls. The girls sat on the floor at his feet listening to stories of, to them, another world. Every now and then he would catch Myrtle listening even though she pretended disinterest as she busied herself in some task.

John knew she listened to every word as he read, "J. D. McCurdy made the first flight in the British Empire at Baddick, Nova Scotia on February 23, 1909. The airplane, named The Silver Dart, is a two seater, with a water cooled engine, flying at an altitude of thiry feet on a clear day." Carefully folding and laying the paper aside, John concluded, "We can be proud that this airplane was designed, built, and flown by Canadians."

"You girls had better get to bed, it is past your bedtime," Myrtle snapped breaking the peaceful mood. Without a word, Leta and Leila quickly scurried up the stairs to their room. Leta tried to imagine what it would be like to fly in the air like a bird. Visions of all sorts of contraptions filled her head as she fell asleep.

Chapter Twenty

Missionaries, called 'Workers', began visiting the Oesch farm. These Workers would stay in private homes as they traveled the country preaching the Gospel. They did not worship in a church building but held their services, called 'Meetings', in private homes. An older missionary and his assistant stopped by late one afternoon to ask if they could hold a Meeting in the Oesch home.

"I am Robert Johnson and this is my assistant, Will Thompson," he said introducing himself.

Giving them one of her rare smiles, Myrtle invited them in for a bite to eat and to warm themselves by the fire. As they ate, Mr. Johnson explained to Myrtle that they were non-denominational missionaries spreading the word of God. Will was an apprentice. "Every Elder takes a young person under his wing, teaching him until he is old enough and knowledgeable enough to become an Elder himself and take on an apprentice of his own. Missionaries always travel in pairs. Two women or two men, but men and women never travel together."

John was impressed at how well these two missionaries knew the Bible without any formal schooling or training. They had explained that they were self taught. Myrtle readily agreed to hold their next meeting in her home. As she bid the missionaries farewell, she was excited about the coming event. John smiled as he thought, "This will be good for Myrtle. Christian teachings might help soften her a little."

To John's chagrin, the more the Workers came around, the worse Myrtle became. She boldly interpreted the Bible to suit herself. What little trust and forgiveness that might have been in her was certainly gone now. John believed she had become even more rigid. She seemed to think in extremes. To her everything was black or white. There was no gray, no middle ground.

This third pregnancy was harder on Myrtle than the other two. Her back ached constantly and she was drained by the end of the day. The more fatigued she became the crankier she got. She was stubborn as a mule and pushed herself as hard as she pushed everyone else. Not one person in the Oesch household escaped her sharp tongue and ridicule. Even accommodating Ione tried to stay out of Myrtle's way.

Early one afternoon John was coming in from the field to fix a broken harness when he saw Myrtle and the girls still slaving over the weeds in the garden. It was very hot and humid. John figured it must be over one hundred degrees. When he reached Myrtle her face was beet red and the sweat pouring down her face left her blouse soaked and streaked with dirt. Her long dark skirt was streaked with mud where she had wiped her sweaty hands. Leila was dawdling as usual and Leta was methodically pulling one weed after another working her way down the long row of carrots. The faces of both girls were red and shinny with perspiration. John was alarmed.

"Myrtle, you are going to make yourself sick. You and the girls need to get out of the sun." He was afraid for her. She looked bad. "Here, let me take that," he said reaching for the hoe.

"I am fine!" She snapped, yanking the hoe away from him. "I have to get this done or the whole garden will be overgrown and we will have nothing!"

"Now, Myrtle, you don't have to do it all today," he chided gently. "It isn't good for you or the baby working out in this heat like this. Put down the hoe now and come to the house."

Throwing down the hoe, she stalked to the house shouting over her shoulder, "If it weren't for you acting like a rutting boar, I wouldn't be having this baby in the first place!" His shoulders slumped; John watched her stomp off, stirring up dust as she went.

Both girls stood and watched their mother's display of temper with wide eyes. They had seen her angry before but never directed at their father in this way. When he turned and saw their dismay he felt a tug at his heart. Picking up Myrtle's hoe he held out a calloused hand to his children.

"Come on girls. Let's go inside and have Ione fix us a nice cool drink."

"Is Mama mad at us?" Leta asked timidly.

"No, Little One. Your Mama is just tired. I think we all are, don't you?" Taking Leta by the hand he said, "Take your sister's hand and let us go cool off a bit."

In the days that followed, Myrtle continued to keep the girls busy weeding the garden, picking vegetables and wild berries, as well as their regular chores. They shelled peas, snapped green beans, and tied string around the cabbage to hang in the root cellar. They carried water for the canning boiler even though they could not carry much at a time. Not one to waste time on romance, Myrtle wanted to get her canning done before Ione and Scotty married. He had asked John for her hand a few months before. John knew they would make a fine pair. They were married in late summer - after Myrtle had her own cupboards laden with canned goods.

Frost always came early, but this year it seemed that summer had just begun when it was time to fill the root cellar with garden produce and butcher the hogs and chickens before the hard freeze. John always brought back elk and moose from his hunting trips so there was plenty of meat. Now that Ione had a home of her own the girls had to take over most of her chores. Both Leta and Leila missed her terribly. Not only because she seemed to be a buffer between them and their mother, but she was always there to help them whenever they needed it. Leta had learned a lot from Ione's kind and gentle ways.

By October the Canadian landscape was covered with snow. Huge feather-light flakes floated silently to the ground without the slightest breeze to disturb their decent. Paths to the barn and privy had to be shoveled every morning. Leta would bundle up in her heavy woolen winter clothes to go out with her father, plowing through waist-high powder along side him as he shoveled.

She loved playing in the snow, rolling and jumping in it until she was white from head to toe. Her Papa always indulged her in these simple pleasures but she was careful never to give way to her urge to dive in the wonderfully soft white blanket when her mother was around. Myrtle would not allow such "foolishness", as she called it.

In the middle of a frigid November night, John gently shook Leta and Leila awake. "Wake up, girls and get dressed. We have to hurry."

Where are we going, Papa?" A sleepy Leta asked. "Just hurry, girls and come to the barn when you're dressed." He answered as he went down the stairs. She knew something was wrong, but without question she quickly got into her clothes as well as helping the dawdling Leila. As they bundled up before going outside they noticed that their mother was still in her bed. Something was terribly wrong and it frightened them both.

Making their way to the barn, Leta held tightly to Leila's mittened hand as they watched their father hastily hitch the team to the sleigh in the dim lantern light. As John lifted the girls into the sleigh Leta asked timidly, "Where are we going, Papa? Is Mama mad at us?"

"You are going to stay with Aunt Kate for a few days," he told her, "No, your mama is not mad."

"Is Mama sick?" Leila asked.

"She is not feeling too good this morning. But don't you worry, she will be fine," he said as he climbed in beside them. Covering their laps with the fur robe, he urged the horses into a brisk trot down the lane. The lantern swinging from the back of the sleigh glowed warmly through the falling snow. Leta's fear began to disappear as she thought of being with her Aunt Kate. The girls always looked forward to being at her house. Aunt Kate would read to them, make them cookies, and even cut out paper dolls with them.

"I like playing with Ruby, Papa, but her little brothers are not fun. Is it alright if I don't play with them much?" Leta asked. Lost in his own thoughts, her father did not respond.

Back in Oesch house Myrtle cried out as another searing pain tore through her. "I will not go through this again!" she muttered to herself through clenched teeth as the pain subsided. "He will not touch me again!"

It seemed like an eternity to Myrtle before she heard John and Granny McTaggart come through the door. He had brought the old woman as quickly as he could. He knew if Myrtle had this baby alone she would never forgive him. As soon as John stepped inside, Myrtle screamed at him to get out of her house. He had never seen his wife so wild eyed. Granny assured him it was just the pain talking but he should keep out of sight until it was over.

As the pain increased and lengthened it seemed as though this baby just did not want to be born. Myrtle had been in labor so long she did not know if it was night or day. Granny McTaggart talked soothingly as she wiped perspiration from Myrtle's brow. John spent the day working in the barn and was numb from the cold when he heard a shrill cry from the house. Smiling as he walked toward the house, he no longer felt the cold. He had another child!

John made a third entry in the Bible that night, 'November 18, 1909. Born: to John Oesch and Myrtle Grace Little Oesch, a girl, Elsie Mabel Oesch'.

Three days later he brought Leta and Leila home. Leila didn't like the idea of her mother and father getting a baby. To Leta she was a beautiful little doll and was surprised as well as delighted that her mother allowed her to tend to the baby. Leta bathed and dressed her. Even when the diaper needed changing, Leta tended to it. She loved her new charge and would sit and hold tiny Elsie for hours. After Myrtle was up and around, Leta was afraid that her mother would not let her continue to care for the baby. She was pleasantly surprised again when most of the care was left to her after all.

It had now become too crowded in Allison's old cabin for the growing Oesch family. John built Leta and Leila space saving bunk beds against the wall. Two month old Elsie occupied the crib now, much to Leila's dismay. If it had not been dead of winter, John had the distinct feeling that Myrtle would have made him sleep in the barn with his horses. Instead he slept on a pallet in front of the small cookstove. He made sure he was up and gone before Myrtle awoke each morning. The embers of her burning anger toward him seemed to ignite into flame whenever he was around her. There seemed to be no end to her anger and no forgiveness in her soul.

The following June they moved back into the Oesch house. Myrtle told John firmly that he would not be sleeping in 'her' bedroom so he quietly made himself a cot in the kitchen. He was still hoping, if given enough time, Myrtle's anger would cool.

Leta readied Elsie for bed each night, and would gently rock the crib, singing to her until she fell asleep. Only when she was sure the baby was asleep did Leta go to bed herself. Elsie never cried. She was a happy, burgling, cooing baby. It seemed she was already trying to talk.

John was proud of Leta, but it saddened him that she seemed so much older than her seven years. He was afraid that she had already missed her childhood. She worried and fussed like a little mother hen over both sisters, but especially Elsie.

It was bath day. Myrtle lifted down a steaming bucket of water off the stove pouring it into the wash tub on the floor. Leta and Leila stood wrapped in towels ready to get into the steaming water.

"Don't stand there dawdling. Get in, and be sure to scrub behind your ears," Myrtle ordered Leila.

Dipping in a foot, Leila quickly pulled it out, whining, "The water's too hot, Mama. It burns!"

"It is not! Now just get scrubbed so Leta can get in. And hurry up or I will get the scrub brush and scrub you myself."

Leila soaped herself hurriedly, softly whimpering as she scrubbed herself with a wash cloth. As soon as she stepped out, Leta climbed in and felt the water burn her skin. She didn't protest as she soaped herself but the water burned like fire. As Leila stood shivering with her towel wrapped around her, Myrtle grabbed it and began to impatiently dry her off. Leila began to cry. Red blotches appeared on her skin as Myrtle rubbed her dry.

"Oh, no!" Myrtle exclaimed. "I got the buckets mixed up. This is the lye water for the wash. Quick Leta, get the soap off you and get out of there!" Leta was only too glad to escape the burning water. "Oh, well," Myrtle reasoned, "it will be good for the Itch." Neither girl had the Itch, but both were minus some hide for quite some time. Fortunately no scars were left. The episode was never mentioned to John.

A few weeks later while Myrtle and Leila were working outside in the garden, Leta was inside busy tending to Elsie. She became tired and drowsy, so she crawled up on the bed with the baby and went to sleep. When Leta awoke the fire in the air-tight heater had gone out and her mother had warned her not to let it go out.

Afraid she would be in trouble, Leta tried frantically to get the fire going again. Laying kindling on the paper, she struck a match to it. The paper burned quickly, but the wood wouldn't catch. It just smoldered. So she blew into the draft hole which caused it to backfire in her face singeing her hair and eyebrows. Now she knew she was in trouble. Her mother would be coming in the house any minute.

"Well, maybe that will teach you not to let the fire go out!" Myrtle snapped when she saw Leta's singed hair and eyebrows. She did not look closely at her daughter to see if Leta was burned. Her main concern was that her fire was out and Leta had disobeyed her. Agitated, Myrtle rebuilt the fire and as she slammed the wood into the stove she berated Leta on how irresponsible she was. Leta stood quietly as she took the abusive words to heart, hanging her head to hide the tears that welled up in her big blue eyes.

That night at supper, Leta picked at her food. She was not hungry and her head hurt. "If you are just going to play with your food, you might as well go up to bed," Myrtle quipped. Leta quietly laid her fork down and left the table without a word. After he had finished his own supper, much to Myrtle's chagrin, John went up to check on Leta. He could not understand why Myrtle was so apathetic and unsympathetic.

Leaning down to kiss Leta on the forehead he could feel the heat radiating from her before his lips touched her head. Quickly feeling her brow and cheeks he turned to Leila. "Leta's sick. Fetch your mother."

Leila jumped off her bed and ran down the narrow stairs into the kitchen. Myrtle was finishing up the supper dishes which were usually washed by Leta.

"Leta is sick, Mama," Leila said. "Papa wants you to come upstairs."

A twinge of guilt shot through Myrtle briefly but she pushed the feeling aside. She realized that Leta had not looked good at supper but had attributed it to the tongue lashing she had given her over allowing the fire to go out. Wiping her hands on her apron, Myrtle ascended the narrow stairs. Entering the girls' room, she could see Leta was burning up with fever before she touched her. A red rash covered her chest and face.

"It's the measles," Myrtle muttered. Returning to the kitchen she grabbed a bottle of quinine and a damp towel for Leta. After giving her a dose of quinine and sponging her off with the towel, Myrtle wrapped her in a quilt and dimmed the lamp. John had already covered the window and told Leila she would have to sleep downstairs for awhile.

The first few days Leta's fever raged. In her delirium she kept saying "I shut the heater off, I know I did." Myrtle was concerned for her daughter, but she never let it show. Leta had been sick before, but never like this. Leila was not happy having to take over most of Leta's chores. She tried her own sick act but it failed to work this time.

Leta's temperature gradually returned to normal, but she was still covered with a blotchy red rash. She wanted to get out of bed and take care of Elsie, but Myrtle told her firmly, "You have to stay in the bed until your rash is gone." Leta would rather have been out doing chores and weeding the garden than stay in her room alone. The only time she saw anyone was when her mother or father brought her meals up. Myrtle would bring the tray and leave it without ceremony. John would try to get Leta to eat a little each time. She really missed baby Elsie. She worried about her.

After her two week quarantine, Leta was up and anxious to be out of the house. John had built a small wagon with side rails so Leta could take Elsie out to the garden with her. After feeding her breakfast and making sure she was dry, Leta would put Elsie in the wagon, wrap cotton netting over it and with Leila's help would pull her out to the garden.

Myrtle had allowed the girls to plant a large flower garden of their own. Every other day or so, they would weed it instead of the vegetable garden. They both preferred working in the flowers. This flower garden was theirs and theirs alone. Some of the plants, like the hollyhocks and snapdragons and sunflowers, were so tall they could park the wagon beside them to shade the baby.

The girls were in their own little world whenever they were in their flower garden. Even though the weeding was difficult, it was not work to them. Even Leila enjoyed it. In this rare time, they could let their imaginations go as little girls are wont to do. However, Myrtle kept a watchful eye on them as she hoed the weeds that seemed to pop up overnight around the vegetables. Even though civilization was taking hold and taming this frontier, it was still a wild country. She was strict and stern with her girls, but she did not want any harm to befall them. School would be starting soon and then they would be under the teacher's watchful eye.

Agnes Linquist came to work for Myrtle just before school was to start. Myrtle begrudgingly had to use some of her egg and cream money to hire the help she would need now that the girls would be in school. Agnes was a large Swedish girl with long blonde braids, huge round blue eyes and spoke very little English.

Chapter Twenty One

"But I don't want to go, Mama," Leila whined.

"I do not want to hear anymore from you! And quit fidgeting," Myrtle scolded as she finished braiding Leila's hair. "You have to go to school and that is the end of it!"

Having braided her own hair, Leta tied a pink ribbon to the end of each honey-colored braid that hung over her shoulders. "I hear Papa with the wagon. Come on, Leila." This was the most exciting day of her life. School! She could hardly wait!

"Don't forget your lunch," Myrtle called as Leta raced out the door still pulling on her coat. Doing an about face, she grabbed the small lard bucket which held her lunch, and was out the door. Still sniveling, Leila slowly and reluctantly pulled on her coat. She took her own lunch pail from the table and followed Leta out the door. It was frigid out this morning and Leila wanted to stay home by the fire. She did not want to learn to read and write.

As John drove the girls the two and one-half miles to the one room school house, he could see the excitement on Leta's face. This was their first day of school and he knew Leta would do well, but he was a little concerned about Leila. Even though Leila was only five years old, Myrtle thought she was ready for school. Leta had been too ill to attend until this year.

She was seven now and seemed to be outgrowing the dropsy just as the doctor said she would.

John pulled the team to a halt in front of the school house. The school teacher, Art Marchant, was standing on the step greeting the children as they arrived. It was the middle of May, 1910 and the Rich Valley School, named by Matt Schmitz, was open for the first time. John helped his girls down from the wagon and introduced them to their male teacher. Leta was beaming with excitement. Leila looked as if she were about to cry.

Climbing back on the wagon, he said, "I will be here after school to take you home. Pay attention to Mr. Marchant and mind your manners." Myrtle thought his taking the girls to and from school was a terrible waste of time. "You will just spoil them!" She snipped. But when he was quietly adamant about taking them and picking them up the first week, she grudgingly kept still about it.

That afternoon when John came to pick up the girls, Mr. Marchant told him the news that on May 4th Great Britain had declared war on Germany. This meant Canada was at war too. All the way home the news weighed on his mind. He was thankful he had only daughters. He would never have to worry about them going off to war. But he was troubled about all his neighbors with young sons. He thanked God that his sister Kate's boys were too young for this war.

As soon as the girls were home from school, chores were waiting to be done. They knew they had to change their clothes and get to work immediately. If their mother had to remind them she would take a willow switch to them. Leta would hurry as fast as she could to finish her chores so she could work on her lessons. She liked her teacher and she loved school.

164

During her first year in school, Leta worked extra hard to keep her grades up. Many nights she burned the midnight oil laboring over the extra lessons Mr. Marchant would give the children. This work was not mandatory, but if it was completed, the children would receive something special from him. These little prizes were always different. Sometimes it would be a hair ribbon for the girls or a handkerchief for the boys. On rare occasions, it would be a bag of cookies or candy his wife had made. Leta was sad when the short school year was over. Due to the severe Canadian winters school could only be held during the summer and through the fall until the hard freeze.

One night just before the school year was over, while John was away on a freighting trip, Myrtle put the three girls to bed as it had gotten quite late before she could finish the milking. When she shut the door it locked itself. When she returned from the barn she could not get back in the house. It was well below zero with a little bit of a wind. She yelled and banged on the door, but the girls were so exhausted from chores and school work, they were sound asleep.

Finally Leta heard her mother and quickly got up and opened the door. Myrtle was furious with them for locking her out. All the while she was ranting and threatening them with the switch, Leta tried to tell her they did not lock the door. Myrtle was sure they had done it on purpose until she realized how easy the door locked when shut hard. "Humph! Well, just get back to bed!" she snapped, with no apology for her error or her anger. Leta and Leila returned to bed in tears.

As the family grew, Allison's old cabin seemed to grow smaller and smaller. To fulfill the requirement that they live on the homestead for six months each year, John would drive Myrtle and the girls to the cabin every night after supper and pick them up every morning before breakfast. They spent their days and ate their meals at the house. John worked Myrtle's inherited section alone. Leta could feel the mounting tension between her parents.

Spring planting had begun as the girls entered the second grade. Leta was now riding Old Buck, a half broke buckskin gelding, to and from school, with Leila on behind her. Old Buck was ornery and would balk at almost everything. Whenever the girls crossed a stream he would try to lie down in the water. One morning Leta could not hold him back as he began to lie down. Both girls jumped off his back and had to wade out of the cold water, soaking both shoes and stockings.

A few days later as they started off to school, Old Buck was plodding along fine until they came to the four corners. All the main roads ran along the section lines so they were aligned perfectly straight - east, west, north, and south. When they came to where the culvert ran under the road, Old Buck refused to go over it. No matter how hard Leta urged him to go on, he refused to go over it. John was plowing the field nearby and saw the girls were having trouble with the horse. Halting his team he went to help, picking up a willow switch on the way. Telling the girls to hold on tight, he swatted at the horse. He missed and hit Leila on the leg. She jumped off and ran squalling back to the house.

"Get off Leta, I'll make him go across," John told her, grabbing the reins. Swinging into the saddle, he smacked Old Buck a good one on the rump with the switch but the horse did not budge. Then suddenly Old Buck started to back up toward the barbed wire fence with John trying in vain to get him to go forward. When Old Buck hit the fence it cut into his rear end and he bolted forward. John yanked him around hard and ran him up the road and back at a hard gallop.

"He shouldn't give you anymore trouble, but watch him," John said as he dismounted the sweating horse and handed Leta the switch. Jumping on the horse's back, Leta took off like a shot down the lane leaving Leila behind. After that experience, Old Buck never balked at anything again.

Mr. Marchant was still standing on the school house steps greeting the children as Leta raced into the school yard. Hastily tending to her pony, she left him in the barn with the other horses. Running up the school steps she noticed there were several new children to get acquainted with. She was elated to be back in school. Each time she stepped into the school room she would close her eyes and breathe deeply taking in all the wonderful smells: the chalk dust, the freshly oiled floors, the books, both old and new. The children kept their lunches by the stove so by lunch time all their lunches would not be frozen in the pails. Most of the heat from the potbellied stove that sat in the center of the room would rise to the ceiling leaving the floors cold and drafty. And no one thought anything of sharing the common dipper in the water pail at the back of the room.

The short school year was passing quickly. The nights were growing colder. John had quietly moved back into the bedroom with Myrtle and life in the Oesch household seemed to be improving.

It was fall before John noticed Myrtle thickening around the middle again. Whenever his questioning blue eyes met her defiant gray ones, she would turn away. Knowing it would be no use to say anything, he would simply walk away staying in the fields until well after dark. He knew this time that she was expecting again but she refused to acknowledge the fact. All summer she had worked twice as hard as usual, helping him break some wild ponies as well as oxen. And she had insisted on plowing up another acre for the garden. Twice, when she had been out working alone, she had come in the house bruised and scratched, her blouse torn and dirty. When questioned she defensively told John she had tripped on the hem of her skirt and fell.

John worried about her constantly but kept his fears to himself. He would not allow himself to think the worst. He remembered her agonies in the last birth with Elsie. The stories he had heard about women who did not want their babies were so horrendous he did not believe them. He had been told some women would smother unwanted babies as soon as they were born. Some reportedly took newborns out and put them into the pig pen for the pigs to eat. These thoughts made him physically ill. The thought of any mother not wanting her child, let alone killing it, was just too much for him to comprehend.

Once again winter was settling in on the Canadian prairie. John was busy working in the barn repairing a broken cultivator wheel when Leta came running from the garden stumbling over frozen mounds of snow screaming, "Papa! Papa! Come quick! Mama's dying!"

Dropping the wheel, John raced out of the barn to meet her. "Calm down Little One. Now tell me slow," he said, gently taking her by the shoulders. "Did she fall again?"

"I don't know." Trying to catch her breath, Leta continued so rapidly John could barely understand her. "We went out to the garden and found her lying in the snow. There's blood everywhere!"

"Oh, God!" Bolting off at a dead run, John felt as if he'd been struck in the chest by an anvil.

Racing into the frozen garden he saw Myrtle crumpled on the ground, blood staining the snow. She had been digging the last of the few vegetables that had not yet frozen in the ground.

"She was too heavy. I couldn't get her to the house, Papa," Leila whimpered.

"It's all right. You did the right thing by staying here with her." As John lifted the semiconscious Myrtle from the ground, fear gripped him like a vise. Leaving a trail of blood in the snow, he gently carried her to the house praying with every step. This time Myrtle would not make him leave her, he vowed. It was much too early for the baby. He knew it would not survive, but Myrtle must. "She must make it," he whispered to God.

Laying Myrtle gently on their bed John turned to Leta. "Go get Old Buck and ride over to get Aunt Kate. Hurry, girl!" Without a word, Leta raced toward the barn.

By the time Kate arrived, Myrtle had lost the baby. It was a tiny, perfect little girl. She did not even weigh a pound. John had delivered her. Kate rushed into the bedroom to find John standing over Myrtle, tears sliding down both ruddy cheeks with a tiny bundle, wrapped in a towel, in his hands. She was not sure if Myrtle was asleep or unconscious.

Slowly looking at Kate as she entered the room he sadly shook his head. Kate's heart was breaking for her brother. She knew how much he loved his children. If only Myrtle...oh well, that was not any of her concern. Right now she needed to tend to Myrtle. "Go build up the fire and put some water on," Kate told him, gently taking the tiny bundle from him and laying it in the crib. Without a word he left the room.

"Is Mama going to die?" Leta asked in a tiny quivering voice. She had never seen her Papa cry before and it scared her.

"No, Little One. Your Mama's going to be fine," He told her, wiping his eyes on the back of his sleeve. "Let's make some tea for her and Aunt Kate."

While Kate bathed Myrtle and changed the linens on the bed, John went out to dig a tiny grave, chipping away the frozen December earth beside the girl's flower garden. When he returned to the house he patiently explained to the girls that the baby had come too early and had been too small to live.

Leaving Myrtle asleep in the bed, John carried the tiny bundle, wrapped in a small quilt, to the frozen flower garden. Kate and the girls walked slowly behind him. Bundled up against the bitter cold, Leta and Leila stood with solemn little faces, with Elsie between them, holding tight to their hands. Kate's heart was still breaking as she listened to John read, his voice tremulous, from the old Bible.

Early the next morning, John hitched his sleigh for Kate to drive home. She had insisted on staying until she knew Myrtle would be all right. "She has lost a lot of blood and will have to stay in bed for a few days, but she will be all right, John. If you need me for anything..."

"I know," he said, interrupting her. "I don't know what I would have done without you."

Patting his arm in farewell, Kate climbed into the sleigh and headed for home. John sadly watched for a moment as she drove away, then went into the house, took the family Bible from the shelf and made a sorrowful entry in it. 'Died at birth, Ethel Oesch, December, 1911.' He did not write in the day, he did not want to remember it. Going in the bedroom to check on Myrtle he was met with hard, defiant eyes. "You will not sleep in my bed again," she told him coldly. Her words were like salt in an open wound. He loved her more than she would ever know, but in his heart he knew that one day she would surely kill that love.

Three days later, still weak from the loss of so much blood, Myrtle was hard at work as though nothing had happened. She drove herself, and everyone else in the family, even harder. Leta and Leila had so many chores to do as well as their school work they could hardly keep up with their mother's demands. Leila whined and complained about everything. Leta did her own work as well as half of Leila's so their mother would not get into a temper. Myrtle's angry outbursts made Leta physically ill, but she held it back, afraid of making her mother even angrier. Many times she hid behind the chicken house, retching, trying desperately not to vomit, swallowing the hot bile that pushed up into her throat as she held back the tears.

Neither Leta nor Leila had missed one day of school this school term. Leila could no longer manipulate her mother into allowing her to stay at home. On one bitter cold morning John helped them hitch Old Nell to the cutter. They did not have a thermometer but it was so cold he felt the children should stay at home, but Myrtle insisted they go to school.

Bundled up in thick wool coats, scarves and caps with only their eyes peeking out, they climbed into the cutter. Placing their feet on a heated brick, which was wrapped in heavy brown paper, they tucked the fur robe around their laps and headed for school. Leta held tight to the reins with gloved hands covered with wool mittens. John had covered the mare's nose with a wool cloth to keep the icy air out of her lungs.

When the girls arrived at the school house, no one was there. So they turned Old Nell around and drove the two and one half miles back home. It was not until much later that they learned it had been fifty-eight degrees below zero that morning.

Soon it was spring and the winter wheat was sprouting in the fields. Large patches of melting snow interrupted the sea of green that was quickly covering the fields. Before beginning his spring planting, John built a small addition onto the back of the house for the setting hens. For the nests he built covered boxes so the hens could not get out. It was Leta's job to take care of these setting hens. There was no door, just a small window that she had to crawl in and out of to take the hens out to eat. Not wanting to chase them to get them back on the nest, she would tie a string to the leg of each hen and fasten them to the fence.

While Leta was busy tending to her setting hens, Leila and Elsie tended to the laying hens, gathering eggs, filling the watering pans and scattering grain on the ground for them to eat. An old rooster had frozen his feet and could not sit on the roost so he slept in a vacated nest. Little Elsie caught the rooster on the nest a few mornings in a row and decided for herself that this chicken needed to be 'set'. So she carried it through the window into the setting shed and put it on a nest with some eggs to hatch.

The next morning as the rising sun painted the clouds on the eastern horizon in shades of deep rose to pink, edged with brilliant gold, Myrtle woke with a start when she heard the rooster crowing through the wall at the back of the house. Jumping out of bed she quickly ascended the stairs to the girls' room. "Leta! Leta! Get up and get that rooster out of the setting shed!" The three girls were awake with Myrtle's first shout. "And I want to know who put him in there!" she demanded angrily, stomping down the stairs. Quickly pulling on her clothes, Leta hurried out to get the rooster.

Myrtle was still fuming when Leta came in with the rooster. Afraid of their Mother's wrath, none of the girls said a word.

"I did it, Mama," Elsie said meekly. "I thought he was a hen. He was in a nest."

Seeing the crippled rooster in Leta's arms, Myrtle began to laugh aloud. "Well, you need to check closer next time. Now you girls get to your chores." With tremendous relief the three girls scurried out the door.

*   *   *

May 10, 1912, John got his land patent. The land was now his and he was using all the horses to clear brush. He seldom interfered when it came to the girls and their chores, but since he knew Leta would have to go after the cows on foot he told Leila to go with her. Leila whimpered and whined with every step. "It isn't fair," she sniveled, "This is your job, not mine." Sometimes Leila's whining would irritate Leta so much she had to fight the urge to pinch her. So she would walk along humming a little tune ignoring her younger sister's nasal whine.

Myrtle had watched to see which direction the cows went when she let them out of the barn that morning and told Leta where to start looking. The two girls were deep into the forest when they came upon a small meadow with a big wild strawberry patch in the center. After herding the cows through it, the two girls stopped to pick a few of the succulent berries while the cows continued on toward home. Leila stopped whining long enough to stuff her mouth full of the juicy red fruit.

"Come on, Leila. We better catch up with the cows." Leta popped another strawberry into her mouth. She started off through the thick forest with Leila trailing behind. After they had walked some distance there was no sign of the cows. Leta started to get scared. She stopped and listened. She could not hear the cow bell.

"Are we lost?" Leila whimpered.

"Hush. I can't hear the bell," Leta told her. When she was on Old Nell she did not have to pay attention to what direction she was going as the horse knew the way back home. Now she did not know where she was and nothing looked familiar. Getting lost didn't scare her half as much as facing her mother's anger for not coming home with the cows.

When they came out of the thick stand of trees, they discovered that they were on the edge of neighbor Hadley's field. They had been walking in the opposite direction from home. Now they both knew they were really in trouble. It would be after dark before they could reach home. Seeing the girls coming across the field toward him, Hadley recognized the Oesch girls and wondered what they were doing so far from home at this late hour.

"What are you girls doing way out here? Is anything wrong over at your place?" he asked as he pulled his team to a halt.

"We got lost," Leila blurted out.

Leta wanted to pinch her. She did not want to admit that she did not know her way home. It was embarrassing.

"Well, it's easy to get turned around in that timber. Come along while I get the horses to the barn and I'll walk you home." After working in the fields all day, he was exhausted but he wanted to make sure the girls got home safe.

John was unhitching the team just outside the barn when Hadley approached with the girls following close behind. Dusk was turning to night, the cows were in the barn and Myrtle was busy milking.

"Appreciate you seeing the girls home, Hadley," John told him. "You girls better get to your chores." Leta and Leila scampered into the barn. Maybe, just maybe, if they worked real fast and got all their chores done quickly they could escape their mother's temper.

"You would do the same for me John should my children get lost," Hadley said with a smile.

"I'll saddle the sorrel mare for you. No sense in you walking all the way back home. Leta can go get her tomorrow," John said, turning the horses into the corral.

After Hadley was out of earshot, Myrtle exploded. "I'll teach you to lollygag on the way home! You can finish the milking and all the rest of the chores tonight!" She stomped off throwing the milk bucket at them. Leta was glad it was empty because otherwise she would have had to clean milk off her only coat.

The girls were so terrified they could hardly get their own chores done let alone their mother's. After finishing the milking they slopped the hogs, fed the chickens, and gathered the eggs. When they were finally finished, Myrtle sent them to bed with no supper. At times John felt she was too severe with the girls but he did not interfere with her discipline.

Early the next morning Leta rode the buckskin gelding over to the Hadley place to bring back the mare John had loaned him. Having ridden through the fields to get there she decided to take the road home. When she came to the bridge she discovered the approach was washed out and the creek was flooded. There was a narrow gap of a few feet between the bridge and the road, but when she tried to get the horses to jump across it the sorrel panicked and nearly pushed Leta and the Buckskin into the raging current. Hanging on to the lead rope with all the strength she had, she yanked the buckskin around away from the roiling creek.

A man who contracted out as a hired hand for many of the farmers in the area was walking toward her and saw she was having trouble. Leta recognized him as he had worked in her father's fields during the harvest several times. Not remembering his name, she nodded in recognition.

"I can help you get them across," he told her. Taking hold of the bridle he led the buckskin to the bridge. "Now, hand me a rein and hang on." The horse followed him as he jumped across the narrow expanse. Leta hung on to the mane with one hand and the lead rope with the other. The sorrel followed the buckskin with no trouble. After leading them across the bridge, the man handed Leta back the rein. "You won't have any more trouble with them. They know it's safe now."

"Thank you." She tried in vain to remember his name.

"Tell your father that I will be around at harvest time again," he said as he walked away in the opposite direction.

Kicking her pony into a lope, she nodded and waved. As soon as she got home she rushed to tell her father about the bridge and the man who helped her. The next day John hitched his team to the stone boat, loaded it with large stones and filled in the approach to the bridge.

A few days later Leta was out on Old Buck hunting the cows. She missed riding Old Nell. The winter before John had loaned Old Nell to a neighbor to haul logs. Using two sleighs, they would haul with one while the other was being loaded. It got dark very quickly in the winter and before the men realized it, night was upon them. In their haste to get the job done they hooked both sleighs together and made the horses pull them, fully loaded, up a steep hill. It injured Old Nell's back and when she got down she could not get up. She had fallen with Leta once and she had to get Reg Barkway to help the old mare up. John did not have the heart to shoot her so he put her out to pasture to die a natural death.

Leta had been riding hard for hours and had not spotted the cows anywhere. As she crossed the bridge she could hear a cow bell, but could not see them. Circling around she finally saw them across the swamp. Seeing she could not get to them she turned around and started for home pushing her pony as hard as she could. Leta knew it was late but did not know it was nearly 10 p.m. as it was still twilight.

John was saddling the sorrel when Leta came galloping into the barn yard. "You really had me worried, girl. I was fixing to come looking for you."

"Sorry, Papa, but the cows are across the swamp and I couldn't get to them," she said breathlessly as she pulled her lathered pony to a halt. "I know Mama is going to be mad but I had a hard time finding them. I looked everywhere."

"Don't worry about your mother. I will take care of it. Looks like you covered some ground. Cool out Old Buck and put him up. I'll go get the cows," he told her as he swung into the saddle.

Leta did what she was told but she knew that her father would be taking the brunt of her mother's wrath for her. Myrtle gave him no more peace than she did the girls. Even though Leta had cooled Old Buck out, rubbed him down and gave him just a small amount of warm water and fed him a little grain, he just stood with his head down. When John returned with the cows he could see that Leta was worried about her horse and felt guilty about running him so hard. "It's not your fault. He is just too old for hard riding. I think it is about time you had a good cow pony. I have some green-broke ponies that I can trade for a fine one," he told her as they walked toward the house.

John Oesch, ferry boat Fort Randall, Nebraska, about 1900

John Oesch, ferry boat Fort Randall, Nebraska

John Oesch driving the grain wagon, 1918

Ed Olsen, 1920

Hunting trip (John Oesch is on the far right), 1920

John Oesch, Milford, Nebraska, returning to Canada, 1920

Oesch family and friends

Hendricks and Oeschs

Bill and Kate (Oesch) Brunner's family

Irwin Oesch holding John Oesch's team

John Oesch

John Oesch's sisters: Mattie, Kate, and Maggie

Myrtle, Elsie and a neighbor, 1920

Thrashing grain on the Oesch farm around 1922

Myrtle, Mrs. Belfry and Hester

Leta and landlady in Spokane, Washington, early 1923

Leta and Ole Olsen, 1923

Verna Keogh, 1923

Leta and a friend on their way to high school

Leta and Verna

Verna Keogh Meeks, 1943

Dan and Leta on their wedding trip, 1923

Leta and Dan Keogh's wedding trip

Leta (Oesch) and Dan Keogh wedding trip

Mabel Oesch Sterling and
Leta Oesch Keogh, 1923

Verna and twins,
1925

Myrtle Oesch and Elsie Oesch with
Keogh twins (Keith and Kenneth),
1925

Reta and Dolly Dee (Olivia)

Leta's first year of
high school

Leta Oesch Keogh and
Liela Oesch Cossairt, 1925

Verna, Keith, and Kenneth (twins), 1927

Keith and
Kenneth, 1941

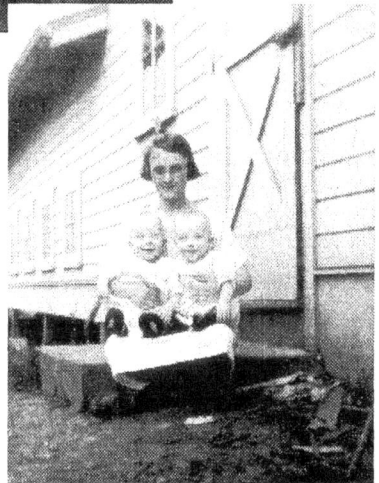

Leta and the twins at Alderwood
Manor Chicken Ranch

Leila Cossairt, Leta Keogh, Kate Brunner and friend in Spokane, Washington, 1928

Oesch sisters: Leila, Leta, and Elsie

Mike, Clem, Ellen, Leila, Elsie and Verna

John and Myrtle (Little) Oesch

Myrtle Grace
Oesch

Myrtle and Leta with Verna
and the twins

Paul Marcie, Howard, Leta, Keith, Kenneth, Dan, and Ellen, 1937

Keith W. Keogh

Leta and Verna Keogh

Ruby and Rid Bruner
(Kate's children)

Verna, Howard, Keith, and
Kenneth Keogh

Chapter Twenty Two

On September 25, 1912, Myrtle received her patent on the homestead she had inherited from her father. She had the cabin and out buildings torn down and used the logs to build another room onto the house. Now they would no longer have to move back and forth. All the land on her section would be used for crops.

Before the hard freeze that winter, John traded several greenbroke ponies for a few head of cattle and a horse for Leta. A Morgan and Quarter horse mix, Buster was a gentle gelding, fourteen hands high with a wide chest and powerful hind quarters. He would make a fine cow pony and he was strong enough to pull just about anything. Leta thought he was the finest little pony she had ever seen and she knew his beautiful silvery white coat would not stay clean for long.

Leta was now spending most of her time working in the fields with her father. She loved working alongside him even though it was hard work for such a small girl. She helped him plow, harrow, and plant. She drove the team, raking the hay into straight rows after John cut it with the scythe. When harvest time came she helped, as everyone did, bundle and tie the cut wheat into sheaves and stack them in long straight rows in the field.

As Leta grew so did her list of chores. It was now her responsibility to milk the cows and muck out the stalls and stanchions. After she had finished with the milking, she took the milk to the house for her mother to strain then she cleaned the barn. She shoveled manure into a wooden wheelbarrow and wheeled it out to a large pile that would be later used to fertilize the fields. Not able to handle a full wheelbarrow, she had to make several trips. As she worked she hummed a little tune she had learned from school. She didn't mind the hard, smelly work. As long as she was working in the barn she was out from under her mother's scrutiny.

As she finished mucking out the stanchions, Leta made her way to the other side of the barn. She needed to turn Buster out into the corral so she could clean his stall before supper. As she approached his stall she stopped dead still. There was a strange horse in the stall next to her pony. His soft dun colored coat and cream colored mane and tail glistened in the dim light of the barn. He was beautiful. With ears pricked forward, he nickered softly at her. She approached him almost reverently and began slowly stroking his neck. Thoughts raced through her head. Where did he come from? Who did he belong to? Oh, how she would love to ride him. Remembering her neglected chores, she gave him a tender pat then, speaking softly to Buster, she proceeded to lead him out of his stall.

Finishing in the barn as quickly as she could, Leta raced out in the field where her father was working. As soon as she caught up with him the questions came tumbling out. "Where did he come from, Papa? Is he ours? Can I ride him?" she asked breathlessly.

Hooking the heavy chains to the stump the two Belgians were about to pull from the ground, John explained. "He belongs to Jule Olsen, your Aunt Phiney's brother from the states. He hurt his leg in the box car on the trip up from Kansas so we will keep him until it heals. As far as riding him, you will have to ask Jule," he told her, urging the team to begin pulling the large stump from its bed in the ground. "We will pasture their other horses for them until they can get their fences built. There are too many range horses still roaming this area to turn them loose. By the way, the Dun in the barn is called Dewey," he finished with a smile.

Later that evening, setting on a pile of straw in the barn, Leta was mesmerized as she listened to her father recount a story of relatives she had never heard of before. As he rubbed linseed oil into the black leather harness he began. "Jule Olsen and his brother, Ed, came up from Kansas a few months ago. Jule's sister, Garfiney - everyone calls her Phinney - is married to my brother Dave Oesch. Bachelors from Kansas, they rented a quarter-section about a mile east of us. They'd been staying with Dave and Phinney until they could get settled on their own land. Ed filed on a homestead eight miles farther east, in Valbrand, and Jule bought a place about half way between. They are both good cooks so they will make out very well on their own.

"Before coming to Canada, Jule homesteaded in Holt County, Nebraska. He sold the homestead and left with Ed to go to Arkansas and the Indian Territory. While there they got word that their sister Elsie - everyone called her Elly - was gravely ill so they sold out and headed back to Iowa. Elly lived eight miles from Council Bluff on the Boyer River. By the time Ed and Jule got there though, she was dying. They were horrified at what they found. Her husband had left her and their three children destitute. There was not enough food for all of them so she went without to feed her children. The boys, William Edward, and Irving Grenville, were so thin Jule swore he could see right through them. Their nine month old baby sister had died of pneumonia three months earlier. Ed nearly ran his horse out riding to Council Bluff for the doctor. But there was nothing he could do. Elly died of consumption complicated by starvation. She was only twenty-seven years old. At the time, William was five and Irving was three."

"What happened to the boys, Papa?" she said, settling herself on the pile of straw next to him.

"Well," John continued, "A few years after Elly died Jule took his two nephews and went south to Tucumcari, New Mexico. Ed came north to Canada. Jule homesteaded in New Mexico two miles from the school so the boys could walk. Not wanting the boys to miss any schooling, he had copied down their birthdays from Elly's Bible before they left Iowa. William was born October 3, 1894, and Irving was born September 26, 1896.

"Education has always been very important to Jule. He spent the money he had inherited from two older brothers on his own education. And he is right. Education is important, always remember that, girl." Soaking the rag with more oil, he went on. "Anyway, after a few years in New Mexico Jule discovered a flaw in his homestead. Discouraged, he packed up and moved to Cold Water, Kansas, and contracted to put up about a half section of hay for some farmer there. When the contract was completed he and the boys moved on to New Haven. Ed wanted him to come to Canada so Jule took the boys to relatives in eastern Nebraska so they could finish school, and he came on to Canada. He came by train this time and shipped nine head of horse."

John looked over at his daughter curled up on the straw, sound asleep. He smiled, "Too much family history at once, eh, Little One? Well, enough for now." His thoughts continued on about the Olsen's as he worked the oil into the rich dark leather.

Julius Olsen was born in Donovan County, Kansas, December 24, 1877. His mother was Christina Marie Peterson, from Aalborg, Denmark. His father, Chris Olsen, also from Aalborg, died in Kansas. Christina lived with her oldest son Peter. John smiled to himself. He could picture the two little boys listening intently to Jule's stories; about seeing Buffalo Bill Cody and of the time the James brothers came through a town where he lived, and he saw the house where Jesse James was shot. Jule remembered vividly the land rush on the Cherokee Strip, September 16, 1893, when hundreds of people raced to get the best piece of land. Many were killed in the wild stampede. Others, with their wagons overturned and destroyed, and their horses bolting in terror, kept racing on foot. When Jule and the boys traveled through Oklahoma in 1907, it became the 46th state. Jule was always teaching and the boys were always eager to learn.

When the boys had asked, Jule told them of their father, John Joseph Keogh. Keogh had migrated from Ireland with his parents and grandparents. Jule used this opportunity to warn the boys about the consequences of a life of drinking hard spirits and fighting. He never told them he always suspected their father had been killed in a drunken brawl somewhere. There was no way to know for sure what ever happened to him, but Jule wanted to impress upon the boys a life like that only led to disaster.

Finished with the harness, John hung it on a peg, set the oily rag and the can of linseed oil on the shelf, and gently woke his daughter. "Come on girl. Time to go in to supper."

Dewey's leg healed quickly. A week after he had been turned out to pasture with the rest of the Olsen horses, Leta was returning from school and saw the entire Olsen herd heading toward Shellbrook at a fast clip, with Dewey trailing behind in the billowing snow thrown up by thundering hooves. Leila had stayed home from school with one of her sick spells so Leta was riding alone. Leta knew she had to catch Dewey but she would need help. Turning Buster around sharply she kicked him into a hard gallop toward the Barkway place.

Pulling Buster to an abrupt halt beside the corral fence she called to Reg who was busy mending the watering trough. "Reg! Uncle Jules's horses are loose. I need you to help me!"

"Let me get a horse," he told her as he laid down his tools.

"If we can catch Dewey I know we can catch them. He's faster than Buster," Leta said hastily as he saddled his Bay.

"I've seen him running in the pasture and he sure is fast alright. Come on, let's go get those horses." Reg swung into the saddle and the two raced after the escaped herd.

Reg easily caught Dewey and quickly slipped the halter off Buster and put it on Dewey. Leta jumped on the Dun's bare back, galloping after the runaway horses. Knowing Buster would go home on his own Reg turned him loose and raced after Leta. Finally catching up with the herd at the railroad station in Shellbrook, Reg laughed when he saw the horses calmly standing around as though they were passengers waiting for the next train.

Reg helped Leta get the herd as far as his place and she assured him she could get them the rest of the way home on her own. He was skeptical but she was determined, so he let her go. Taking off like a shot, laying flat on Dewey's back to keep from being clobbered with chunks of flying snow from galloping hooves, Leta ran the herd at a hard gallop the rest of the way home. Hearing the thundering hooves, Myrtle and Agnes ran from the house to see what all the ruckus was about.

All they could see was Jule's horses racing toward the corral in a billowing cloud of powdery snow.

The next day Leta was busy mucking out the stalls and did not hear Jule enter the barn. A stab of fear went through her when she looked up and saw him standing in front of her. She had not met him yet and was sure he would upset about her riding Dewey without permission.

"Hello there, you must be Leta." The big man put her at ease instantly with his soft kind voice. The twinkle in his gentle blue eyes warned her he was a tease. "I am your Uncle Jule."

"Hello," she answered, timidly pausing for a moment. "I rode your horse," she suddenly blurted out.

"So I hear. Dewey needed a good run and if you had not brought those horses of ours back they would have caught the first train back to Kansas," he told her with a smile.

She giggled at the image of horses getting on a train like regular passengers. "I meant to ask first. Papa said I should, but...," she trailed off.

"We will just pretend you did. You can ride him whenever you want. Here, let me finish this," he said, reaching for the pitchfork she still held in her hands.

She hesitated. "I better do it. Mama won't like it if I don't."

"We won't tell her then. Besides, I need someone to go push some hay down to the horses. I have a little bit of the hay fever and it really gets me to sneezing." She saw that twinkle again and smiled as she handed him the pitchfork.

Chapter Twenty Three

When the fences were up on their respective farms, Jule allowed Leta to help him and Ed drive the horses to their new home. As of yet there were no barns but the Olsen's had constructed shelters and large corrals. Each brother had a small cabin to live in and enough land had been cleared to start planting in the spring.

The Olsen brothers had barely settled on their own land when they received word from their brother Peter that he was sending their mother to Canada. Peter had hired a nurse to travel with her as she was not in good health. She was a determined woman and had insisted on going to Canada. Christina Marie Peterson had two sons and a daughter in Canada and wanted to see them all before she died.

When she arrived, Jule and Ed took her to their sister Phinney's and offered to pay for her care. But Phinney refused to accept their money, so the brothers bought a washing machine for her to show their appreciation. Phinney was pleased and proud to be the second woman in the entire area to own a washing machine.

When John suggested to Myrtle she could use a washing machine also, she pointedly told him a contraption like that was a waste of good money.

As his girls grew older, John became more involved with the school and was elected to the School Board. One day in May was set aside for a work day at the school. Men brought their teams and plows to clear the school yard of brush and other unwanted growth while the women cleaned the inside of the building from top to bottom. A patch of ground was plowed for the children's vegetable garden. Late in the afternoon when the work was completed everyone enjoyed the potluck supper prepared by the women.

As always, the school house was the activity center for the district. All special events were held there; school plays, box socials and the Christmas program. But Myrtle would not allow the Oesch girls to participate or attend any of the events. They were never allowed to celebrate any holiday, not even Christmas. There were no presents, no Christmas tree, and certainly not a special dinner. John had hoped with the missionary Workers stopping by every other month or so, Myrtle would soften and begin to celebrate the Holidays. It saddened him that the girls had never even celebrated their own birthdays. The only way they knew what day they were all born was the notation their father had written in the family Bible.

A few weeks after the school yard had been cleaned and the garden planted the annual School Fair was planned. The teacher had praised Leta on her beautiful hand writing and wanted her to enter a sample of her penmanship. Myrtle surprised her daughter by telling her, "Since you have an entry, you can go to the Fair." To perfect her entry, the teacher had Leta write the same phrase over and over until Leta hated the sight of it.

When the big day came, Leta hitched up the pony and cart to drive the teacher into Shellbrook where the Fair was to be held. When they arrived, a sheepish Leta discovered she had accidentally left her paper at home. It was too far to go back for it. Her teacher had a strong suspicion it had not been left behind by accident. Leta enjoyed her day at the Fair even though she knew she would have to face the music when she got home for forgetting her entry.

That evening, as soon as Leta returned from the Fair, she quickly changed her clothes and ran to the barn to begin her chores before her mother noticed she was home. Hastily unhitching the pony from the cart, she turned him out into the corral and noticed elfin-like Elsie standing in the calf's pen. "I hope she hasn't tied the calves' tails together again," Leta whispered. Her youngest sister was so mischievous and was always pulling some kind of prank.

When Leta entered the pen Elsie was giggling as two calves struggled to free themselves of each other. "Elsie, you better get them separated before Mama sees them. You know she will have a fit." Leta barely got the words out when they heard the sharp sound of their mother's voice.

"Who tied the calves together?" she demanded. Neither girl said a word. "Well, since neither of you will admit it, both of you will be punished," Myrtle snapped, shaking her finger in their faces. "Tomorrow after your regular chores are done, you both will clean out the chicken house. If this happens again you will get the switch." She turned and stomped toward the house.

Leta hated cleaning out the smelly chicken house. Trying to shovel and hold your breath at the same time was hard. But at least this time Elsie had to do it too.

A few days later a neighbor sent for Myrtle since she was recognized as the best mid-wife in the area. Preparing to leave, Myrtle gave strict orders the girls were to cultivate the garden.

It was a tremendous job that took a full day even with the girls taking turns pushing the small hand cultivator up and down each long row. They were crestfallen. They had hoped to spend the day with Aunt Kate.

"Do we have to work in the garden all day, Mama?" Leila whined. "We wanted to go to Aunt Kate's."

"All right, you can go to Kate's if you finish the garden," amending her order as she rushed out the door.

There was a ray of hope and for the first time Leta was thankful for Leila's sniveling. Somehow they had to get the garden finished by afternoon. After some collaboration the three girls hooked the single tree to the cultivator and hitched the pony to it. Leta led the pony down the rows while Leila handled the cultivator with Elsie brushing out any telltale tracks.

Early that afternoon Myrtle returned home as the girls were leaving for Kate's. She was instantly furious. "I told you to finish the garden before you went anywhere!"

"We did, Mama," Leta told her. "We cultivated every row."

Without another word and puffed up with anger, Myrtle stormed out to the garden. She was certain they were lying to her. When she reached the garden she stopped short. Her mouth agape in stupefaction, she stared at the neat cultivated rows. She wasn't sure how they had managed it but they had completed the laborious task.

Storming back into the house Myrtle demanded, "Did you use the pony to pull the cultivator?"

Icy fingers of fear gripped Leta around the chest. Nausea threatened to overwhelm her. "Well...yes." Leila and Elsie stood fearfully behind her, eyes like saucers. They were all terrified of what was coming next.

"Humph! I guess I can't stop you from going then. I saw the tracks you missed and if you had lied to me I would have skinned you all alive," she said angrily. "But you better be back here early tomorrow."

Relief washed over them. Without another word the three girls hastily grabbed their coats and rushed out the door. Scrambling into the buggy, Leta grabbed the reins urging the pony into a brisk trot before her mother could change her mind. Leila and Elsie barely had time to get themselves seated.

The Oesch girls loved visiting Aunt Kate and Uncle Bill. Kate was quiet, warm and loving. She patiently taught the Oesch girls how to embroidery, tat and other hand work. Uncle Bill was a big burley man. He loved his family and farming his land. He was as kind and gentle as he was big. To stay overnight with Aunt Kate and Uncle Bill was a rare treat their mother seldom permitted. The ride to Parkside was pleasant for the girls. Pretending to be grown up ladies going to tea, their daydreams took them out of their harsh world into a softer, more genteel one.

The next day when the girls returned home a little late they hastily unhitched the buggy, turned the pony lose into the pasture and raced into the house to change their clothes. They knew their mother was going to be in a temper. When they entered the house, much to their relief, both parents were gone. Quickly throwing on their work dresses, making sure their good ones were neatly hung on their respective hooks and hearts pounding with trepidation, they raced outside. They split up, one toward the barn, one toward the chicken house, and the other to the garden. Wanting it to look as though they had returned earlier, they all worked as fast as their little bodies allowed.

Two hours later the chickens were fed, eggs gathered, the pigs slopped, hay forked down for the cows and one-third of the garden had been weeded. The three girls were in the garden working diligently when Myrtle came back home. She had been helping John pull stumps. Immediately suspicious, she knew something was amiss because even Leila was steadily hoeing without looking up. Checking the barn and chicken house to make sure they had done all their morning work, she was surprised to find that it was all finished. Not able to find fault with anything she dismissed her suspicions, took up a hoe, and headed for the garden. She was expecting a migrating family to arrive soon and there was still so much to be done.

At supper that evening when the Oesch girls learned they were having company they were excited. They loved having people stay with them as families frequently did until they could get settled. Myrtle seemed to be happier when there were other people around. Life on the Oesch farm was more enjoyable for everyone during this time.

Days and weeks flew by in a stream of activity. Jule and Ed needed to move the last of their horses from the Oesch farm. Leta and Elsie were thrilled when their father told them they could help. Saddling up an old gentle mare for six year old Elsie and the frisky Buckskin for Leta, John told the girls they could bring up the rear to help keep the herd moving. After rounding up the horses and driving them out of the pasture, they were steadily trotting across the field when the herd stirred up a hornets nest in the ground. Every horse bolted.

Suddenly the girl's ponies lurched and began bucking furiously, jumping and kicking, attempting to rid themselves of the swarming, stinging insects. Elsie was slipping off the panicked mare when Jule galloped up beside her and grabbed her off. If she fell off he knew she would be trampled. Quickly putting Elsie in the saddle in front of him, he grabbed the Buckskin's bridle and yelled for Leta to hang on. Plunging straight into thick brush the bees were left behind, leaving several big red welts on their intruders.

Leaving the girls in the brush, telling them to stay put, Jule galloped off to help round up the spooked herd. Her heart still pounding, Leta slid off her horse to comfort Elsie who was rubbing the swelling bee stings on her tiny arms and whimpering. "They hurt, Leta."

"I know," Leta said. There were several large red welts burning her arms. "Here let me put some mud on them," she said, digging a handful of mud from the marshy ground. When John returned with the mare Elsie had been riding in tow, he found both girls had covered their arms and faces with thick slimy mud. The horses were soon rounded up and they continued on, with the girls trailing well behind.

As soon as they returned home that evening, Myrtle washed the mud from the girls, checking to make sure all the stingers were out before plastering fresh mud on them. She left John to take care of his own stings.

The bee incident was soon forgotten as the fall work began. There were fields to harvest, canning to be done, and produce from the garden to be stored in the root cellar. As the days began to grow shorter, everyone had to work twice as hard to finish before winter set in. It pleased Myrtle that Agnes could out-work most men.

During the previous year, a railroad siding had been built one-and-a-half miles from the house. Now John could charter a box car whenever he had a carload of wheat to ship. Late one afternoon he sent Leta to see if the car was on the siding. Not taking time to saddle Buster, she swung up on him bareback, guiding him with just a halter rope and headed for the tracks at a leisurely lope. Finding the siding empty she pointed Buster toward home.

When she was about one half mile from the house, John looked up from his labor to see three coyotes following her. Grabbing his rifle he ran to meet her. Rabies was his greatest fear. As soon as he was close enough he took aim, but the coyotes bolted off before he could get a shot at them. Seeing her father running toward her with the rifle, she looked around and saw the three coyotes racing for the timber. She quickly urged her pony into a hard gallop.

That evening Leta and Agnes were searching for the cows in a stand of thick timber and had not noticed the same coyotes following them. Then Old Dog caught their scent and raced off after them. Before the girls realized what he was after he already had one of the coyotes by the tail and was rolling it over and over. The other two wild curs were snarling and snapping at the dog. Old Dog turned the coyote lose and grabbed another by the tail and rolled it on the ground. Suddenly all three coyotes ran off a short distance, sat down, raised their muzzles to the sky and began to howl. Certain the wild canines were calling for help, the terrified girls kicked their horses into a hard run for home with the aging dog racing close on their heels.

Jumping off her pony just outside the barn, Leta ran inside to find her father. "Papa! Papa! The coyotes followed us! They are still out there!" Leta told him, trying to catch her breath.

Dropping his hammer he grabbed a bridle, "Go to the house and get the gun." Quickly putting a bridle on the horse in the stall he was repairing, Leta raced for the house. Astride the horse bareback, John met her as she came out of the house, rifle in hand. Handing it up to her father Leta watched, her heart still pounding, as he galloped off.

Later when John returned with the cows, he had one dead coyote hanging in front of him across the horse. "Had a little trouble calming this pony down when I slung this varmint on his back." He said as he slid off the still skittish horse. Leta led the pony to the barn while her father hung the coyote up to skin. She knew her mother would make good use of the fur.

A few days later Leta and her father were picking up roots in one of the fields that needed cleared before winter set in. Dark pewter clouds rolled overhead. They could hear the thunder in the distance. Lightning bolts flashed from the rumbling clouds to the earth. "We had better head for home, girl," John told her as he threw a large root on the wagon.

Leta scrambled onto the wagon as her father quickly climbed up beside her. Urging the team into a fast trot, John remembered a close neighbor that did not heed a storm's warning and continued plowing his field. He was plowing with four horses abreast when lightning struck the outside horses in his hitch killing them instantly as well as a colt that was following close beside its mother. Thereafter, every time there was a thunder storm, the man would suffer from terrible headaches.

Not even a faint breeze stirred the warm dense air as the black clouds tumbled across the sky. Blinding bolts of lightning connected them to the horizon in every direction. "Hang on, Leta." John slapped the reins on the horses' rumps and they galloped toward home. He had to get the horses in the barn and unhitched. The metal rings and chains on the harness could be very dangerous. John also feared this storm would stir up a cyclone.

Driving the team into the barn, John jumped off and began unhitching them from the wagon. Without a word, Leta quickly helped her father get the potentially dangerous harness off the horses. Leaving the wagon in the middle of the barn they put the team in their respective stalls. Making sure the wet horses had grain and water before making their way, bent against the now blustering wind, to the house. Thunder rattled the windows and shook the earth. Bolts of lightning flashed in the black sky the entire night. To everyone's relief no cyclone developed but the rain poured down in sheets for hours.

The next morning dawned calm and fair. The bright sun glistened on the wet grass. Leta and Leila were taking their father's one-and-a-half horse power motor to the Schmitz farm to earn extra money sawing wood for him. As soon as they had completed their chores, the girls had hitched a pony to the small wagon, loaded the motor, and left before their mother could change her mind about letting them go.

John had traded work for the small motor which was also used to run the washing machine he had bartered for. Myrtle was such a stickler for cleanliness the girls would rub their knuckles raw scrubbing the laundry in strong lye water. Reluctantly she had to admit the machine with its hand cranking wringer got the clothes much cleaner.

After Leta and Leila had finished sawing nearly a cord of wood, Mr. Schmitz asked the girls, "Would you two like to ride into Shellbrook with me. Thought you might like to spend some of your money," he said with a twinkle in his eye. He knew the girls seldom got an opportunity to go to town. "Mrs. Schmitz needs a few things and we won't be long." Since they had finished early they both eagerly agreed to go with him.

Arriving in Shellbrook the first automobile either girl had ever seen was parked in front of the general store. As they walked around it in awe, gazing at the shiny black fenders and spoke wheels, the owner came out and asked if they would like to go for a ride. Mr. Schmitz knew the man well and knew the girls would be safe with him and his 'contraption' as he called it. "You enjoy your ride now. I will meet you back here shortly," Mr. Schmitz told them, entering the general store.

The girls climbed in and sat gingerly on the edge of the shiny new black leather seat. Cranking the motor, it started with a loud back-fire scaring the horses across the street. Prancing and yanking back on their halter ropes they tried in vain to escape from the explosive noise. When car settled down to a noisy chug-a-chug, shaking from side to side on spindly wheels, the driver climbed in beside the girls. "Scoot back and hang on." He told them with a grin as they lurched down the dusty street. Eyes wide with excitement, the girls grinned from ear to ear as they rode down the short rutted street and back at a tremendous speed of 15 miles per hour.

On the way home from the Schimtz' the girls agreed they better not tell their mother about going into Shellbrook and certainly not about the automobile. But Leta could hardly wait to tell her father about their adventure.

That February, on a cold clear day, John came home leading a beautiful lively stepping bay with the conformation of a quarter horse. He had four white stockings and a white blaze down his face. "He is only green broke so you will have to train him to harness." Her father told Leta as he handed her the halter rope. She was thrilled with her new pony and promptly naming him Pat. By the middle of March Leta was driving him to school hitched to the cutter with Buster. Leila did not want to ride with her but it was either that or walk to school. She complained that Leta drove too fast. But walking to school appealed to Leila less than a wild ride with Leta in the cutter.

During the summer to earn extra money for themselves, Leta and Leila hauled cow manure to the neighbors' fields and spread it for 35 cents a load. By fall they had nearly $6.00 each to spend, a real fortune. After school each day they spent hours searching through the Timothy Eaton catalog for hair pins and other feminine notions.

The following spring, Leta saw a perfect match for Pat at the Bersinger's. When she told her mother about the horse, Myrtle surprised her by telling her, "If Mr. Bersinger is agreeable to it, you can have 40 hens to trade for him." Leta did not waste any time catching the hens. She packed them in crates, loaded them on the wagon and hauled them over to the Bersinger's. Leta knew Mr. Bersinger would be more willing to trade if she had the hens with her.

Leta found Mr. Bersinger working in his barn and he stood patiently smiling down at her. She was talking as fast as she could without taking a breath. She seemed afraid if she did not get her rehearsed speech out all at once she would lose her nerve.

"Well, that sounds like a right fair deal to me. The Missus could use more chickens." He said with a twinkle in his eye. "We best get these hens in the coop and go catch your horse." Leta beamed up at him as she breathed an audible sigh of relief.

Tying her new pony to the back of the wagon, Leta waved to the Bersingers and she pointed Buster toward home. Looking back at her prize prancing along behind the wagon she quickly named him Dick. She would need her father to help her train this one since he was barely halter broke. When she got home with her new horse, her father examined him closely and told her proudly, "You made a fine deal, girl. A find deal indeed."

That same afternoon Dick's training began. John put a saddle on the lively pony and with a long rope attached to his halter made him run around and around in a circle. When he showed signs of fatigue, John put Leta in the saddle, and she would ride him around in the corral.

Convincing Leila she needed her help, the next day Leta saddled both Buster and Dick, fastening Dick's halter rope to Buster. Leila climbed up on Buster and when Leta mounted Dick she glimpsed her mother watching them covertly as she hung out the clothes. Grabbing up the reins, Leta kicked Dick in the sides and away they charged. Dick took off ahead of Buster pulling them all straight toward the barbed wire fence. Leta heard her mother scream, "Stop them John! They're going for the fence!"

Before John could put down his shovel, Leta yanked Dick to a sliding stop inches from the hazardous wire. Swinging him around, she slapped his rump with the end of the reins and he bolted down the road with Buster trying to keep up. Precariously perched astride Buster, Leila was hanging on for dear life.

When the two girls charged past Mr. Bersinger's field, he looked up from his plowing to see a large dust storm billowing up the road. Pulling the six horses he had hitched abreast of his plow to a stop, he laughed when he saw that it was only Leta on Dick dragging Leila and Buster along behind her.

It wasn't long before Leta had Dick broke to ride and trained to the harness. One icy morning the Oesch girls were on their way to school, Leila and Elsie riding Buster and Leta riding Dick. As they trotted down the road, Dick's feet went out from under him nearly hanging Leta on the barbed wire fence. Telling her sisters to go on to school, Leta led the limping pony back home.

"He's strained a tendon in his hind leg. You will have to leave him out in the pasture until it heals," her father told her after examining the pony.

By late summer, Dick had been out to pasture for about four months. John needed Leta to help him drive some cattle to the railroad station in Shellbrook and she planned to ride Dick. He was feeling his oats and started to buck as soon as Leta was mounted. Every time he came down on all fours John would yell, "Hang on, Leta! Hang on!" By the time they had covered the 15 miles to Shellbrook and back, Dick was not quite so frisky.

While in Shellbrook, Leta and John stopped in to see Dr. French to remind her of the long awaited upcoming fishing trip with them and the Bersingers at their favorite lake about 50 miles from Shellbrook. Everyone liked and respected Dr. French. She was a big and rather masculine woman. She was an excellent doctor who would go through the worst storm to tend to her patients. She hailed from England, bringing along two thoroughbred horses and two Airedale dogs.

There was a fairly good road to the lake that could be traveled by car, but the last 7 miles had to be traveled by horse and buggy or team and wagon. It had been planned that Myrtle and the Bersingers would be going the entire way by wagon so they were going on ahead. Dr. French would bring John and Leta in her car, meet the others at the end of the road and go the rest of the way in the wagon.

The week they spent at the lake was a rare experience for the Oesch girls. Not once did they get a stern look from their mother nor a harsh word. They fished with their father, explored around the lake and, for once, were allowed to be children.

A few days after returning from the fishing trip, Myrtle rousted the girls out of bed well before daylight. It was berry picking day and she was going to make sure all their chores were completed before they left to pick berries. Leta hitched Pat and Dick to the democrat. They would be picking up Mrs. Barkway and her daughter-in-law Mabel on the way. Myrtle packed a hearty lunch into a large basket. They always made a full day of picking as many different varieties as they could find; blue berries, black berries, goose berries, and raspberries. The strawberry season had already come and went.

Leta did not argue when her mother insisted on driving the team. She knew better than say a word even though she did not relish the idea of anyone else driving her team particularly her mother who drove with a heavy hand. Hiding her unhappiness as she always did, Leta climbed into the back of the democrat and sat on the box that replaced the rear seat, next to her sisters.

The sun was barely peeking over the horizon when Myrtle jerked the team to a halt in front of the Barkway's house. Mrs. Barkway and Mabel were waiting on the porch with their berry baskets stacked beside them. Leta and Elsie jumped down and loaded the baskets in the back as the two women seated themselves beside Myrtle.

"How is your sewing coming along, Leta?" Mrs. Barkway asked.

"Fine, thank you," Leta replied politely. Mrs. Barkway had been a tailor in England and was teaching Leta. Leta loved tailoring. Myrtle approved of her learning a practical skill such as sewing. She even seemed pleased with the delicate embroidery work Leta did on the cuffs and collars of some of the blouses she had made.

Keeping the team at a steady pace, Myrtle held the reins firmly, taping the horse's rumps now and then when they started to lag. Dick was still being trained to harness but did well along side Pat. Suddenly a rabbit darted across the track in front of the team. Startled, both horses shied then bolted. Trying to stop the terrified team, Myrtle pulled back on the reins with all her strength but they were out of control. The buggy hit a stump at the edge of the track, throwing everyone, and everything, through the air. As she flew out, Leta caught her head between the rear wheel and the buggy box pulling out a clump of hair. Human screams intensified the horses' terror and they took off like a gun shot with the empty buggy bouncing crazily along behind them.

Still stunned, her head bleeding and throbbing, Leta struggled to her feet. Leila was sitting on the ground squalling. Elsie was trying to comfort her. Myrtle and Mabel were struggling shakily to their feet. Still dazed, they rushed to Mrs. Barkway who was lying motionless in the bushes beside the track.

Leta's only concern was for her horses. They were gone, up over the sand hills. She started after them with her head throbbing and dizziness nearly overwhelming her. "If you find them, you wait until I get there." Myrtle called after her.

Leta found the trembling team several hundred feet away standing in the swamp. She was pulling off her shoes and stockings when Myrtle caught up with her. The tongue was bent under the buggy, the horses were tangled in their harness and the water was nearly up to their bellies. Wading waist high in the murky water, Leta led them out. They were so jumpy she had a hard time controlling them. Leta knew Dick would be more skittish than Pat. The horses were marked almost exactly alike and she hadn't noticed that they had switched sides.

Myrtle helped Leta lead them back to where Mabel was tending to Mrs. Barkway. Elsie and Leila were setting in the grass beside them, pale and shaken. Elsie helped Leta hold the horses while Myrtle and Mabel got Mrs. Barkway settled under a tree so they could see to her injuries. She had a bad heart and they were afraid for her. Myrtle snapped at Leila, "Quit sniveling and go find the water jug!" Wiping her eyes and sniffing, Leila reluctantly did what she was told.

"Leta, you will have to go get Reg. Tell him to bring our wagon." Obeying her mother's command, she swung up on a muddy horse not realizing it was Dick. He was so jumpy she could barely control him all the way to the Barkway's. Finding Reg in the field he quickly unhitched his team from the plow when Leta told him what had happened. He swung up on one of the horses and rode at a fast clip to the barn with Leta racing along side.

Tying Leta's team to the back of his wagon, Reg took Mabel and Mrs. Barkway home first, then Myrtle and the girls. They would go get the buggy later. By this time Leta had begun to shake all over, her head ached terribly and she had a large red lump where the mass of hair had been pulled out. Mrs. Barkway had a sprained ankle and the others had minor scrapes and bruises.

John was coming out of the barn when Reg pulled the team to a halt in the yard. Reg quickly related to him what had happened. After making sure his family was all right, John unknowingly hitched Dick up with one of his big mares to go after the wrecked buggy. The skittish horse gave John a bad time but John held him firm, the mare almost dragging him along. By the time John got back with the damaged buggy, Dick had been effectively worn down. After that episode, Leta didn't have much trouble with him.

Chapter Twenty Four

Most families now owned an automobile and the versatile blacksmith had established the first garage in Shellbrook. To the Oesch girls delight, John bought a new 1916 Model T Ford. As was most of the new cars, it was open to the weather. A thunderstorm would quickly turn a dirt road into a quagmire as well as soak the inside of the car and everyone in it before they could put the top up and fasten the side curtains.

Both the towns of Shellbrook and Prince Albert were growing too fast for John's liking. Prince Albert had grown from a little over 3,000 to well over 6,000 in population from 1906 to 1911. And now the figure was well over that. John was glad he had quit the freighting business years earlier and no longer had to go into Prince Albert. He had never liked cities.

During this same year, John's brother Dave and his family moved from Kansas to Canada. Dave's daughter Elsie and Leta quickly became fast friends even though they lived in separate districts. Leta lived in the Rich Valley District and Elsie in the Silver Cliff District. Every chance they got they would spend hours together. Since the Olsen's lived between both Oesch families, and much to the girls delight, the Uncles would frequently concoct some chore they would need Leta and Elsie to help them with so the girls could spend some time together.

Leta taught Elsie to crochet and they would spend hours hidden away making all kinds of doilies and such. Leta knew if Myrtle ever found out that she and Elsie were wasting their time with such 'foolishness', as her Mother called it, both girls would have felt the sting of a willow switch.

But when Elsie's mother Phinney died suddenly, Myrtle picked a huge bunch of wild flowers and made a beautiful wreath for the plain casket John and Dave had made of Tamarack wood. For a small moment in time, Myrtle allowed a faint flicker of compassion to show through her emotional armor. She knew all too well the pain of losing ones mother. But Myrtle snuffed out the emotion so quickly, Leta thought she had imagined it.

In the weeks after Phinney had been laid to rest, Myrtle allowed Leta to go every day to help with the extra burden that now fell on Elsie. Leta and Elsie became even closer friends during this difficult time.

Leta won a Brownie box camera at school in the fall of 1917. Both Leta and Elsie were in the seventh grade and quickly learned how to be photographers. They coerced everyone they could to stand and pose for their pictures. The flash unit was a teaspoon of gun powder on a tin pan. After they posed their subjects, a match was touched to the gun powder, it flashed and that moment in time was captured forever. The girls tried taking pictures of the animals, but the furry creatures would not cooperate by standing still long enough. When Leta's teacher helped her develop the film she told her she should stick to human subjects for her photographs.

Later during that school year, Leta brought a month old newspaper home to her father. In it he read that the U. S. had declared war on Germany. He knew it would be the beginning of a world war. He was thankful he had daughters and they were all far away from those troubles.

Another year had slipped by and it was haying time again. As usual Leta was helping her father rake and haul the hay to the barn. John wanted to get all the hay in the barn before dark. He could smell rain in the air. It was still early afternoon when ominous dark clouds began rolling overhead and the wind began to blow. The distant deep rumble of thunder could be heard. John quickly scanned the far horizon for lightning. When he saw a funnel cloud forming, he yelled to Leta, "We had better get to the barn!"

Quickly unhitching the team and leaving the rake in the field, each leaped astride a Belgian and galloped toward home. Just before they reached the safety of the barn, the cyclone started touching down, skipping across the field. As they neared the barn yard, the powerful wind sucked the water tank up spraying water like rain as it disappeared into the black funnel cloud. Leta could not hear her father's shouts above the roar of the wind. Tree limbs, brush, and debris were flying everywhere.

Dismounting inside the barn, he grabbed Leta by the arm and shouted, "Get in the root cellar. I better stay with the horses." He knew Myrtle would already be there with the other two girls. Leta wanted to stay and help him with the horses, but obeyed her father without question. Fighting against the wind as she made her way to the root cellar she nearly fell down the stairs when she reached them. Pulling open the heavy plank door she saw Myrtle and her sisters huddled together in a far corner.

The next day they heard that their water tank ended up a half mile away in a neighbor's field. Another neighbor lost the new addition he was building on his house, but the old original part was left untouched. Everyone was thankful no lives, including stock, had been lost. But most of John's hay had disappeared along with the funnel cloud and that was bad enough.

After assessing the damage, families went from farm to farm helping each other rebuild everything that had been destroyed in the storm. What one neighbor lost, another shared. John and Myrtle had lost nearly all their hay crop. Another family had lost their entire vegetable garden so the families swapped vegetables for hay.

It was 1919 and John wanted a better education for Leta so he and Myrtle decided that she should go to the collegiate school in Prince Albert. Her sister Elsie still attended the small country school in the Rich Valley District. Leila went so seldom anyway she had quit attending school the year before.

"I'm so excited, Elsie. But I'm a little scared too. Prince Albert is too big." Leta and her cousin sat in the shade of the narrow porch shelling peas. "I won't be able to come home until Winter break."

"You will be so busy, the time will fly by. And when you come home you can tell me all about it." Elsie smiled. "You might even meet some handsome young man that will sweep you off your feet just like Frank did me."

At 16 Elsie seemed much older than her years and had encouraged Leta to go to Prince Albert when Leta had voiced her fears as well as her excitement to her friend. A few months before, Elsie had married Frank Johnson, a quiet man of 32, and they were expecting their first child. The couple had moved in with the Oeschs until Frank could get a cabin built.

"No young man for me. You know I want my teaching certificate."

Two days before she was to leave for school, Leta sat behind the wheel of the Model-T while John jacked it up and spun the rear wheel to get it started. The crank had broken and she was on her way to Shellbrook to buy another. When the automobile started with a chug-chug, John quickly kicked it off the jack and yelled to Leta as she lurched down the road, gripping the steering wheel in both hands. "Don't kill it, Leta!"

Half way to town she was still merrily chugging along with the wheels in the deep ruts which were like reversed railroad tracks. Once the wheels were in these ruts there was no getting out. Suddenly she spotted a cow in the middle of the road. Knowing she couldn't stop for fear of killing the motor, she closed her eyes, gripped the wheel, gave the cow a sound thump and kept right on going. Quickly glancing back she saw the cow standing dazed at the side of the road. Later, on the way back from town, she looked for the same cow but did not see any sign of her. When she arrived home and told her father about the cow he laughed, "That cow will probably stay clear of any automobiles from now on."

The big day had arrived. It was time to go. Leta felt a huge lump in her throat as she climbed into the Model T. Her father was driving her to the train station in Shellbrook. In her small valise she had packed the two new dresses she had made for herself, and few personal items: a comb and brush, a small hand mirror, hair ribbons of various colors, hair pins, a small picture taken of the family with her Brownie camera, and her crochet hook. She had used nearly every penny she had saved to buy the material for the dresses. She wanted something new for school this year. After all, she was in high school now.

John looked over and smiled at his grown up daughter sitting beside him and felt a tug at his heart as he put the Model T in gear. Leta looked back at her sisters, a tear started to form, but she smiled at them and waved. She would miss them terribly. Leila and Elsie stood on the front porch waving as they drove away. Myrtle did not interrupt her chores nor did she even step outside to see her oldest daughter off.

In no time, it seemed to Leta, they were at the train station in Shellbrook. "I'm going to miss you, Papa." She said climbing aboard the train to Prince Albert, the lump in her throat growing larger.

"I will miss you too, Little One." He had not called her that in many years and a lump was growing in his own throat. "But you will be home again before you know it."

She nodded, afraid to speak. The train started to move as she made her way into the passenger coach, found a seat and waved from the window. Not wanting to cry in front of strangers, she held back the tears, but then she was used to holding back her emotions. As the landscape rolled by she began to think of school and the people she would meet. The feeling of excitement returned and she was looking forward to the new school year.

When Leta arrived in Prince Albert there was no one to meet her, but she had the address of the boarding house where she was to stay, tucked in her pocket. Arrangements had been made for her to work for her room and board and the rooming house was close enough to the school so she could walk. After asking directions she started off carrying her small valise. She had not been in Prince Albert in over two years and the town was so much bigger than she remembered. Leta began to feel a little nervous and very much alone.

About thirty minutes later, Leta stopped in front of a large white frame house with blue shutters and a blue door. A sign hanging from the porch read, "Henderson's Boarding House". She breathed a sigh of relief as she mounted the stairs to the front door. She was beginning to feel a little weary as she knocked on the enameled wood. A stout gray haired lady opened the door wiping her hands on a clean white apron. "You must be Leta," she said with a smile. "Come in, my dear. I am Mrs. Henderson. Oh, my. You are early. I did not expect you until later. No matter. Let me show you to your room." Mrs. Henderson spoke in a constant nervous chatter as Leta followed to her new room. She did not stop speaking until they reached Leta's room in the back of the house.

"Well, this is it. I hope you like it. As soon as you are unpacked come on in to the kitchen and you can help me with supper. Oh, yes. The bath room is just down the hall here." Mrs. Henderson finished, scurrying down the long narrow hallway back to the kitchen.

It only took Leta a few minutes to unpack. She loved her room. It was small but cozy with flowered wallpaper and a large braided rug on the floor. The single bed was covered with a thick blue and white quilt. Beneath the yellow lace curtained window was a small table with one chair that was perfect for her studies. On her way to the kitchen Leta peeked in the bathroom door. It was the first indoor bathroom she had ever seen and could hardly wait to use the large claw footed bathtub that gleamed snowy white against the cobalt blue tiled wall. As soon as she entered the kitchen Mrs. Henderson handed Leta a clean white apron and had her peeling potatoes before she could even say "hello".

The next two months were extremely difficult for Leta. Her days were long and full. She labored over her school lessons for hours every night after finishing her chores at the boarding house. She was up again before dawn, studied for two hours, did her morning chores, then walked to school. Never having known anyone who talked so much, let alone being around them in close proximity, was exhausting in itself. The adjustment of being away from familiar surroundings, the noise of the city, the hustle and bustle was a cultural shock to Leta.

Her work at the boarding house coupled with her school work began to take its toll. Leta had so much to do for Mrs. Henderson she did not have sufficient time for her school work. It was a struggle every day trying to keep up with it all. When her grades began to fall, she knew she had to find another place to room where she would not have quite so much extra work so she could spend more time on her lessons.

As soon as she had the opportunity she asked one of her teachers, "Do you know of someone who could use some help in trade for room and board that would be close to the school?"

This kindly teacher knew how hard Leta worked and told her of a friend that owned a restaurant with a small furnished apartment above it. She suggested that Leta go talk to her friend that afternoon. Leta was elated when her teacher's friend, Mrs. Johansen, agreed to let her stay in the apartment in exchange for working in the restaurant mornings only. It was a longer walk to school but Leta did not mind at all.

The single room apartment was roomy with a small bay window dressed in cream colored lace curtains that held a small writing desk and chair. Leta was thrilled when she discovered the apartment also had its own private bathroom. The narrow single bed was against the wall opposite the bay window. There was a small wood stove just inside the door, and a bright floral rug covered the floor. "This is perfect," Leta said to herself and moved in that same day. The room was perfect. The job was perfect. And, Mrs. Johansen was a woman of few words. Everything was perfect.

As soon as she was settle in, Leta sat down at the small desk in the bay window of her apartment to write her parents of her address change. As she began the letter, Leta felt the old anxiety she always felt at home when she had to tell her mother something Leta was sure she would not approve of. "At least Mama is far enough away the worst thing she can do is write me a stinging letter," Leta reassured herself.

The response to her letter came quickly. Leta's hand shook slightly as she opened the envelope written in her mother's hand. Relief washed over her as she read the words, "I am pleased you are doing well and your accommodations are more suitable for your studies." Tears of happiness began to slide down her face as she continued on. "Your father will be coming to bring you a pony and cutter so it will be easier for you to get around..." Papa was coming. Her heart was so full she thought it would burst.

The load she carried was nearly staggering but Leta loved every minute of it. She amazed Mrs. Johansen at the amount of work she could accomplish before going to school each morning. Then, after walking the two miles over ice and snow covered roads and back home every afternoon, she would pour over her mountain of homework far into the night.

She loved learning new things and absorbed the knowledge like a sponge. In studying current events in the United States she learned that this year, 1919, the 19th Amendment was passed giving the women there the right to vote. Also in January of this same year the United States Prohibition Amendment had been proclaimed.

John arrived in mid-December driving a sleigh with Elsie following in the cutter. Leta was elated when she saw them both. She had not realized until that moment how terribly homesick she had been. A surprise from her mother was a box full of home-canned goods. She discovered moose meat, sauerkraut, blueberry jam, strawberry preserves, stew, and vegetable soup. She was delighted with the familiar foods even though she ate all her meals at the restaurant.

After paying Mrs. Johansen board for the horse he would be leaving with Leta, John led the pony and his team to the small barn behind the restaurant. Mrs. Johansen refused his offer to pay to house his own team for the night.

That evening as John and his daughters were eating their meal in Mrs. Johansen's restaurant, conversation between them was lively and light. But Leta was stunned into silence when her father suddenly said, "We are going to Missouri. If we like it we will buy a farm and re-settle down there. Sold the stock last week and the farm has been rented out."

Leta's head was spinning. Her family was leaving Canada? Her father loved Canada. It was home. She knew how hard both her parents had struggled to carve a home out of the Canadian wilderness. This had to be her mother's doing. She knew her father would never go otherwise.

To lighten the dark mood that had suddenly overwhelmed Leta, John began to tell her of the plane that landed in Shellbrook. Elsie giggled and cut in, "Papa came to school and got us and Leila didn't tighten her cinch. The saddle started to fall off and her pony got scared and took off. She looked so funny hanging from his neck."

"Well, thank God she was not hurt." He continued with a little chuckle, "That pony took off like a streak of lightning. Didn't catch up with her till we got to town. He had banged her up pretty good with his knees but she hung on." Finishing his last bite, he laid his fork and knife across his plate and pushed himself back from the table.

"You want some pie, Papa?" Leta asked.

"No room left. You were sure right about Mrs. Johansen being a good cook. But I think we had better turn in. Need to be headed home early tomorrow and I still have supplies to pick up." No more was said about the move to Missouri.

Early the next morning John and Elsie were bundled up against the bitter cold ready to head back home. They would make one stop for some supplies then would be on their way.

"I wish you could stay longer." Leta said, tears stinging the backs of her eyes.

"We will be on our way to Missouri before you know it so you will be seeing us again soon." He assured her. "And remember, it's just another blackberry winter." Leta remembered throughout her childhood whenever she hit a big bump in life's road her father would tell her, "The blackberries are always the biggest and sweetest after a long, hard winter. And it's the same in life. It's the tough times that make us better and stronger." But nothing lifted the dark gloom hanging over Leta. They might not be coming back from Missouri and she knew she could not bear that. Elsie turned and waved. Leta felt emptiness in her soul and a tug at her heart as she watched them drive away. Tears streamed down her cheeks.

Leta slowly walked up the stairs to her room with a big empty place in her heart. She was so afraid if they left Canada she would never see them again. Suddenly her life was taking too many new roads.

Chapter Twenty Five

Early in January Leta woke with a pounding headache. Lifting her head from the pillow, the painful throbbing intensified. She lay very still for a few minutes hoping it would go away. But after dozing a few minutes she felt much worse. Her entire body ached terribly. Even her skin hurt...it felt dry and hot and her eyes burned. With great effort she rose and poured a glass of water from the green glass pitcher on the table. After a few sips she was sure the water would come back up. Suddenly she began to chill. Shaking uncontrollably she made her way back to the bed and pulled the quilts tightly around her. She wanted to build up the fire in the heater but was afraid if she got up again she would faint.

When Leta did not appear for work on time, Mrs. Johansen became worried and came up to check on her. Upon finding Leta burning up with fever and a rash spreading over her, she quickly called the other hired girl. "Go hitch up Leta's cutter and bring it around front. We have to get her to the hospital." Having lost two children with Scarlet Fever, Mrs. Johansen knew what was wrong immediately. Wrapping Leta tightly in wool quilts she had the handyman carry her out to the cutter.

Arriving at the hospital, a doctor carefully lifted Leta out of the cutter and carried her inside. "It's scarlet fever, Doctor. I know it is," Mrs. Johansen said, wringing her hands as she scurried alongside him. Even before examining Leta the doctor knew Mrs. Johansen was right. He quickly carried Leta into a small empty ward and gently laid her on one of the beds. "Now don't you worry, Mrs. Johansen we will take good care of her," he said, trying to reassure her. "Where are her parents?"

"They are in the States," she told him.

A young girl in a nurse's uniform entered the room and quickly began assisting the doctor. Leta was barely conscious as the doctor gave her a spoonful of medication. "Keep her as comfortable as possible and see to it she takes this every two hours. It will bring down the fever and help her sleep," he instructed, handing the bottle to the nurse. "Watch her temperature. If she gets delirious, call me immediately." Turning to Mrs. Johansen he said, "You need to get along home now, Mrs. Johansen, and don't worry. She is in good hands." The strange voices sounded far away and everything seemed to be spinning as Leta slipped into a deep sleep.

Two days later Leta woke and saw a girl not much older than herself, dressed in white, setting in a chair beside the bed knitting. Leta tried to speak but her throat was dry and raw and her head was still throbbing.

"Are you feeling any better?" the young woman asked, rising to give her some water. After a couple of sips Leta nodded. "But still not quite ship-shape, eh? Here, take some more of this." The nurse spooned the bitter-tasting medicine into her mouth.

"Where am I?" Leta asked, confused.

"You are in the hospital. They brought you in a couple of days ago with the scarlet fever. I am your nurse, Miss McIntyre, and we are going to be here awhile. We have been quarantined together so I will be taking care of you." Leta nodded and tried to smile as she fell asleep again.

The entire 30 days she was in the hospital, Leta was the only patient. Whenever the doctor came in he brought the crochet thread and books she had asked for. Not accustomed to asking for anything it took the doctor awhile to get it out of her what she would like to have to occupy her time.

To help pass the time, Leta taught Miss McIntyre to crochet. The two young women made fancy collars for their dresses with matching cuffs, and doilies for chairs and side tables. At times the nurse would read to Leta while she crocheted. Leta's favorite poem was *The Homesteader*, so Miss McIntyre would read it in the evenings just before she lowered the lights for Leta to sleep. As she read, Leta would recite it in her mind along with her...

"It was in snow plated Saskatchewan
          In the Northern Frigid Zone,
It is hard to hold down a homestead
          When a fellow is all alone.
In the winter, out in this frozen land,
          The jack rabbits all turn white;
And look like a lot of phantoms
          When they parade around at night.
The aurora borealis lights up the northern sky,
          Huge owls with snowy plumage
Sound like angels flitting by.
The days grow short, and shorter,
          And the mercury drops very low
The wind, as it hurries southward
          Picks up great drifts of snow.
The homesteader, in his lonely shack,
          Stirs the fire until it roars,
And swearing softly buttons his coat

It is time to do the chores.
He hurries through his nightly chores
  The wind blows through his clothes,
And when he gets back to his fire
  He has a badly frostbitten nose.
He buried his face in a handful of snow
  To take out the frost and pain,
And swore if he got out of this country alive
  He would never come back again.
The days and weeks and months crept by
  And spring was long over due
The homesteader prayed and cursed, by turns
  He was frozen thro' and thro'.
One day from the great Southwest
  A Chinook wind began to blow
It warmed the heart of the lonely man
  As it melted the drifts of snow.
One day the homesteader was up at dawn
  As the sun was turning back the dark
When he heard the sweetest music ever heard
  It was the song of a meadow lark.
He looked around for the little chap
  And his face was wreathed with smiles
As he threw him a handful of grain to eat
  After the flight of many miles.
They became great friends, the man and the bird
  And they filled the days with cheer,
As the big man whistled, and the little bird sang
  And the music was good to hear.
The weeks and months and years rolled by
  Every spring the bird came back,
The big man had proved up on his claim,
  And had made a home of the homestead shack.
One day in the fall when the work was done,
  The bird and the man took wing
To spend the winter in the sunny South

But they both promised to come back in the spring.
The next spring, when the Chinook had melted the snow
        The man and the bird came back.
And with them the girl who had waited so long
        To share their lot in the homestead shack."

As Leta drifted off to sleep she could see the unknown author, the meadow lark, and the homestead shack in her minds eye.

Having missed so much school, Leta would not be able to go back again until fall session began. She regained her full strength and energy within a few weeks. Mrs. Johansen told her not to worry, she could utilize her full-time in the restaurant. Leta would be able to keep the apartment and earn a little extra money as well. Every Sunday, as no one worked on Sundays, she would hitch up her cutter and explore the city and surrounding countryside.

One crisp, cool, Sunday afternoon as she trotted along beside the railroad track there were two cutters, one on each side of the road, coming toward her. She could see the train coming in the distance but did not think anything of it as she approached the other cutters. She smiled and nodded to each driver as she began to pass between them. The moment the three cutters were lined up, the train blew its blaring whistle. Her horse panicked. He squatted, trying to run away from the terrifying noise. First he jumped one way and then the other as Leta struggled to hold him down. The men in the other cutters stopped their ponies, holding them with a tight rein so their horses would not bolt. Suddenly, in the cramped space, Leta's pony turned around between the two cutters and bolted back toward town. Both men watched the spectacle in disbelief.

By the time he had raced to the outskirts of town, Leta had slowed the horse to a brisk trot. When she finally pulled him to a stop in front of the barn she was shaking all over. She vowed she would not ride along the tracks again.

Fall session was about to begin again and Leta could hardly wait to get back in school. Before returning to classes she went home for two weeks as her family had returned from Missouri. The move had turned into an enormous disaster. Her father decided that Canada was not so bad after all.

When Leta arrived home she was pleasantly surprised to find that nothing had changed. Everything was just as she remembered it. Her happiness soon dissipated as Myrtle's bitterness and anger toward John was now directed toward Leta and her sisters. Myrtle had all three girls working the vegetable garden as soon as their regular chores were completed each morning. They barely had time to finish their evening chores before supper.

The work load was nearly overwhelming but working in the garden all day, every day, became a refuge for the girls. The tension between their parents was stifling. It was becoming so bad Leta could hardly wait to get back to school. Her father had become quiet and withdrawn and hardly spoke to anyone, staying in the fields longer and longer each day.

Never having the opportunity to speak privately to her father, Leta learned about the trip to Missouri from her sisters. Elsie told her the story as they hoed weeds in the huge garden, working parallel in their respective rows.

"Papa strapped the extra baggage to the top of the Model-T and we made sure the tube repair kit was all there and the three spare tires had enough air in them. Then we piled in the car and bumped down the road."

"It was an awful trip," Leila whined, leaning on her hoe. "I'm glad to be home."

"It was fun," Elsie said continuing. "We went through the Dakotas the same way Mama and Papa came up here. Only it was much faster than the wagons." With barely a pause she snapped at Leila, "Leila you better keep hoeing or you will have Mama out here after us." Grudgingly Leila continued to chop at the stubborn weeds.

Leta smiled at the aggressiveness of her youngest sister as Elsie continued with the story. "When we got to Missouri we visited Florence, Mama's half-sister, and then we went on to Papa's sister Maggie's. Papa got awful sick there. The doctor told him it was the Dakota water. As soon as Papa got better, we went to stay with Aunt Mattie in Milford, Nebraska. Oh, Leta, the Ozark Mountains are beautiful. I wish you could have been with us." Elsie's eyes were shinning.

"So do I. Hurry and tell me the rest before Mama comes out here," Leta told her, keeping her head down so her mother would not see them talking.

"Anyway," Elsie went on, "as soon as we arrived at Aunt Mattie's, Papa got sick again. It was Small Pox and we all got it. I got it after Papa then everyone had it, even Mama and Aunt Mattie and all her family."

"Aunt Mattie said she just thanked God that no one died." Leila recounted, adding, "As soon as we got well enough, Papa packed everything up and we came home." The girls worked silently for a time staying abreast of one another.

Giggling, Elsie continued. "The water there is stored in a large cistern and worms got into our drinking water. Aunt Mattie told us they were only mosquito wigglers but Papa said that was the last straw. We were going back to Canada. The States were not for him. He was a Canadian and he would live in Canada for the rest of his days."

After a pause she added, "Mama was furious when he would not change his mind and stay in the States. For once he stood up for himself. He told her he had hardly been sick a day in his life and in the few months they had been in the States he nearly died. And then he told her she could come with us or stay behind. But he was taking his girls back to Canada. Leila and I thought she was going to have a fit and fall back in it. But she clamped her jaws shut, you know how she does, and never said another word to him or us for the whole trip back home."

"So that's why she keeps us working out here. So we don't have a chance to talk to him either," Leta said sadly.

Elsie nodded and went on, "I was glad to get back home."

"Me too," Leila said. "It was too cold and wet there. Papa said the dampness crept right to the bones. We could never get warm. There was a coal strike going on and since everyone heated their houses with coal, they were all freezing cold. I would rather be here with all the snow. It is warmer."

"I thought I would freeze to death too but I loved eating at the restaurants we stopped at. They had so much wonderful food, we couldn't stop often enough for me," Elsie added. Myrtle usually cooked hearty one dish meals that could be left simmering on the stove all day. Only when company was expected could the Oesch girls expect more than a one course meal.

Now that her family was back on the farm, Leta didn't feel so homesick when she returned to school. Mrs. Johansen had rented out the room above the restaurant, so Leta found herself a small apartment. It was fully furnished, clean, and very modern with two rooms and its own private bath. There was a stove for cooking and heating, and a small dry sink. It was light and airy with large windows to let in the sunlight.

In order not to take her first year over, Leta had made arrangements with her second year teacher to make up all the courses she missed when she was ill. He told her she would have to maintain an acceptable grade average on all the studies she missed as well as her new studies. She was determined to do it because she did not want to take the year over.

Her father helped with her apartment expenses and would bring several boxes of food with him on his rare visits to the city. She still had a heavy work load. Each morning before school she set up tables in a large restaurant near her apartment. Every day after school and long into the night she spent hours pouring over her studies.

The work was hard and the hours long, but Leta loved every minute of it. There was so much to learn and she absorbed her new knowledge like a sponge. She was a whiz in math and english but her favorite subject was history. Memorizing facts and dates became a daily challenge.

Settling in for a long evening of study, Leta climbed into bed, fluffed her pillow against the headboard, pulled the quilts up around her, turned the lamp up on the night stand and began to read her history book. She learned that on September 17, 1878, secret ballots were used for the first time in a Federal general election. Turning page after page, she read that on February 8, 1879, Standard Time was invented by Sandford Fleming. He divided the world into 24 equal zones and this idea was adopted by 25 countries in 1884, and on New Year's Day, 1885, it went into effect.

She read on about the Metis leader, Louis Riel, Jr., an educated twenty-year-old who spoke English, French and four native languages. And as a self-proclaimed prophet, he led the Metis rebellion in 1884. It was crushed at Batoche, Saskatchewan, May 12, 1884, and on November 16, 1885, Riel was hanged for treason. Leta quickly jotted down some notes in her small notebook. She wanted to learn more about this amazingly unusual man.

Absorbing fact after fact, she learned in 1905 the territories of Assiniboia, Saskatchewan, and Athabasca were formed into the Province of Saskatchewan with 243,382 square land miles and 8318 square water miles. Total population in 1901 was 91,279 and by 1911 it was 492,432. After reading about the Hudson Bay Company monopoly, she fell asleep and began to dream about the people and events that had passed into History.

All Leta's time was taken up with work, school, and studies. There was no time for socializing. She was so shy and reserved it had taken daring for her to ask any of her classmates if they would like to ride to school with her in the cutter. Thinking they just did not like her when they always refused she was surprised to learn no one wanted to ride with her because they thought she was reckless and drove too fast. She was a good driver and she knew it. She knew just how to slide the cutter around the icy corners without turning it over. So she kept to herself and continued to study hard.

As the year wore on she slowly began to get acquainted and make a few friends. One afternoon after class, a girl that had befriended Leta asked if she would like to go on a picnic with her and some friends. Thinking it would be with a group of young people, Leta was surprised when her new friend Eunice showed up at her apartment with two nervous young men in a rattling, chugging Model-T. Leta climbed in the back seat beside a very homely young man who had the reddest hair and biggest ears she had ever seen on a human. He sported more freckles than she thought a person could have on one face. Introductions were made and the conversation was polite but a little strained.

All Leta could think of was the terrible stories her mother had told her about men. Her mother's bitter words came back to her, "Men are not to be trusted and are worse than animals". Leta was never quite sure exactly what Myrtle was talking about. She knew her father was not like that at all. The boys at school all seemed to be just roughnecks and smart alecks. But this young man they called Red was very nice and remained a perfect gentleman.

They spread their picnic lunch in the warm spring sun beside a sparkling stream. Not being accustomed to socializing with people her own age, Leta took some time overcoming her shyness. Soon Red had Leta feeling completely at ease. It wasn't long before the red-headed young man had Leta laughing and thoroughly enjoying herself. Red had brought along a ball and bat and after they had eaten, they all played a modified game of softball.

Too soon it was time to head back for town. Packing up the remains of their picnic, they all climbed into the car and were on their way. Taking a corner too fast, Charles yanked the wheel back too quickly losing control of the car. To the horror of the occupants, the vehicle shot down the slope toward the river that was nearly overflowing with the spring thaw.

Opening the rear door, Red shouted as he leaped from the car, "Quick, Leta! Jump! Jump!" Leta followed suit jumping out on her side. At the same time Eunice jumped from the front seat. Charles stood on the running board steering the car all the way down the slope. The vehicle finally stopped just before plunging into the swollen, swift current. By then the motor had died. Checking to make sure the girls were not injured, Red ran down the slope to help Charles get the runaway automobile started. There were no more mishaps the rest of the way home and they all took a vow of silence. If Charles' parents ever found out he almost wrecked their automobile they would never let him drive it again.

There was little time for picnics and social events after that memorable day. Charles' father apparently found out about the incident with the automobile as Leta did not see him driving it again. Red had been in Prince Albert visiting his Aunt and had returned to his home in Saskatoon. Before he left, he told Leta he would like to write to her. She felt he was sincere about the promise but really did not think she would ever hear from him. He was a nice young man and they had had fun together. This reinforced her opinion that you could not tell a book by its cover. She liked Red and smiled as she thought of him. She now knew that men were not at all like the creatures her mother had warned her about.

Chapter Twenty Six

The first day of December, as Leta packed a few things to go home for Christmas break, she remembered it was her mother's birthday. But there would be no mention of it when she got home. Birthdays and holidays were still not celebrated in the Oesch household. The one and only time, when they were first married, John had given Myrtle a small birthday gift. She gave him such a dressing down on what a wastrel he was, he never forgot it. He also never gave her another gift. He did not agree with her not allowing the girls to have any birthday memories. But in order to keep the peace, he kept still about it. And this year, the same as every year, there would be no Christmas celebration. Every day in December was the same as far as Myrtle was concerned, including the birthday of the Christ Child.

Leta had been home about a week when her father asked if she would like to visit her cousin Elsie while he helped Ed and Jule Olsen finish some shelters for their stock. Since Myrtle was at a neighbor's lending her skills as a mid-wife, Leta knew she would have the entire day. Leaving Leila and Elsie to tend to the house, Leta and her father left as soon as the morning chores were done.

Not one cloud interrupted the deep blue sky that stretched from horizon to horizon on this crisp, cold, clear day. The frozen snow crunched under the horses trotting hooves as they pulled the cutter smoothly along. Leta and her father were bundled up in heavy wool coats and caps, the fur lap robe tucked over their legs with the heated stone at their feet. Daylight was short on these winter days so they were anxious to be on their way. Leta had not seen much of Elsie since her marriage and had not yet seen Elsie's baby.

As John pulled the team to a stop in front of the Olsen cabin, Leta waved at Ed who greeted them from the front porch. He invited them to come in for tea and meet their nephew who had just arrived from the States. Leta was anxious to get on to Elsie's but she did not want to appear rude by rushing off. However, to her dismay, John quickly accepted the invitation as he stepped from the cutter.

When they entered the small cozy cabin, a handsome young man with sandy brown hair, deep set blue eyes, and a strong jaw line sat at the table as Jule was pouring strong tea into heavy mugs. Ed made the introductions. "John, Leta, this is our nephew, Dan."

Dan rose from the table, nodded and smiled warmly at Leta. She smiled back and nodded in greeting as her father shook Dan's extended hand. John was impressed by Dan's politeness and good manners. When his sister had died, Jule took his nephews, Bill and Dan, and raised the boys himself. Being a gentleman of the old school, Jule had made sure the boys learned proper manners.

Dan, having traded his given name, Irving Grenville, with a horse, kept steering the conversation to Leta, asking her questions about Canada. John was proud of her as she quietly responded, embellishing facts with stories of her own about the colorful homestead life. He noticed how Dan seemed to hang on her every word.

Sipping his tea as he watched them, John knew Dan was definitely smitten. He also knew Leta was naively unaware of the young man's inclinations. At the same time John felt a melancholy fatherly twinge for what he knew would be inevitable one day. And, looking a Leta, it was not too far in the future she would have a home and family of her own. He remembered when he first saw Myrtle and the emotions and desire he felt years ago, before she had snuffed them out one by one.

Finishing her tea, Leta politely excused herself, "Elsie is expecting me so I had better get going. I will be back before dark, Papa." Jule and Ed cleared the table as Dan walked Leta outside. Driving away she thought, *What a handsome young man. And so polite.* Dan was nearly as tall as John but had a more slender build. "Elsie and I will have a lot to talk about today." She smiled as she urged the horses into a faster trot.

Chapter Twenty Seven

During the next few months Leta thought very little about Dan. She was kept busy with her studies and part time job. But when she came home again in June for the summer break, she was surprised to find Dan working for her father.

As she worked alongside both men in the fields, a friendship quickly formed between Dan and Leta. Leta laughed when Dan told her, "I thought you would be stuck up since you were away going to that fancy school and all." Then he added with a twinkle in his eye, "But I am sure glad you're not." He liked to tease her and make her blush. In fact he liked everything about her. Soon the two young people were courting on the sly.

John liked Dan and turned a deaf ear and a blind eye to the budding romance. Myrtle did not like Dan at all. She did not understand or like his teasing ways. Most of the time she was openly hostile toward him, but her attitude did not hinder him from teasing her just the same as he did her girls.

It was difficult this time for Leta to return to school in August. For the first time in her life she was in love. And she knew Dan felt the same even though neither had said the words. More than once Dan had hinted about them having a life together, telling her, "I can make a living for the two of us." They said a quick farewell in the barn while Dan was hitching the horses to the wagon. Even though her father was nearby

Leta could feel her mother's hawkish eyes watching from the house.

Walking back to the house to collect her things, Leta hoped Dan would not be seduced by Leila's underhanded tricks. *No telling what she might pull*, Leta thought. She knew Leila had had her eyes set for Dan from the beginning. Leta felt a little sorry for her sister knowing that Dan's affection was not for Leila. Leta did not know, however, that he only tolerated Leila because she was her sister, and that he hated her conniving, whinny ways.

As the team pulled the wagon out of the yard, Leta turned and waved good-bye, quickly glancing at Dan as he repaired a wagon wheel near the barn. She could feel him watching her even while his head was bent over his work. Winter break seemed a lifetime away.

During the months she was at school, Leta and Dan did not correspond with each other for fear of alerting her mother of their relationship. A day did not go by that Leta did not think of Dan. In December when she came home for winter break and Dan greeted her with a teasing remark, she knew nothing had changed between them. It wasn't long until their courtship was renewed and began taking on a more serious tone. As Dan continued to make comments about his making a living for the two of them and referring to a future together, Leta began to join in with his dreams and plans.

Dan had served in Army during the World War and received a monthly pension from injuries he suffered, so she knew that no matter what, their future would be secure. When he asked her why she had never said anything before, she told him she wanted to make sure of his intentions first.

Privately, they began to plan their future together, but publicly they were merely polite friends. Myrtle watched them constantly with a stern, suspicious demeanor. She was still angry with John for hiring Dan. She did not care whose nephew he was, she did not want some "rutting young buck", as she called Dan, around her girls. John took her verbal abuse in silence. He had no intention of letting Dan go as he was a good worker and a great help to him. A good mechanic, Dan kept the thresher John had bought a few years back as well as the Model-T, in good running condition.

Leila became so jealous of Leta and Dan's relationship Leta was afraid she would cause him to be fired. "But then," Leta reminded herself, "If Dan was gone, Leila couldn't flaunt herself in front of him."

Leila tried every trick she knew to get Dan's attention. She would faint and have dizzy spells that caused her to fall into him so he would have to catch her. Without fail, he was always the perfect gentleman which frustrated Leila even more. One day while Dan was working in the barn alone, Leila came up behind him so quietly he did not hear her until she touched his arm. He turned around just as she had removed her coat and began to unbutton her blouse, smiling provocatively up at him. Fear gripped Dan's heart. He knew if she placed them both in a compromising position, Myrtle would have him horsewhipped, fired, or worse. Dan had no desire to marry Leila, but he knew of similar situations that had led to hasty marriages. He wanted no part of this.

Knowing she was as vindictive as her mother, Dan had to handle the situation very carefully. He was not attracted to Leila, in fact she repulsed him, but he could not anger or insult her either. As gently as he knew how he told her he loved Leta and was going to marry her. To soften the blow, he said, "Leila, you are a very pretty girl. Any man would be proud to call you his own. I'm sorry, but Leta has already stolen my heart."

Seeing she was embarrassed by his rejection, he quietly told her he was flattered by her flirtation while resisting the strong desire to haul her over his knee and give her the spanking she deserved. "You had better put your coat on, Leila. You don't want to catch your death." He said with a steady smile and turned back to his work hoping he had put an end to her advances.

The next morning before the girls had come down for breakfast, Myrtle ordered Dan to hitch up the sleigh. When Leta came down to the kitchen her mother told her, "You go catch some laying hens before they are off the roost. We need to take them over to the Barkway's. A fox got into their hen house. They lost most of their chickens."

After catching several hens and loading them onto the sleigh, Leta picked up her mother and Leila at the house. Elsie was told to stay home and finish the morning chores.

Not taking time to visit, they delivered the hens and promptly headed back home. Halfway there the tongue came loose from the sleigh and the team bolted, nearly running away with them. Leta managed to hold them back but they were skittish the rest of the way. Dan came out of the barn as Leta pulled the horses to a stop in the barnyard. Without a word to Dan, Myrtle and Leila went directly to the house.

As Dan began unhitching the team Leta told him, "When the tongue came loose they almost ran away with me. It was all I could do to control them."

Dan laughed. "I can't believe you let a little team of horses run away with you." After unhooking the tongue and getting the neck yoke lose, he reached for the lines when both horses bolted. Quickly grabbing a handful of mane he was swung up onto Big Red's back by the momentum of the charging horse. Hanging onto the one line he reached over grabbing the other pony's bridle. When he finally got them under control and back to the barn he was grinning sheepishly. Leta smiled triumphantly at him. "Just a little team of horses, huh?" she said, snickering as she walked back to the house.

That night at dinner John said, winking at Leta, "I hear you had quite a ride today, Dan."

"Yes, Sir," Dan replied glancing at Leta, his face turning pink. "That team is still pretty jumpy. They are almost too much for Leta to handle. If you don't mind I'd like to work with them a bit."

"Well, Leta's used to driving green broke teams, but if you can find extra time to settle them out that would be fine."

"Humph!" Myrtle grunted, "He doesn't need waste his time on those ponies. Leta needs to be driving them more instead of her fancy team." With her cutting remark the conversation ended abruptly. Dan glanced over at Leta who was concentrating on her plate. In his entire life he had never been around anyone as negative as Myrtle. It frightened him to think of what kind of mother-in-law she would make. To fill the awkward silence, John began to discuss the spring planting and adding to his herd of cattle.

Leta silently wished her mother didn't always embarrass her in front of Dan. She knew Myrtle did not like him, but could not understand why. He was a hard worker, never said or did anything out of line, always showed respect, and was always the perfect gentleman. She knew her mother disliked his teasing ways, but that was not a reason to dislike someone.

Leta choked down the last few bites of her stew, forcing it past the huge lump that had formed in her throat. She knew better than to not clean up her plate.

To keep the peace, Leta took over the task of working with the troublesome team herself. She loved all the horses but this team was so ornery she hated driving them. They spooked at the slightest thing. Leila had assigned herself to help Leta. Wherever Leta was, Dan was always close by watching, so that was where Leila wanted to be also.

Every morning, as soon as Leta got the skittish team harnessed and had hooked up the last tongue, she and Leila quickly jumped in and off they sped. Leta missed driving Pat and Dick. They were the only perfectly matched team in the area and she was proud of them. Dick was a little feisty when ridden, but he was fine as long as he was hitched alongside Pat. Dan admired the way Leta handled the horses and didn't tease her about anymore runaways.

Just before Christmas, Leta had a bout with the whooping cough. She was confined to her small room above the kitchen for nearly two weeks. Leta missed Dan terribly. He was the only man, other than her father, that made her feel special. She knew her mother would not allow him to visit her and knew better than ask. Now that they were older, no man was allowed in the girls' room, not even their father.

When Leta was finally allowed to get out of bed, she caught Pat early one morning and was hitching him to the cutter when her mother stormed out of the chicken house, "And just where do you think you are going?" Myrtle demanded.

"I promised Elsie I would take her some butter and eggs before I got sick," Leta answered calmly, belying the fact her knees were shaking and her insides were quivering.

"Oh." Her attitude quickly changing, Myrtle added, "Well, you had better take her a few jars of meat and soup broth."

Relieved, Leta quickly finished hitching Pat to the cutter, packed a box full of goods for Elsie and was on her way before Myrtle could change her mind. Leta had so much to tell Elsie. She hadn't dared to put it in a note for fear Myrtle might see it. Not only did Leta want to tell Elsie about Dan, She needed to know more about married life. She needed to know how to be a wife. She knew how to work the fields, plant a garden, train horses, and every other outside chore, but knew nothing about running a household. Myrtle had never allowed the girls to cook or even clean the house, with the exception of sweeping the floor and washing the dishes.

Elsie was standing on her porch with her arms full of wood as Leta pulled Pat to a halt in front of the small cabin. "Leta. What a wonderful surprise. How did you ever manage to come alone?" Elsie knew how strict and watchful Myrtle was. "Come in. Come in. Frank," Elsie called toward the barn, "Look who's here."

Leaving Frank to tend to the horse and carry in the box of canned goods, Elsie took Leta by the arm, saying proudly as they entered the cabin, "Come see the babies." When Frank and Elsie married, Leta had thought he was much too old for Elsie. But seeing them together, Leta knew that age was really not important when two people were as compatible as the Johnson's were.

After the babies, Louise and Viola, were put down for a nap, Leta brought out a ball of string she had hidden in her coat, "Mama would have a fit if she saw what we made with this string." She said as she handed a crochet hook to Elsie. "I got an extra one in Prince Albert for you." With their hands busy -

Leta would always hear her mother's voice admonishing her, "Idle hands are the Devil's workshop." - turning the thread into delicate lacy doilies, Leta haltingly began asking Elsie about love and marriage.

"My mother never talked to me either," Elsie told her. "She taught me how to cook and clean and to tend babies, but nothing else. I wasn't prepared to be a wife."

"Elsie, I never planned it this way. I always wanted to be a teacher. I still do." Leta was so grateful that Elsie was the first to marry. There was so much to know. Living on a farm, Leta knew how babies were born. She had assisted her father in pulling calves more than once. And she had figured out on her own how they were conceived. However, she could not hide her shock and embarrassment at some of the information Elsie was sharing with her. With trepidation, she now was not at all sure she wanted to get married. But she had to admit she was irrevocably and hopelessly in love with Dan, and knew she would never get him out of her heart as long as she lived.

The winter days were very short and soon it was time for Leta to start for home. She still had chores to do before dark and she had stayed much longer than she had intended. The two young women shared their hopes and their dreams as well as their fears.

"Mama's going to be furious at me for being gone so long," Leta told Elsie. Saying their good-byes with promises to see each other more often, Leta snapped the lines over his rump, urging Pat into a brisk trot. She had a lot to think about on the way home.

Driving the cutter into the barn, Leta quickly unhitched Pat, put him in his stall, threw a forkful of hay in his manger and promptly headed for the house, bracing herself for the fury sure to come from her mother.

To Leta's relief, Myrtle had been called away to assist a neighbor in childbirth and she had taken tattletale Leila with her. Myrtle had served as a mid-wife ever since Leta could remember, taking over the job for Granny McTaggart. Leta always thought it odd that her mother would help other women have their babies when she detested childbirth herself.

Without Leila to slow them down, Leta and Elsie had all the chores done before their father and Dan came in to eat supper. Elsie helped Leta dish up the stew Myrtle had left simmering on the stove and the four of them, Elsie, John, Dan and Leta sat down to enjoy a rare, pleasant meal together.

The peace and serenity quickly was replaced by tension as they heard Myrtle and Leila returning. Myrtle entered the house muttering what beasts men were and went directly to her room. She was always in such a foul mood when she delivered a baby that Leta wondered why she did it at all. Leila took a plate from the cupboard and heaped it with stew and sat down beside Dan.

"I'll go take care of the team," Dan said, quickly rising from the table.

"I'll come along," John said pushing his plate back. He knew it was best if he steered clear of his wife when she was in this frame of mind. "There are a few things I need to finish up in the barn."

A few days later, as they were eating supper, Dan boldly asked Leta to go with him to the Christmas program at the school in Shellbrook. Every member of the Oesch family stared at him dumbfounded. Myrtle's eyes narrowed and she glared at Dan.

"I...I don't think I could," Leta said haltingly, quickly glancing at her mother.

"Of course you can. I'll promise to not keep you out too late," Dan teased.

As Myrtle opened her mouth to protest, John said quickly, "I think that is a fine idea. You can take the cutter." Her face scarlet with rage, Myrtle stormed from the table without a word. With gratitude overflowing in her heart, Leta smiled at her father. She knew he would pay dearly for this.

"But we all won't fit in the cutter, Papa," Leila whined.

"Dan asked Leta to go, not you and Elsie," John said gently.

"I didn't mean to cause trouble," Dan said quietly.

"You haven't," John said to Dan. "Leta, you go with Dan and have a good time."

The three girls quietly began clearing the table as the two men went outside. They knew Myrtle would be in a snit for days and everyone would feel the cold blade of her anger. But to Leta, it was well worth the price she would later have to pay.

Late the next afternoon, bundled up against the cold, Dan and Leta set off for Shellbrook in the cutter. There was no warmth in the bright winter sun and the temperature was below zero but to Leta it was like a beautiful spring day with the winter sun sparkling on the snow like a million tiny diamonds. She was so happy she could hardly speak. Dan kept Pat at an even trot and soon they were in Shellbrook. The town had grown from a single two-story log building to several new businesses along with the hotel, general store, church, and school. Out buildings and lots of houses clustered about. In five years the population had doubled. As her father told her, "People are discovering Canada."

It surprised Leta when Dan pulled Pat to a stop in front of the general store instead of going straight to the school house. Even though it was still early Leta knew the Christmas program would be starting soon. Tying the pony to the hitching rail, Dan helped Leta from the cutter and held her arm as they entered the store. Assuming he needed to buy something for himself she didn't ask why they were stopping. Her eyes widened in surprise and her breath caught in her throat when Dan asked, "May we see your stock of wedding bands?" To the couple's disappointment none of the rings were small enough for Leta's tiny fingers. "Well," Dan assured her, "We will just have to keep looking." Her heart was so full, tears of happiness welled up in her eyes.

When they arrived at the small school house it was filled to overflowing with proud parents. Babies slept in their mother's arms and toddlers sat in quiet attention. Throughout the program Leta was transfixed. It warmed Dan's heart to see her enjoy herself so much. He knew she did not have many pleasures at home. Not for a moment did she take her eyes off the young actors. Having only read the Christmas story at Aunt Kate's as a child, she had no idea it was so beautiful. Now it was all brought to life by these children. Despite the little ones forgetting their lines, and singing off key, Leta loved every minute of it. Her mother had always preached that everyone was going to Hell no matter what. This fire and brimstone attitude frightened her and she was afraid of God. After seeing the pageant and watching the children's faces, she began to feel differently toward Him now.

Shortly after the Christmas pageant, with Dan's encouragement, Leta announced that she would not be returning to school this term. Myrtle crisply stated, "If you are doing this because of Dan and want to waste your life on some man, I guess I can't stop you."

"I'm not going to waste my life, Mama," Leta said quietly, "We love each other and want to build a life together."

"Humph! Love! There is no such thing! Men are no better than rutting boars," Myrtle spat. "If you marry him you will regret it just as ...." Stopping in mid sentence, Myrtle quickly retorted, "If you are going to get your chores done before dark, you had better get to it." Turning her attention back to the simmering stew on the stove, Myrtle abruptly ended the conversation.

Leta slowly pulled on her coat, stepped outside, and quietly closed the door. Her mother's words echoed in her mind as she joined her sisters who were already busy milking the cows. "Well, maybe Mama regretted marrying Papa, but I will never regret marrying Dan," Leta muttered to herself.

In the kitchen Myrtle choked back a tear that began to well up as the bittersweet memory of Claude nearly overwhelmed her. The emotion took her by such surprise she turned and slammed a coffee mug down on the table with such force it shattered. Clenching her fists and gritting her teeth she forced the memory from her mind. Anger and bitterness once again buried the softer emotion.

Chapter Twenty Eight

Starlight glistened on the frozen snow as Leta watched Dan walked quietly, but quickly, to the barn to hitch Pat to the cutter.

"Hurry," Elsie whispered. "Leila's waiting at the front door. Mama and Papa could wake up any minute. And don't worry, I will handle Mama."

Leta's heart was thumping as she turned from the window and pulled on her jacket. She had made her wedding suit at Cousin Elsie's and had smuggled it home. She placed the stylish wide brimmed hat she had made on her head, pulled on her thick wool coat, and made her way quietly down the stairs. Once outside she and Leila hurried toward the barn.

As the three pulled away from the Oesch farm every sound seemed magnified in the stillness of the early morning; the horse snorting, hooves crunching the snow, the runners of the cutter skimming over the icy snow, the leather and chains of the harness squeaking and rattling. Heart pounding, Leta was afraid to look around for fear of seeing a light blink on in the house. Even though she knew her mother would not stop her, fear and anxiety gripped her. Leila looked back and whispered, "No lights. We made it."

Later as the early morning sun sparkled on the snow, tears of happiness welled up in Leta's eyes as she heard the minister,

Cyril Phillips say, "I now pronounce you man and wife. Before you kiss the bride this is my blessing to you both.

"May you live well, laugh often, love much. May you gain the trust of pure men and women, and the love of little children. May you fill your niches; and accomplish your tasks. May you leave this world better than you found it. May you never lack appreciation of earth's beauties, nor fail to express it. May you always look for the best in others and give the best that you have. May your lives be an inspiration; and your memories a Benediction." Closing his Bible and removing his wire rimmed glasses he smiled, "Now you may kiss the bride."

Taking Leta firmly in his arms, Dan kissed her for the first time as his wife. She was his. Now and forever. He loved her with all his heart and he promised he would always take care of her. As she looked up at him her eyes and heart were bursting with unspoken happiness. Now she would have a real home. A happy home. With Dan beside her there was nothing she could not do.

She felt a small twinge of regret of losing her dream of being a teacher. She was only four months short of getting her teaching certificate, but quickly reminded herself she would be able to finish her schooling later. Leta loved Dan more than anything else in the world. She had made her choice.

Trying to hide the envy and jealously she felt, Leila hugged and congratulated Leta. After paying the minister the customary amount, Dan helped Leta into her coat. The Presbyterian minister and his wife waved from their porch as Dan drove away with his new bride beside him. The sun was shinning brightly in the cloudless azure sky on this 13th day of January, 1923.

When the newlyweds returned to the Oesch farm later that afternoon, John hugged his daughter and congratulated Dan. Earlier that morning as they sat down to breakfast Elsie had announced the news that Leta and Dan had eloped and Leila had gone with them. A faint smile played on John's lips. He was pleased. Myrtle was incensed but held her tongue. Elsie knew as soon as Leta returned, Myrtle would vent her wrath on her sister and Dan.

Leta's knees shook and her heart pounded as she entered the house with Dan beside her. With a look of utter contempt Myrtle said coldly, "Now that you have married and thrown away your future, you will suffer the consequences." Without another word she stomped into her room and slammed the door behind her.

Leta's eyes were swimming with unshed tears. Her mother had ruined every important event in her life, why did she think that this would be any different. Why couldn't she, just for once, be happy for her?

"You two go gather up your things. It will be all right. She will come around," John said comfortingly.

Dan and Leta moved into Shellbrook. Dan soon found a job as a mechanic at the only garage in town. They rented a small room from an eighty-year-old Danish widow. The room was attached to the back of her house with its own entrance. The tiny room was impossible to keep warm even with the small air-tight heater. The newlyweds thought they would freeze to death. When a room upstairs became available, they quickly moved into it. It was above the kitchen so it remained cozy and warm with the heat from downstairs coming through the floor. It also had a small cook stove in it that would hold a fire longer than the air-tight heater.

Work at the garage was slow and Dan wasn't working too steady so they decided to move to the States where he could make more money. The thought of leaving Canada frightened Leta and gave her a pang of sadness. However, the prospect of living in the States was exciting too. She had never been further than Prince Albert in her entire life, but she felt as long as she was with Dan, everything would be all right.

In March, with Leta expecting their first child, and after saying their good byes to the family, Leta packed what she could and they caught a train in Prince Albert. Spellbound, Leta watched the landscape slip past the train window as they passed through rolling prairie farmland and the towns of Roddick, Waldheim, Hague, and Clark. With a four hour lay-over in Saskatoon, Dan took Leta to a Jewelry store where he found a wedding ring that fit her tiny finger. She didn't pick the smallest one, but selected a plain gold band with a little room to grow in.

In Regina they got on a different line called the Canadian Pacific, and continued south. The changing scenery was beautiful. Leta couldn't tear her eyes from the window. Waves of homesickness ebbed every now and then but she would push the feeling aside and think ahead of an exciting new life with her young husband. Familiar looking settlements, town and communities were quickly left behind. She wanted to etch the landscape and every town in her memory forever; Moose Jaw, Mortloch, Chaplin, Herbert, Rush Lake, Beverly, Antelope, and Sidewood.

After passing through Maple Creek, they crossed into Alberta, stopping briefly to take on passengers in Medicine Hat, and then passing through Lethbridge. They crossed the U.S. border at Gateway and continued on through Kingsgate, Idaho. There were high mountains with snowy crags, rushing rivers and huge evergreen trees that seemed to touch the sky. Dan knew the proper procedure at the border so they had no trouble as he had Leta's papers in order and she was now married to a U.S. citizen.

The honeymoon trip continued on the International Railway to Sandpoint, Idaho, and Rathdrum, and then finally their destination, Spokane, Washington. After finding a furnished apartment, Dan went to search for work while Leta set up housekeeping. The apartment was light and roomy and Leta loved it, even though the rent was more than they had planned to pay. Good mechanics were in such demand that Dan was hired by the first garage he applied for work.

After his first day of work, Dan told Leta excitedly, "A car salesman came in the garage today trying to sell the boss a new luxury Cadillac." Trying to mimic the salesman, Dan continued, "For only $290.00 you can own one of these beauties. If you don't want to spend that much cash right now, you can pay it off in easy payments of only $5.00 a week." Dan added thoughtfully, "Anyone can own a luxury car nowadays."

Incredulous, Leta asked, "Why would anyone want to go into debt for something like that?" For an instant she was afraid Dan was thinking of buying a new car.

"Too fancy for me. And too much money to spend on an automobile," Dan said, sitting down to the simple supper Leta had prepared. The meat was a little overcooked and she was still trying to perfect her biscuits but Dan ate hungrily as though everything was cooked to perfection.

Before the month was out Dan found a smaller, more affordable apartment for them. Their new landladies, Myrtle and Goldie Laird, took to Leta instantly like two mother hens. When they found out Leta was expecting, the two spinsters were delighted. Myrtle promptly took Leta under her wing and began sewing tiny clothes for the anxiously anticipated baby. Due to all their traveling and moving, Leta had nothing prepared. So Myrtle took Leta to the Dollar Day sales at a nearby emporium to buy material they would sew into gowns and diapers.

Evenings Dan and Leta poured over the Sears catalog, ordering baby things they could not make themselves. Leta blushed at the shocking ads for the new swimsuits that showed women's bare limbs. She thought the one-piece suits without sleeves and leggings were daring and a little indecent.

Every week the newlyweds enjoyed the local vaudeville shows. Leta was mesmerized by them. They would go to the Pantages Theater where the show changed every week, and alternate with the show at the Hippodrome which changed every two weeks.

Married life was more wonderful than Leta had dared dream it would be. And soon they would be a family of three.

Chapter Twenty Nine

On September 15, 1923, Leta gave birth to a healthy girl, Verna Evelyn. She had the luxury of giving birth to her first born in a hospital. While recuperating from childbirth during the customary ten day stay in the hospital, Leta studied Morse code between feedings. Dan was attending telegraph school on a government program and was teaching Leta Morse code so she could help him study. She learned so quick he teased her about being his competition.

Before Leta and the new baby were out of the hospital, Dan was transferred to Naples, Idaho, for his first job as a railroad dispatcher. The railroad was moving a lot of fruit and it was a busy time. So the Keogh's loaded their meager belongings in the second-hand car Dan had bought, and left for Naples. Leta and Verna would follow later by train.

Verna was barely a month old when Leta boarded the Spokane International with one small suitcase and her newborn. When he had completed his job in Naples, Dan was hoping to complete his training. However, the government could no longer fund him and Dan and Leta lacked the money to pay for the training themselves. So Dan opted to work with the section crew on the same railroad but the job only lasted less than a year. During that year, Leta's sister Leila, accompanied by Uncle Jule, came to stay with them. With his job finished, Dan purchased a good team of horses and wagon for the move. Dan and Jule loaded most of their belongings in the wagon. Everything else was stuffed inside and piled on top of the Model T. Since Uncle Jule did not know how to drive a car he drove the wagon and Dan followed in the Model-T.

After the two men struck out for Washington, Leta, Leila and Verna, who was now a toddler, boarded the train to go back to Spokane. Leila had met a nice young man in Naples and Leta believed it was just a matter of time before they married. Asa Jay Cossairt was all she talked about during the entire trip. Now thirteen months old, Verna could jabber a blue streak, almost keeping up with Leila. A woman sitting next to Leta refused to believe Verna was so young.

A few years back, Ed and Jule Olsen had purchased twenty acres in Deer Park, a small community just outside Spokane. Jule convinced Dan that they could make the necessary improvements on the property and move onto it. So Dan and Jule located a log building with long narrow windows and moved it onto the property. After a little remodeling, the cabin was livable.

Soon after they moved into the log house Leta drove the bumpy, deeply rutted road, twenty miles into Spokane and bought dress scraps from a dress factory managed by Russell Meeks. Leta had become friends with his mother, Myrtle while in Naples. At twenty-three, Russell had proved to be a responsible young man and had been promoted to manager in record time.

Leta felt her life was about as perfect as it could be. But that only lasted until she received a letter from her mother, who announced she was coming to visit. There wasn't one word about how long the visit, or why she was coming. After reading the letter to Dan she told him, "I will be so glad to see Elsie though."

"Well, yes...it will be nice to see Elsie," he commented.

They both had a sense of foreboding about this visit. Leila had already returned to Idaho and Dan silently hoped Myrtle did not plan on staying long. He was determined for Leta's sake to get along with that impossible woman. After all, she was his mother-in-law. He had heard many mother-in-law jokes but Myrtle was no laughing matter.

Too soon it seemed after the letter arrived, Dan and Leta were meeting Myrtle and Elsie at the train station. Myrtle said very little during the trip back to Deer Park but Leta and Elsie didn't seem to notice their mother's silence. They chatted happily away as the Model T bounced and chugged along. Leta was proud of their small log house and what she and Dan had accomplished with so little money. Dan gritted his teeth and Leta cringed as Myrtle criticized everything. Elsie loved the little house saying excitedly, "This looks just like a doll house." Her few positive words helped to overshadow Myrtle's numerous negative comments.

In the days that followed, Leta learned that her mother had left her father for good. "I will no longer live with a man like that," Myrtle stated venomously. She voiced several reasons why the separation was inevitable, all of which neither Leta nor Elsie believed. They had never known their father to even think of the things their mother accused him of, let alone doing them. He was a good man, a good father, and they knew how hard he had tried to be a good husband.

In the days that followed Leta grew tired of her mother's constant harping about the bare windows so she suggested they make curtains with some of the scraps she had bought from the dress factory. After Leta sewed the long, multi-colored and various patterned strips together on the treadle machine, Elsie and Myrtle hemmed them by hand. When Dan came in that night Leta showed off the new window coverings. "What do you think of our fancy curtains?" she asked him proudly.

"Well, I think they look like hell," he said with a hint of a grin and a twinkle in his eye. Leta knew he thought they were grand. Elsie also knew his off-hand remark was a complement.

But Myrtle took it to be a personal insult. Her face turned beet red and she puffed up like a banty rooster ready to fight. "Well! That's the thanks we get for trying to make this shack livable!" Myrtle spat.

"Now, Mama, he didn't mean it like that," Leta said, her heart sinking. Dan gave Leta an "I can't take much more of her" look and without a word, went out the door. *Why does she always have to throw cold water on every spark of happiness?* Leta thought to herself as she slowly folded the left over pieces of material and put them away in a drawer.

As the weeks went by, Leta became huge with child. It seemed she was nearly as round as she was tall. Leta's belly was so large Myrtle kept insisting the baby was due any time and would not allow Leta to satisfy her ravenous appetite.

One damp, drizzly May morning Myrtle shook Dan awake. "You better go for the doctor!" In an instant he was up and pulling on his pants and racing out the door. Leta was having a hard time and Myrtle did not want to deliver the baby herself.

Elsie wiped the perspiration from Leta's brow with a cool cloth and Myrtle bathed her arms with cool water as they both anxiously waited for the doctor to arrive. Myrtle secretly feared the baby was too large for Leta's small frame. Hearing Dan drive up, Myrtle scurried to the door.

"She's having a hard time of it doctor," Myrtle told him as he and his wife quickly began tending to Leta.

Bending over Leta the doctor said quietly, "Well, looks like we made it just in time. Here comes the little one now. You are doing just fine, Missus. One more push and that ought to do it." Leta groaned and the baby slipped into the doctor's waiting hands. "Looks like you have a fine boy this time." Exhausted, Leta smiled and closed her eyes.

As the doctor was tying off the umbilical cord, Leta cried out with another pain. "Something's wrong!" she cried.

Not looking up from his task the doctor told her, "Everything is fine. It is just an afterbirth pain. It will pass."

"She needs attention, Doctor!" Myrtle told him firmly.

"Yes, in a moment. I have to finish tying this cord," He told Myrtle patiently.

"Doctor, it looks like there is another one!" his wife exclaimed. He quickly turned his attention back to Leta just in time to deliver another baby boy.

Two identical tiny red-faced squalling baby boys, bundled in soft flannel blankets, were placed on a soft feather pillow and laid gently on the open oven door to keep them warm. Soon Leta and her babies drifted off to sleep. Myrtle made a fresh pot of coffee; the doctor recorded the amazing births in his register book. While his wife cleaned up, the doctor wrote as he sipped the scalding strong coffee, 'May 27, 1925. Identical twin boys born four minutes apart. The first weighing 6 3/4 pounds, the second weighing 6 1/4 pounds.' Elsie and Dan stared down at the sleeping babies in awe.

"She's done a fine job. Yes a fine job indeed," The doctor said as he and his wife prepared to leave. "Keep her in bed the rest of the week and I will be out on Monday to check on her and the babies."

Later when the babies awoke demanding to be fed, Dan said teasingly to Leta, "If I'd known there were two, we would have let you eat more. That's a lot of babies for someone so small." Myrtle laid one of the babies in Leta's arms and he greedily began sucking on the offered nipple. "We need to name them," Leta said smiling up at Dan. After a few suggestions they agreed the first born would be Keith William and the second, Kenneth Donald.

The next day Dan tore apart the new baby bed he had made in order to remodel it for two. When twenty-month-old Verna saw the twins for the first time, she peeked into the crib and exclaimed, "Oh, lots of babies!"

A week later Dan's brother Bill and his wife came to visit from southern California. Bill's wife was baby Verna's namesake, but was nicknamed 'Spike'. Leta had never met them but, having heard so much about them both from Dan, she was delighted to see them. Bill and Spike had no idea Dan and Leta had a family until they walked in the door and was greeted by a little tow-headed jabber box. "My name is Verna. I have an aunt with the same name. Would you like to see my two baby brothers?" The words flowed out of her tiny mouth like water running over stones. Having no children of their own, Bill and Spike loved her instantly.

It was a little crowded in the small house, but Dan and Leta enjoyed having Bill and Spike there. Spike was so energetic and absolutely the most positive person Leta had ever known. The two women took to each other instantly. Bill was much like Dan and enjoyed helping his brother with the outside work. To Leta's amazement, Myrtle behaved herself and remained in a fairly decent mood. Leta was grateful for the temporary peace. She was heavyhearted when it came time for Bill and Spike to go back to California.

Each week the doctor sent his nurse out to check on Leta and the twins. The nurse belonged to the Eastern Star which had a layette the organization loaned out to new mothers. She brought it for Leta to use. Not knowing there would be two babies, Leta did not have enough clothes for them. She had made only two gowns. A few days before the babies were born she decided she should make more. She had two pieces of outing flannel a yard square and made two more gowns. With only four gowns for two babies, Leta was grateful for the borrowed layette. She took good care of it so she could give it back for someone else to use later.

When the twins were 10 days old, Myrtle became angry over a teasing remark Dan made about Leta's cooking. In a rage, she packed up herself and Elsie and stormed out of the house. Elsie begged to stay with Leta and help with the twins, but Myrtle would not allow it. Later Dan and Leta learned that Myrtle had went to Spokane and rented a room from a Mrs. Peats. With her mother out of the house, Leta wrote to her father expressing her love and support. She knew in her heart he would be much happier living alone.

A week after Myrtle left, Dan began working with a logging crew in the woods and was gone twelve to fourteen hours a day. He was driving a team and would have to get his horses together, harnessed, and get them to the logging site before daylight every morning. With Dan gone so much of the time, a neighbor girl would come once a week in her old car, load up Leta and the three children and all the laundry. She drove them to her house and washed the clothes for her. Leta did not have a washing machine and had been washing everything by hand.

When the twins were barely a month old, Dan moved his family back to Spokane. After they were settled into a tiny cabin, he went to work for Independent Garage. They lived there nearly eight months and then again, packed up all their belongings and traveled across the state of Washington to Alderwood Manor which is situated between Seattle and Everett. The back seat of the car was loaded nearly to the roof with just enough space behind the front seat for a bed for the children. What would not fit inside, Dan strapped on the outside of the car. The trip took several days. Each evening they camped beside a clear, cold stream. While she cooked the fish Dan caught, Leta heated water to wash clothes, diapers, and children.

Once they had settled in Alderwood Manor, Dan entered into a government training program on a poultry ranch learning to raise chickens. By autumn they owned 375 laying hens. They had moved onto a five acre plot with a roomy house four miles from Puget Sound. Leta loved the house. She had never lived in one so nice. She hoped and prayed that they would stay there.

She enjoyed the peaceful life away from her mother. Myrtle was residing in Spokane with Elsie and Leila who had moved back from Idaho. Elsie was attending Business College and Leila was working in a candy factory. Asa Cossiart, Leila's young man, came to visit Leila often, much to Myrtle's dismay. One night, September 3, 1926, they went out to a dance and returned married. That very night Asa packed Leila up and took her back to Payette, Idaho. Myrtle was furious. She packed up and went back to Canada. This time Elsie refused to go with her. When Elsie wrote and told Leta the whole story, she did not leave out a single detail. Leta smiled as she read the letter. Elsie was always very descriptive.

But the following spring, March of 1927, Dan got itchy feet again and decided to return to Spokane and work for the same garage. He was such a good mechanic they were more than happy to have him back. At this time Leta was seven months pregnant with her fourth child.

She was terribly disappointed that they left their chicken ranch and lovely home in Alderwood Manor. But Leta remembered the Bible verse in Ruth 1:16, "for whither thou goest, I will go; and where thou lodgest, I will lodge". She willingly would do whatever Dan decided. She did not complain or lament on what was left behind. And she did not reveal how increasingly difficult each move was becoming for her. Bundling up her children, she followed her husband where he led. As long as she was with him, she knew everything would be all right. He was always good to her and the children. She knew he loved her and their children without his ever having to say it.

Dan rented a small house near the garage where he worked and they had not been there long when Kenneth developed pneumonia. The doctor came and gave Leta medicine to give him but she knew a mustard plaster would bake out the infection. Not having made a plaster herself, she had to think hard to remember how her mother did it.

"She mixed one pint of powdered mustard to seven or eight parts flour, mixed with water to make a thick paste...the chest must be greased first so not to burn the skin," she recalled as Dan wrote down the ingredients they would need.

Stirring up a mild mixture, Leta carefully spread the mustard plaster on Kenneth's tiny greased chest. A cloth was put over the mixture to hold in the heat and it had to be changed often.

Dan and Leta took turns getting up in the night with Kenneth to change the plasters. Leta told Verna and Keith that Kenneth was very sick and they would have to be careful of him. The two toddlers would go out and pick flowers, a collection of weeds and grass, to help their brother feel better. Leta proudly placed these weedy bouquets in a glass of water by the crib. After two weeks of changing a mustard plaster every few hours, the crisis was over and little Kenneth was on the mend.

Most evenings while Leta prepared dinner, Dan usually read the news paper to her. She never had time anymore to read it for herself. The year before, when Dan read about Charles Lindberg flying the Chicago-St. Louis mail route, she had commented, "Imagine, getting mail that fast." Now Mr. Lindberg had flown around the world solo. This news was more than she could imagine. The only plane she had ever seen did not get very far off the ground. She could not fathom how it was possible for a man to go all around the world in one of those things.

When Dan read about Al Jolson starring in the *Jazz Singer*, the first 'talkie', they both would have loved to go see him but money was tight now that they had three children and another on the way. So luxuries like going to the movies would have to wait.

Chapter Thirty

Another son, Lloyd Howard, was born on May 3, 1927, in the small hospital in Deer Park. The required ten days Leta was in the hospital was the last rest she would get for a long time.

During that summer, Leta was overjoyed when her father and his sister Kate came for a visit. She had not realized how much she had missed her father until she saw him. She was so happy to see him and Aunt Kate it nearly brought tears to her eyes. She had been faithful in writing to him so he knew about the children, but was awe struck when he saw his four beautiful grandchildren for the first time. The children loved their Papa John and Aunt Kate instantly and the feeling was mutual.

It relieved John greatly to see that Leta was, in fact, happy and that Dan was good to her and the children. But he furtively wished that Dan would stay planted in one place, instead of continually moving his family all over the country. But he could see that they were happy and that was the important thing. They all enjoyed each other's company immensely and the visit was over much too soon. The children cried when their Grandpa and Aunt Kate said goodbye. Leta had a huge lump in her throat and felt an old familiar tug at her heart as the train began pulling out of the station carrying Grandpa John and Aunt Kate back to Canada.

A few days after John and Kate left for Canada, Dan packed up his family and drove to Payette, Idaho for the apple season.

"I can make more money picking fruit than here at the garage and you will have a chance to visit Leila and Asa," Dan had told Leta convincingly. She was beginning to get weary of the constant moving. It was especially difficult now that she had four small children. He had traded the Model-T for a larger touring car and the vehicle was packed tight, from stem to stern. "All this packing and unpacking is wearing everything out," Leta told Dan jokingly.

"If it wears out I will buy you new things," he chided her.

In Idaho, the Keogh family stayed with Leila and her new husband, Asa, while Dan worked in the apple orchards. Now and then he would take Verna along with him and she would play beneath whichever tree Dan was picking. One day the field boss laughingly told him, "That little tyke never stops talking unless a apple falls off the tree and hits her on the head...then that only stops her for a minute or two."

By the time the orchards were picked clean, Leta was more than ready to go back to Washington. Leila had seized the opportunity of Leta's visit to have one of her 'sick' spells leaving Leta with all the household chores as well as caring for her own children. Asa was a kind and patient man and both Leta and Dan enjoyed getting to know him, but she would be glad to get home. When Dan decided it was time to go back to Washington it didn't take Leta long to pack.

In October of 1927, Dan got the wanderlust again and decided they needed to go to Nevada. "Nevada is a growing, prosperous state and we will do very well there. There have been several gold and silver strikes. The state is booming." Once again Dan convinced her he would find the pot of gold at the end of the rainbow. This time he knew he would find it in Nevada for sure. So, once more, Leta began packing for another long journey.

Uncle Jule and Ole had traveled down from Canada the month before and they were both eager to try Nevada too. The two bachelors had tired of the harsh winters in Canada, but their brother Ed had chosen to stay behind. So, on a balmy autumn day, the Keogh's and the Olsen's packed up, leaving many of their belongings behind, and headed south. Neither Olsen brother knew how to drive so on the long trip to Nevada, Leta taught them both.

Dan penciled in the route they would take connecting the towns like a child's dot-to-dot game on his well worn map of the United States. Leaving Spokane they traveled to Sprague, through Ritzville, Lind, Pasco, and down to Wallula. Turning west, following along the banks of the Columbia River on the Washington side, through Plymoth, Carley, Columbus, White Salmon, then Stevenson and on to Vancouver. Jule and Ole chugged along behind Dan and Leta in their slightly battered Model T. When the road got too rough they would stop and Leta would drive them through it.

During the long days in the car, the miles slowly slipping behind them, Leta listened and learned along with her children as Dan told them about the railroad being built through the mountains in western Canada with mostly Chinese labor. "The western terminus was changed from Moody Bay to English Bay which upset many speculators and investors. The town used to be known as Gastown. It was named for the saloon owner called Gassey Jack Deighton, but was changed to Vancouver in a hurry." Before he had finished his story, all the children had fallen asleep.

"It's going to be getting dark soon so we had better stop for the night," he told Leta.

Pitching camp on this trip was a little easier on Leta as Jule did most of the cooking. He was a good cook and was very good in a kitchen or over a campfire. He had taught Leta how to cook as her mother never had the patience nor would take the time to teach any of her girls. With Jule and Ole tending to the camp chores, Leta washed clothes in the stream, throwing the sodden laundry over the bushes to dry, and caught up on some mending. Leta was still nursing Howard and Jule fussed like an old mother hen making sure she didn't over-do.

When the campfire was blazing, Dan and the three oldest children returned from the river with enough fish for dinner, most of which he let the children catch themselves. Proudly handing their catch over to Jule to clean and cook, the three little towheads scampered off to play.

Before daybreak the next morning, in the cool, crisp air, the travelers continued on their journey. Crossing the Columbia River at Vancouver into Oregon, they drove through Portland, Oregon City, Salem, Harrisburg and Springfield. Mountains bordered the Eastern and Western horizons of the Willamette Valley. The wide valley floor was dappled with huge Douglas Fir trees clustered between large farms. There were so many rivers and large creeks that Leta couldn't keep track of them all. Dan told her the largest river was the Willamette which they had followed most of the way from Portland.

At Cottage Grove they began climbing more mountains, winding through tiny bergs called Drain and Yoncalla. The children giggled at the funny sounding names. Both cars overheated climbing the steep grade at Rice Hill and the men had to fix a flat tire on the Olsen vehicle. Dropping down into Oakland, Dan told the children, "This is Oregon's oldest town and the first public school was built here."

Continuing on through the mountains on the rough, narrow winding oiled dirt road to Roseburg they followed the Umpqua River to the villages of Myrtle Creek and Canyonville. It was another long climb over steep mountains before dropping down into Wolf Creek and Grants Pass. At Wolf Creek the mini caravan stopped at the old stage stop to refill the canvas water bags and replenish supplies. "Did you know Jack London stayed here while writing *Call of the Wild*?" Dan told Leta as he strapped the water bags on the fenders. She had read the book and could see how the author would be inspired by the beautiful mountains covered with thick forests of huge Douglas fir trees and the wild crystal clear streams.

At Ashland they began climbing the Siskiyou Pass. After several stops to let the cars cool off and fix flat tires they were finally over the mountains and crossed the state line into California. The sight of snow capped Mount Shasta made Leta a little homesick for Canada. But she shook off the feeling as the mountains gave way to gentle rolling hills spotted with scrub oak and carpeted with waving golden grass. Redding and Red Bluff were the next towns she marked off the map.

The miles seemed endless. Every four or five days, Dan would rent a cabin for a night to give everyone a break from pitching camp. Seeing a sign that read 'Cabin to rent, 25 miles', Dan said to Leta, "I think that would be a good place to stop for the night."

"We could all use a good nights rest," she agreed. It had been a long, dusty, hot day. But when they reached the cabin the entire area was deserted. There was no one around for miles. It would be dark soon and they were all nearly exhausted so they decided to stay anyway.

Hanging a lantern in the middle of the room over the small square wooden table, Dan Helped Leta spread blankets over tarpaulins on the floor while Jule and Ole started a fire in the cookstove. After dusting off the stove, Jule put the vegetable bean soup on to heat. It was the last jar of Leta's canned stock she had packed. As soon as the young ones finished eating, she tucked them into their quilts on the floor by the stove. A cool gentle rain began falling and they were all grateful to have a roof over their heads.

The next day they turned southeast to Chico and on to Marysville. Turning due east to Grass Valley, they passed through Emigrant Gap, Truckee, over the Donner Pass, and down into Reno. They had followed, in reverse, the wagon train route to California. When they reached the top, Dan stopped where the Donner party had spent the winter. All that remained of the crude cabins they had built were the rotting log foundations. "The only ones to survive that terrible winter were the ones that lived off the others," Jule told them sadly.

"You mean they..." Leta could not believe what she was hearing.

"Yes," Dan explained. "They were starving and it was the only way. They reasoned when someone died those who were still left would have a chance to make it to spring. Few of them made it anyway."

The tragic story of the Donner party filled Leta's head as they continued their journey. She thought of the mother who fed her children but refused to eat the soup made of human flesh.

Of all the mountains that they had traveled over, to Leta, these Sierra Nevada's were the highest. From the top of the mountain, Donner Lake looked like a small deep blue shield far below. The road was very narrow with nothing but sharp switch backs down the face of the mountain. Many times Leta did not dare look down. She feared that they were going to fall off and not stop rolling until they came to the lake. And she was afraid to look back to see how Jule and Ole were faring. She just hoped and prayed they were alright as she knew she could not drive down this narrow ribbon of twisting mountain road. It seemed to her an eternity before they had safely descended the mountain and had reached their destination.

Reno was nestled in a wide dusty bowl with treeless mountains on all sides. It had taken a little over three weeks to make the trip from Washington. This was desert country and Leta was not accustomed to the hot, dry arid heat. But she did not complain of the heat or the hardships.

As soon as the family was settled in the white-washed four room frame house that Dan had rented, he went to work in a garage. Jule and Ole found themselves a room in a nearby boarding house and quickly found jobs as cooks for a local mining company.

After living in Reno for nearly a year, Dan and Leta moved to Sparks, a small community just outside Reno. With every move, Leta learned how to make something from nothing, whether it was a meal or clothing for her children.

Since she had never known an abundance of anything, Leta always made do with whatever she had on hand. When Verna needed a new coat Leta took some wool scraps she had and fitted them together to make one. One sleeve had seven different scraps that she had fitted together so well it looked like one piece.

She cut up old shirts that Dan's brother Bill had given them and made short sleeve shirts for the twins. Bill was a policeman in Los Angeles and couldn't wear the shirts after the collars or cuffs were frayed so he sent them to his brother's family as he knew Leta would make good use of them.

She also learned the many uses of vinegar and always kept a gallon on hand. She used it for nearly everything, such as: furniture polish, to clean windows, remove mildew, remove perspiration odor from the clothes. A bowl of vinegar setting on the kitchen counter would remove cooking odors. It was used to remove the chalky mineral film on jars, and to cut the grease in her dishwater. And she wiped the kitchen counters with it to keep the ants off. In Canada she had used it in the animal's water to deter fleas and ticks. The amount of water she mixed it with depended on what she was using it for at the time.

Dan went to work in Lindsey's Furniture store in Sparks. He and Leta became good friends with the owners, Frank and Mary. The Lindsey's had no children of their own and really enjoyed the Keogh brood. The children loved the Lindsey's little black and white Pomeranian which Frank had taught to do tricks. When he had her sit up and wear his glasses, the children giggled and clapped, begging for her to do it again.

Whenever a piece of furniture came in damaged, Frank would let Dan buy it at a bargain price. He would take it home and repair it. They obtained several pieces of new furniture this way. Leta was thrilled when Dan brought home a silver gray bedroom set that had been damaged as well as a rose colored taffeta bedspread with matching pillows that had been torn. Dan repaired the furniture to look like new and when Leta finished patching the spread and pillows no one could tell they had ever been damaged. Dan also brought home a floor model Trebbe radio. Verna and the twins were awe struck as they listened to the voices coming from inside the radio.

"Do the little people ever come out, Daddy?" Verna asked mesmerized by the new contraption. "Will we get to see them?" the Twins wanted to know.

"If they came out, how could we listen to the radio?" their father countered. With that question, three wee heads leaned closer trying to get a glimpse of the little people the children knew were living inside this fancy box.

The winter of '28 passed quickly and summer was turning into fall. Family life for the Keogh's was what Leta had always dreamed it should be. As she went about her daily chores she hoped and prayed they would not have to move again.

Finishing the last piece of ironing, Leta set the hot iron on the high window sill in the kitchen to cool while she put the starched and pressed clothes away. She was grateful to have a new electric iron so she did not have to keep a fire in the stove to heat her flat irons. After hanging the clothes in a closet she started to return to the kitchen when she heard Howard making a funny little noise that sounded like it was coming from just outside the kitchen window. At fifteen-months, he was climbing on everything. Instinctively she knew he was hurt. "He's fallen off the porch!" Leta started to run outside then she heard him again. The noise was coming from the kitchen.

Rushing into the room she saw that Howard had managed to pull a chair over to the window and had knocked the iron over onto his arm. The hot iron had adhered to his arm from the back of his tiny hand to his elbow. Grabbing the iron she quickly pulled it off him. A layer of skin had stuck to the bottom of the iron and when Leta pulled it off his arm, the skin pulled apart like cotton. Howard did not cry. He just made that same funny little sound. He didn't even cry when she smeared butter on his arm and wrapped it in a clean white cloth. But he would carry a scar from his fingers to his elbow his entire life.

A few weeks after Howard burned his arm, Leta took all the children with her to do the weekly shopping. Walking the short distance to town, Verna and Howard were close on their mother's heels with the twins bringing up the rear. Before going into the bakery she instructed the four tots to sit on the bench out front and to stay put. After buying what she needed, Leta went out to gather her brood and head for home. Coming out of the bakery she saw a woman across the street had Howard by the hand and was walking away with him. Disregarding his siblings protests, he had climbed off the bench and wandered down the street.

Dropping her bundles on the bench beside the other children, she shouted, "Howard!"

Turning at the sound of her voice, Howard called back, "Yes, Mama?"

Without taking her eyes off him she instructed the other three not to move and ran across the street.

"Where are you taking him?" she demanded of the woman. Leta's knees were shaking and her heart pounding. She believed the woman was trying to kidnap her child.

"I'm taking him home," the woman answered belligerently.

"Not in that direction," Leta snapped, grabbing Howard by the hand. She marched across the street, gathered her bundles and children and hurried home. Howard never wandered off again.

A few weeks later Jule came to the Keogh house very ill. He was having stomach problems and had been to a Chinese doctor who had given him some bitter medicine that tasted so putrid he had to chew raisins before he could swallow it. It did not seem to be helping so he went to Leta. He was sure she would have something that would help.

Jule was so thin and weak that it scared both her and Dan when they saw him. Leta fixed up a cot in the kitchen for Jule to sleep on. She fixed custard and milk toast for him making sure he did not eat too much at one time so it would stay down. The Chinese doctor had told him that his stomach muscles were too weak to hold the food long enough to digest. They found out later that he had contracted food poisoning.

While Jule was recovering he taught the children how to catch grasshoppers. Early every morning Verna and the Twins would follow Uncle Jule out to the garden to capture a bunch of these green insects. They kept these creatures in the boy's room in a can with a cloth over it. Periodically, of course, some of the insects escaped.

The first time one jumped out at Leta while she was sweeping the floor, she let out a loud yelp and jumped nearly as high as the grasshopper. She made such a sight, her children laughed and laughed. The mischievous three loved this game that had been invented by accident and would let one or two grasshoppers loose in the house on purpose so they could watch their mother jump and holler. Of course Jule enjoyed it as much as the youngsters but he feigned innocence.

Uncle Jule was always making all sorts of games that were educational as well as fun. Jule's keeping the children entertained was a big help to Leta as well as helping her with the cooking. And when all the children came down with the Chicken Pox, he became a nursemaid. The children missed Uncle Jule terribly when he went back to his brother Ole's.

The day after Labor Day, 1929, Verna started First Grade in Sparks. Leta walked her to school the first day and had a time convincing the teacher the tiny towhead was old enough to attend. Two weeks after Verna started school, Dan suddenly decided to move to Fresno, California, uprooting his family again. Packing everything that would fit into a small trailer and the car, the family headed west traveling back over Donner Pass. At Sacramento they turned south to Fresno. Leta was thankful they could stay in auto courts instead of camping out on this trip. Even though she had no babes in diapers, Howard still had 'accidents' and she would have to wash out his clothes every night.

Soon after they arrived in Fresno, Dan found a small rental house and he went to work picking fruit. Leta, once again, set up housekeeping. Times were getting tougher for the Keogh family. All the children came down with the Whooping Cough. The Great Depression had begun and jobs were getting scarce. The Coolidge promise of prosperity had soured. The roaring 20's were over and so was the Jazz Age. Leta was grateful for Dan's $25.00 monthly compensation from the government. His lungs had been burned with mustard gas during WWI and the paltry sum helped buy staple groceries for the family. Most families did not have this much security.

Jobs had always been easy for Dan to find but now they were scarce. Even in the fruit industry. May of 1930, he decided they should go back to Spokane. Once again Leta would leave behind what could not be packed in their '24 Essex, and a small trailer. What was not sold was given away. The back seat of the car was loaded from the floorboards to the top of the front seat. A tarpaulin was strapped over the heaping load in the trailer.

Long before the promise of daylight streaked the sky, the grass still heavy with dew, Dan and Leta loaded the children in the packed Essex and headed north. Kenneth was still recuperating from the Whooping Cough so Leta kept him in the front with her. The other three children rode on top of the load behind the front seat.

Trying to save what little money they had, they camped out for most of the trip. Only when the weather was too rainy did they stay in an auto court. Kenneth's racking cough was still so bad Leta feared he would come down with pneumonia again.

When they arrived in Spokane both Leta and Dan were stunned and dismayed to find things were bad there also. "We will go on to Deer Park. We can live in that little house of Uncle Jule's. If I remember right it's on five or six acres. We can plant a garden and when I get a job, we'll make out just fine." He told Leta optimistically.

After six weeks of searching for a job, any kind of job, for the first time in their marriage Dan was unsuccessful. The Great Depression had spread throughout the country like a cancer. The newspapers were full of discouraging news. In the cities there were long bread lines; three and four men abreast and over a block long. Men in total despair shuffled along in the slow moving lines. If lucky enough not to be at the end of the line, one could get soup, bread, a room for the night and maybe a rumor of a job. Men in business suits stood on street corners selling apples.

"It has to be better in Canada," Dan said, laying the paper down. "I know your mother and I don't see eye to eye, but maybe she would let us stay with her until we could find a place of our own."

The children were asleep and Leta was cleaning up the supper dishes. Dan spoke so quietly she wasn't sure she heard him correctly. "You know she would not turn us away. And I'm sure she could use help on the farm since Papa left." The thought of going home excited Leta. When her father had written telling her he was moving off the homestead and giving it to her mother, Leta was stunned. He had put it simply, "I just can't deal with your mother's bitterness and anger any longer. It is eating her alive and I want a little peace and happiness with what life I have left." It did not surprise her when her parents separated, but she never thought her father would give up his homestead.

Stacking the dishes in the cupboard Leta said chuckling, "Besides, Mama would never turn down free labor."

Chapter Thirty One

Traveling to Idaho on their way to Canada, the Keogh family spent two days with Leila and Asa then continued on their long journey north. Crossing into Canada at Gateway, they turned east through British Columbia and Alberta. From Regina, Saskatchewan, they continued up to Saskatoon and on to Prince Albert. As they passed through each town, getting closer and closer to Shellbrook, Leta realized for the first time how very much she missed her homeland. She could hardly wait to see her father and Cousin Elsie.

The constant bouncing and swaying of the car made Leta a little seasick and she was grateful when they would stop for the night. Dan had bought a folding table and a small gas camp stove for the long trip so setting up camp each night was much easier. Leta set the camp stove on one end of the table, spreading the plates and food on the other end. They sat on whatever they could find: a large rock, a stump, a log, or on the ground to eat their simple meal.

After washing out a few clothes and diapers in the creek and laying them over bushes to dry, Leta helped Dan spread the tarpaulin on the ground, arranging the bedding on top. Dan and Leta slept on the outside like book-ends with the four children between them.

After a cold breakfast of leftovers from the night before they broke camp, piled into the car and continued on their long journey. To amuse themselves the children had crayolas, pencils, paper and Verna's beloved Colored doll to play with. Leta showed them how to pin one of Dan's hankies to the roof lining in the car to make a hammock for the doll. As they continued north, Verna quickly fell asleep watching her doll swing back and forth in its make-shift hammock.

Turning off the main road to the town of Frank, Dan told the children it had once been a gold rush town and had been buried by a mountain. "The Indians had warned the white people not to build the town at the foot of their mountain. Ignoring the warning, the white people built it anyway. The three houses that were built on the outskirts of town were the only buildings to survive the avalanche that hit at noon one day, burying the entire town and killing most of the people in it."

Parking the car near one of remaining long deserted houses they all climbed out and walked over the town buried under tons of rock and dirt. "The white man would have been better off to have listened to the Indians in most everything," Dan mused.

"You've given them a history lesson they won't forget, Dan," Leta told him quietly.

After nearly three weeks of camping along small streams, and occasionally staying in tiny tourist cabins, the family was nearing their destination. The last cabin they stayed in was located on a farm beside a river. After Dan paid the farmer $3.00 for the night, Verna and the twins tumbled out of the car. They walked shyly over to the farmer's young son who was standing beside his father.

"Hello," he said to the three towheads. "Want to see my fish?" Three small heads bobbed in unison. Following the boy around behind the farmhouse, their eyes widened when they saw several large trout swimming in a washtub.

"Where did you get all those?" Verna asked.

"Come on. I'll show you." They followed him to the river directly behind the house. Whenever the farmer irrigated during the day it lowered the river so much that it left big puddles full of marooned fish that couldn't get back into the mainstream.

Without a word, the three Keogh children quickly pulled off their shoes and stockings and waded into the closest puddle. They started grabbing fish and tossing them out onto the bank as fast as they could. If one of their catch tried to flop back into the shallow water, one of them would smash it in the head with a rock.

In the meantime Dan had finished unloading what they would need for the night and Leta was preparing supper on the small wood cookstove in the cabin. Howard was sitting at the table drawing a picture with a crayon on a brown paper sack.

"Where are the Twins and Verna?" Dan dumped an armful of wood in the wood box.

"I thought they were with you." Leta quickly stepped outside and began calling. The young explorers answered from the direction of the river. Sliding the skillet to the back of the stove, Leta went to gather her brood.

Leta laughed when she saw her children trying, unsuccessfully, to stack slippery trout in their arms like stove wood. After counting seventeen fish, she found a stick and showed them how to string the trout on it so they could carry every single one back to the cabin. They were very proud of their catch.

Dan laughed and shook his head when he saw the procession coming. Laying his grease rag down, he shut the hood of the car and went to help carry their catch. Leta and Dan cleaned fish until midnight, and then she cooked them all so they would not spoil.

The last day on the long road north they traveled until about 2 a.m. It never became completely dark at this time of year and there was still a streak of light in the Northern skies. They'd had so many flat tires that the last few miles, Leta had to ride with her head out of the window to watch if the tires were going flat. That way, Dan could stop and pump them up before they deflated completely.

Leta had written to her mother to let her know they were coming. She was not anxious to live with Myrtle again but Dan had assured her it would only be for a short time. He promised he would build a house for them as soon as he could get some land.

When Myrtle heard the car coming down the lane, she stepped out on the porch. She was glad they had come. Even though it wasn't completely dark on this August night, Myrtle held up a glowing lantern to welcome them. She smiled as Dan pulled to a stop in front of the house.

Suddenly Leta was struck with an overwhelming feeling of homesickness. She had not realized how much she had missed this place until now. It was good to be home.

"Hello, Mama." Leta stepped out of the car.

"Myrtle," Dan nodded as he came around the car. There were no hugs, no show of affection whatever. They greeted each other like polite strangers.

Dan carried the sleeping children to Leta's old room above the kitchen. They barely stirred as Leta removed their clothes and shoes and tucked them under the thick quilts. Even though it was August the nights were quite chilly.

Myrtle offered steaming vegetable soup and bread for them to eat. Much to Leta's surprise, Myrtle seemed happy to see them. The conversation was pleasant as they ate and Leta prayed her mother and Dan could get along this time. She knew her father had bought a small farm in Choiceland with his share of the money from the sale of one of their sections of land and lived there alone. Leta could hardly wait to take the children to see him but knew better than mention him in her mother's presence.

The house that always seemed so big to Leta when she was growing up now seemed so small. As the days quickly passed everyone seemed to get along, on the surface, but Myrtle had little patience with the children. Despite their tender years, she kept them busy with some kind of chore every waking moment. Dan found himself biting his tongue to keep still as she barked orders to his children. Leta was proud of his restraint, but she did not know how long it would last. Or how long she would last. The tension was getting to her, and she knew Dan was at the breaking point.

Soon after the Keogh family arrived in Shellbrook, Leta enrolled Verna in Mrs. Lindsay's Second grade class. Every morning Leta hitched Old Babe to the buggy and drove Verna to school. As she picked up neighbor children along the way she thought about her own school days at the same school house. At that time there were no other children between the Oesch farm and the school house.

Early one frosty morning, Leta was keeping Old Babe trotting along at a fast clip when suddenly a rabbit jumped out of the brush alongside the road. The aging horse shied, breaking the buggy shaft. After calming the quivering mare, Leta untied the halter, rope then tied the shaft together with it and they continued on to school.

Occasionally, Leta would take the twins and Howard along for the ride. On this particular morning Old Babe was trotting briskly along when they came upon a Model-T noisily chugging along. The vehicle scared Old Babe so bad she bolted, passing it like a shot. Leta hollered, "Hang on!" and off they flew with the three little round eyed towheads hanging on for dear life.

A few days later, Dan decided it was time to hunt partridge. After the grain had been shocked the fields were thick with game birds. Taking Verna and Howard with him, he stopped the buggy at a spot where he could see a large flock of partridge out in the field. They were so thick they looked like a feather blanket spread out in the field. Aiming the .22 caliber rifle carefully he got three with one shot.

Old Babe did not flinch when the gun was fired but when Dan gathered up his kill to load it in the buggy, one of the birds began to flutter. Babe spooked and bolted with two screaming children clinging to the seat. The old mare headed straight for the barn with the buggy bouncing wildly along behind her. With the rifle in one hand and three partridge in the other, Dan ran after them as fast as he could yelling, "Whoa, Babe. Whoa."

Hearing all the commotion, Leta ran out of the house with a paring knife still in her hand. Myrtle was right behind her. They stepped off the porch just as Old Babe passed the barn, ran over a pile of fence posts, and Howard flew out. Verna had grabbed the reins and was hanging on for dear life when Old Babe took another sharp turn. Verna flew out still clinging to

278

the reins and was dragged several feet before she finally let go. The terrified mare headed straight for the garden.

Dan's sweater had somehow gotten tangled in the buggy wheel and Leta feared the large tangle of wool was one of the children. With her heart in her throat, she ran into the garden directly in front of the runaway horse. Myrtle was racing close behind Leta shouting, "Don't let her get in the garden!" Leta grabbed the bridle as the mare sped past her yanking the frightened horse to a stop. The instant the horse stopped Leta raced to the rear wheel. Tears of relief streamed down her cheeks when she saw it was only Dan's sweater wrapped around the spokes. Still shaking she led the horse out of the garden and back toward the barn.

By this time, Dan, still trying to catch his breath, held both skinned and bruised children in his arms. Verna was howling. Howard lay too quietly against his father's chest. His tiny face was as white as a sheet. Seeing her stricken face Dan reassured her, "He just had the wind knocked out of him. I had a time getting him to move his legs though."

Myrtle put up the horse and buggy while Dan and Leta carried their bruised and battered children to the house. Leta could not remember seeing Dan so frightened.

The time to move out of Myrtle's house and into one of their own was long overdue. Dan was afraid that he would be pushed to do bodily harm to Myrtle due to her venomous mouth. He was still amazed that Leta had such a positive attitude growing up with such a negative woman as Myrtle. In the seven years he and Leta had been married, he had never seen her lose her temper. He knew she had one, but he had never seen her lose it. She had an incredible ability to control her emotions, too much at times and it took its toll on her.

Much to his astonishment, Myrtle agreed with Dan that he should build a cabin for his family. "You're welcome to the timber you'll need and I will give you a plot of ground to build it on." He planned to start on the cabin immediately before she changed her mind.

So every day, after the chores were done and the fields were tended to, Dan would take Verna and the twins out with him while he cut the trees and skid them to the cabin site. The three youngsters rode perched on Old Babe's back as she pulled the skid. They loved "helping" their father build their new house. Since Howard was prone to accidents, Leta kept him with her. Making sure he did not feel left out, she gave him little jobs to do for her.

Dan always made sure the children were out of harm's way when he was felling the trees. They waited from a safe distance on Old Babe's back while she grazed on the lush green grass. All was well until one day the old mare decided to go back to the barn. Starting off at a brisk walk, the aging mare ignored the children's alarmed shouts of "Whoa! Whoa!"

Throwing down his ax, Dan bolted after the horse shouting, "Jump! Jump off her!"

Verna was terrified to jump. It was an awful long way to the ground. "Jump, Verna, or we will to push you!" Keith and Kenneth said in unison. Holding tight to the mane, Verna apprehensively began sliding off. With Verna dangling from the mane, afraid to let go, Old Babe stopped. Dan caught up with them as the twins were trying to pull their sister back up onto the mare's broad back. Dan quickly grabbed Verna and sat her in front of the boys. Verna's tiny hands remained entwined in the thick mane, her lip trembling, tears about to spill. She was still terrified. Dan quickly defused the situation with a few reassuring words.

Within a few weeks Dan had peeled the bark off the logs, notched the ends and fitted them together to form the walls of a nice large cabin for his family. He framed in the windows and tar papered the roof. He planned to put the shingles on later. The logs had not yet been chinked when the family moved in their new home. Unfortunately winter set in the same night with howling winds forming huge snow drifts and the temperature plummeting. When the Keogh clan woke the next morning snow covered all of their beds. Verna thought she had been thrown outside in a snow bank when she tried to crawl out of her quilts. It felt colder inside than outside the cabin. Dan and Leta hastily bundled up their children and went back to Myrtle's.

Upon arriving at Myrtle's they saw that the snow had drifted over the fences around the barn and the pigs were not in their pen. After getting the children settled in the house Dan and Leta went hunting for the missing pigs. When Leta spotted steam rising from a large snow bank they quickly investigated. Finding a small hole emitting steam they dug down and found the pigs huddled beneath the crusted frozen snow.

Neither Dan nor Leta wanted to be confined with Myrtle all winter so early one morning they left the children with Myrtle to get their cabin chinked before nightfall. The day was clear but frigid. Working as fast as they could they still could not keep the mud, straw and ash mixture for the chinking from freezing. Reluctantly they gave up trying to finish their cabin and returned to Myrtle's for another night. "At least it's warm there," Leta said as they trudged back to her mother's house.

In order to tolerate life with Myrtle, Dan went hunting and fishing as often as he could. Leta and Myrtle cleaned the fish and he butchered the game, hanging it in the ice house to freeze. When he wasn't out hunting or fishing, Dan worked in the barn repairing harness and making small chairs for his children.

On one of his hunting trips, Dan trapped a skunk by accident and knowing Leta would make good use of it he brought it home. After scraping and tanning the skunk hide, she made a lovely fur collar for Verna's coat. Verna loved it. She felt so grown up wearing it. She wore the coat everywhere. Leta could hardly get it off her. That is, until she wore it in the rain and the fur got wet. When skunk fur was wet, it still smelled like its original owner.

One cold, sunny afternoon, as mother and daughter silently worked at the table her father had made, Leta thought as she glanced over at Myrtle, *Nothing has really changed here, it is still as primitive now as it was when I was growing up.* Leta was sewing quilt pieces together with tiny even stitches while her mother carded the wool that would fill the quilt by hand. The two women worked mostly in silence just as they had done when Leta was a young girl.

Leta's eyes scanned the room from the coal oil lamps to the wood cook stove. "*All of us living here, mostly in one room to stay warm in winter, the privy outside, and thunder mugs still under the beds.*" She smiled inwardly at that thought.

Leta had experienced the luxury of electric lights, indoor bathrooms, and kitchens with large sinks and running water. Even with all its hardships, Leta still preferred this land. It was part of her father. It was part of her. If only Papa were here, it would be perfect, she thought sadly.

Chapter Thirty Two

Life at Myrtle's seemed to be going along smoothly until one evening at supper Dan made a teasing remark to Leta about the food she had prepared. "You should be grateful you have food to put in your stomach," Myrtle snapped at him.

This was the last straw! Without a word, Dan slammed his coffee mug down with a bang, shoved his plate back, and slowly and deliberately rose from the table. He stood clenching his fists at his sides glaring at Myrtle who still stood at the stove.

The children watched, terrified. Leta's face paled, afraid to say anything. She suddenly felt the same as she did when she was small. Her mother's wrath churned up her insides and she could feel the bitter bile rising in her throat. Dan had ignored Myrtle's sniping remarks all evening and now he had had his fill. "You are the most cantankerous human being I have ever known. And I have heard enough of your snide remarks." Dan's voice was hard and cold.

Myrtle grabbed the boiling tea water off the stove, her face purple with rage. She held the pan ready to throw the scalding liquid on him. He glared at her and said evenly through gritted teeth, "Go ahead, by God, go ahead."

They stood facing each other like raging bulls in a standoff. Myrtle slammed the pan down on the stove. The spilled water sizzled as it danced across the hot surface. "Get out of MY house!" she screeched and stormed into her bedroom, slamming the door behind her.

"Come on Leta," he said his chest heaving with anger, "pack up the children. We're leaving. I will not stay another minute on any part of her property." The cabin they had worked so hard on would be abandoned.

Since Jule was still in the States with Ole, Dan took his family to his Uncle Ed's. "It will only be temporary," Dan told Leta. "If I don't get away from your mother I swear I will end up killing her."

In all his life Dan had never seen such an unstable human. One minute, she was agreeable and half-way pleasant. Then the slightest thing would ignite her like a keg of dynamite. And one never knew what was going to set her off. Now Dan understood why John left everything he had worked so hard for behind.

The Keogh family had not been at Uncle Ed's very long when Leta became ill. She was unable to stay in the house when Uncle Ed was cooking and she didn't eat much for a couple of weeks. It seemed to the children she was in the privy vomiting most of the time. They began to get anxious about their mother.

"Now don't you fret. Your mama is going to get you a new brother or sister in the spring," Dan told the children. "Why does it make Mama sick to get a new baby?" they asked. "Well, that is just the way Nature intended," their father explained. Totally confused, the children did not ask any more questions.

Soon the morning sickness passed and Leta took over the household chores. The children liked it much better at Uncle Ed's. He did not make them work all the time like their Granny did. Even with the chores they were assigned, Uncle Ed made sure they had time to play. Dan and Ed made a long wooden toboggan for the children. Soon they were all sliding down the small snow covered hill in back of the house near the barn. Then Uncle Ed showed them how to pour water down it every day turning the slope to solid ice. When they all jumped on the toboggan they would go flying down the hill. But it took them a few times of struggling up the icy incline to figure out that if they went around the ice and walked in the snow it was a lot easier.

After supper one evening Uncle Ed popped some corn to make popcorn balls. The children were so eager to try this new treat, Ed had more help than he needed. So he took the syrup and popped corn out the back, set the lantern on the stump beside the door, and proceeded to finish the treat. The popcorn balls formed very quickly in the icy air and in a short time all four Keogh children had their mouths stuffed full of the sweet treat.

Every day in order to give Ed some peace and quiet, Leta would take the children and walk to Cousin Elsie's as the Johnson place was not far from Ed's. Ed enjoyed having the children around but Leta was afraid her rambunctious brood would wear him out.

When they had first married, Elsie and Frank Johnson had stayed with John and Myrtle. Elsie had been only 16 and still needed to learn many things. She enjoyed being able to share everything with Leta each day but life with Myrtle had been too much for the newlyweds. As soon as he could, Frank built his family a house on their own land. They would have stayed with Elsie's parents who lived in Scotty Lauder's old cabin just a half mile north of the Oesch place, but it was so small there was barely enough room for two people.

At this present time, Leta and Elsie were both expecting. Leta was due the last of April as near as they could figure, and Elsie's baby would be born in early February. Frank and Elsie had a girl child about every two years. After 5 girls, Frank, like most men, was hoping for a boy this time. But he loved all his girls - Louise 10, Babs 8, May 6, Alice 4, and Dolly 2 - and would not trade any one of them for anything. All the Johnson and Keogh children had a great time playing together, and even though the boys were out-numbered, they did not seem to mind.

Dan and Frank had moved an old building that had once been a granary onto the Johnson property next to the house and the men were fixing it up for the Keogh family to live in. The old granary was only one large room, but it was big enough for Dan's growing family.

When the granary house was finally livable, the Keogh's loaded what little they had onto a wagon and hauled it to their new home. After everything was unloaded, Frank and Dan set up the simple beds Dan had made from scraps of wood. Leta put the few dishes and pans in the cupboard Dan had nailed to the wall between the only two windows in the room.

"After I get some curtains on the windows it will be homier," Leta told Elsie as they made up the beds.

Soon the Keoghs were all settled in their new home, but the building was so difficult to keep warm they ate most of their meals at Frank and Elsie's and only slept in the drafty converted granary. It seemed a good arrangement for everyone. After all, they were all just one big happy family.

When time permitted, Dan and Frank went hunting and ice fishing to keep Frank's small ice house stocked. It took a lot of food to feed the two families. And Dan was not about to ask Myrtle for any of the meat he had left hanging in hers.

Leta and Elsie didn't have a wool carder or a spinning wheel so they pulled the raw wool by hand then twisted it into yarn. With this yarn they knitted heavy socks for Dan and Frank to wear inside their low rubber shoes. The powder dry snow shook off easily so their feet never got wet and the thick wool socks kept their feet from freezing in the sub zero temperatures. Every day the women washed, mended, and knitted the wool yarn they had rolled by hand into socks, caps, scarves, and mittens. They kept large pots of soup or stew simmering on the stove as well as attending to the many crises that arose among their nine children.

One day while cutting fire wood, Dan missed his aim with the ax and sliced a big gash in his foot ruining one of the socks that Leta had just finished knitting. He came in the door trailing blood with each step. Elsie quickly shooed all the children upstairs. They reluctantly obeyed, grumbling as they ascended the stairs. Every time there was a crisis or disturbance that Elsie felt the children were too young to understand or be witness to, up the stairs they had to go. However, Elsie was not aware of the large crack in the floor of the children's room so they watched what was going on anyway.

Leta carefully pulled off Dan's blood-soaked sock as Elsie poured hot water in a basin. After they had washed the wound in hot soapy water and poured alcohol over it, Elsie dipped her needle and thread in alcohol and began to sew the gaping flesh together. Through the entire procedure Dan gripped the edge of the chair, knuckles white as his face. Leta felt she would faint but kept swallowing hard while she held the edges of the deep wound together for Elsie. When she finished the last stitch, Elsie poured alcohol over the entire foot again and wrapped it tightly with clean white rags.

Peering down from directly above the procedure, Verna and Louise quit watching as soon as the first stitch was taken. The twins thought it great to watch, but Howard and the girls did not.

As Leta grew larger with child, her feet and ankles began swelling until she could not be on her feet for any length of time. So Dan decided that Verna and the twins could help by doing the dishes on the few occasions they ate at their own place. They were still too short to reach the table so he put the dish pan on one of the benches. Verna washed, Kenneth rinsed, and Keith dried. They stacked the dishes on a chair and Leta would put them away. Sometimes they didn't get completely clean, but Leta never scolded.

During her entire childhood, Leta missed being allowed to celebrate Christmas. However, in the years since her marriage, the Keogh family celebrated it every year. Not having the money to buy gifts, Leta always made something for everyone. She knitted wool slippers, caps and scarves, made flannel shirts for the boys and a new flannel gown for Verna. Dan carved toys and made slingshots for the boys. Leta made a doll for Verna from one of Dan's worn-out wool socks. They may have been poor in material things, but they were rich in family.

The first Christmas they spent at the Johnson's was an exciting time. Leta's father, John, came in his sled from Choiceland. He had a gentle black colt tied on behind, a gift for the children. Elsie and Leta and their children decorated the large cedar tree with the ornaments they all had spent hours making. The finishing touch was the popcorn and paper garlands. The children had made Christmas cards for everyone and hung the festive cards over red yarn strung on the wall above the organ. When they finished, they all stood back and admired their work.

On Christmas Eve everyone piled into John's large sleigh and sang Christmas carols on the way to the Christmas program at the Silver Cliff School. They all snuggled together, adult laps full of children covered with fur lap robes and feet on a heated bricks. At the school the students put on their traditional Christmas play, singing loud and a little off key with the teacher prompting them with their lines, to a roomful of proud parents.

On Christmas day, the two families feasted on roast goose, baked ham, mashed potatoes, yams glazed with brown sugar, mashed turnips, and boiled carrots. The women had made mincemeat and pumpkin pies as well as berry cobblers. There was plenty of fresh, warm bread, spread with sweet butter and jams, along with fresh baked cookies and rare home made fudge.

After dinner Frank played the organ and they all joined in singing every Christmas carol they knew. When the hour grew late the sleepy Keogh and Johnson children were put to bed. The adults stayed up until the wee hours. The men played cards at the kitchen table while Leta and Elsie crocheted by the fire.

With so many playmates the youngsters had no trouble amusing themselves. Digging in the snow around the Keogh house they found several small stones that contained fools gold. Thinking it was real gold, the children put the rocks on the back of the heater to "melt out the gold" they told their mother. Leta patiently accommodated them, cooking around their treasure for weeks.

After a few weeks, Kenneth decided that the gold was not going to melt out and carefully rolled the stones off the stove onto a large spoon and proceeded to take them outside. Seeing Howard playing alone at the corner of the house, mischievous Kenneth crept up behind him and poured the hot rocks down his back. Howard had a bad habit of yelling whenever one of the other children would get too close to him and they would get the spanking for making him holler. But, unfortunately, this day Dan was trying vainly to mend a buggy wheel and his patience was at an end. When Howard started squalling, Dan stormed over, bent Howard over his knee and proceeded to give him a long asked for spanking. After several swats, he stood Howard on his feet, "Now you have something to cry about."

Howard sobbed, "But, Daddy, he...he...he put hot rocks in my shirt," pointing to Kenneth who was quickly trying to make himself scarce. Lifting up Howard's shirt, he cringed with regret as he could see the blisters already forming on his small back. "Come back here young man!" Dan barked at Kenneth. Turning back to Howard he said, "Sorry son, I didn't know. Now go in the house and have your mother see to your backside."

A few days later, Leta moved in with Frank and Elsie. Dan and his children slept in their own house but now ate all their meals with the Johnson's. In this late stage of her pregnancy Leta could hardly walk to the outhouse. Her legs and feet swelled until she could barely stand. She sat with her feet elevated most of the time doing the mending for both families and making tiny gowns for the new baby. Elsie's baby was nearly three months old now and she placed the cradle next to Leta so she could tend to the baby while she sewed. Elsie did not mind that most of the other household chores were left to her.

Dan made a low ironing board so Leta could sit and iron and she could use it as a small table to peel potatoes and cut up vegetables for the stews and soups. The children were given the jobs of bringing produce and canned goods from the root cellar as well as feeding the chickens and gathering the eggs.

Late one cold April afternoon the children watched as Dan shaved the corners off an orange crate making it oval shaped. After sanding it smooth, he made sure there was not even a speck of sawdust left on it. When it was finished it looked just like a big basket. "There," he told the children, "this will be a fine bed for the new baby." When he took the finished bassinet to Leta she lined it with soft flannel and made a small thick quilt to pad the bottom.

A few days later, Frank rushed in the cold one room house and shook Dan awake. "Dan, wake up. Leta's having a hard time. You have to go after Myrtle." Quickly pulling his clothes on, he roused the children. Bundling them up, they followed Frank to his house, barely noticing their father racing toward the barn. Still half asleep, they were quickly hustled up the stairs and put in bed with the Johnson youngsters. They knew something important was happening and tried in vain to stay awake to find out what it was.

The next morning when the children woke they tiptoed down the stairs and found a new baby in the tiny bed their father had made. Dan had circled the date on the calendar on the kitchen wall...April, 29, 1931. Peering at the baby's red squalling face, Verna exclaimed, amazed, "We got us a Indian baby!" Eyes wide with curiosity and amazement the Keogh children gathered around to get a better look. This new addition to the Keogh clan was kicking her feet and waving tiny fists in the air. Verna was sure the baby was waving at her and decided then and there this Indian baby was just fine after all. "This is your new sister," their father informed them.

"Can we name her Tommy, Daddy?" Verna asked.

"She already has a name. Ellen Joyce, after my mother," Dan told them.

Elsie shooed the curious brood to the kitchen where she and Myrtle had steaming bowls of mush ready for them to eat. Verna did not want to leave her mother. Leta's face was chalky gray and there were dark circles around her sunken eyes. Verna was afraid her mother was dying.

During the birth of her fifth child, Leta nearly died of a hemorrhage. When Frank had told him the urgency of the situation, Dan forgot the anger and animosity he felt for Myrtle and gladly went after her. When Myrtle and Elsie finally got the bleeding stopped, Leta was so weak she could barely hold the baby.

When Myrtle felt that Leta was out of danger and had helped Elsie wash the soiled linens from the birthing she asked Dan to take her home. "I have stock to tend to," she told him.

"I will take care of the stock for you, Myrtle. I...I want to thank you for your help," he said humbly.

"No need to thank me. She's my daughter." Myrtle's voice was barely above a whisper. Dan thought he saw a tear in her eye but she quickly turned away.

The day Ellen was born, Elsie allowed the children to stay home from school but the next morning she insisted they go. As young as Verna was, she knew her mother was very ill and was afraid to leave her, so she feigned a stomach ache.

"Well then, I will give you castor oil and you can stay in bed," Elsie told her. After the other children left for school Verna took her dose of castor oil, gagging and swallowing quickly to keep it down. It was a small price to pay in order to stay with her mother. It wasn't long before she was out of bed wanting to help Elsie take care of her mother and new baby sister.

The following morning Verna informed Elsie she still had her stomach ache. "I'll get the castor oil again. That will fix you up," Elsie said. "I'll give you two doses today so you can go to school." Suddenly Verna's stomach ache disappeared. Dressing quickly she joined the other children at the breakfast table.

Hearing the clamorous children leave the house, Leta remembered her own school days. The small country school remained unchanged since Leta had gone herself. Closing her eyes as the baby nursed she could see in her minds eye the one room school house. All eight grades met in the single room, the teacher dividing his or her time among the grades, making sure each grade received an equal amount of attention. The room was heated with a large potbellied stove which stood in the center of the room. It was the older boys' job to bring in the wood and keep the fire going and they took turns mucking out the barn where the horses were kept. In this North Country it seemed as though time stood still.

By the time Ellen was three weeks old, Leta still had not fully recuperated. Elsie would only allow her to do light household chores, most of which she could do sitting down. Ellen was such a good baby, she required very little attention. If her stomach was full and her bottom dry she was content.

The days were full with never ending chores. Elsie had spent most of the day outside washing clothes on the scrub board. With eleven children and four adults the laundry piled up quickly. It was still early spring and the weather had turned unseasonably warm. She finished hanging out the last tub of clothes and hoped the laundry would dry before she had to bring it in. They had spent the entire winter with damp clothes hanging in the corner behind the stove.

Carrying the empty laundry basket into the house, Elsie could hear the older children returning from school. They walked the two miles to Silver Cliff School on the days that weather permitted. Leta had taken them in the cutter before her condition had confined her to the house. During that time, Dan took them when the weather was too severe.

May came running into the house yelling. "Mama, Mama, it's snowing!" The others trailed in after her wide-eyed and excited. When Elsie saw the gray-white flakes on their coats, fear shot through her.

"It's ashes! Not Snow!" Without another word she bolted out of the house, picked up the large washtub brimming with dirty soapy water, raced around the house and dumped it on the smoldering fire in the manure pile against the back of the house. Elsie was short, stout and strong. "Quick! Go get a pitchfork! We have to make sure this is all out." She ordered Louise. In no time the fire was completely out, averting a disaster.

In late fall, manure was usually banked around the house for insulation to help keep it warm. It would freeze and remained covered with snow all winter. Dan and Frank had been busy with the spring planting and had not hauled it to the fields before it had thawed. Before the men returned from the fields, Elsie and the children had all the manure shoveled away from the house, ready to be hauled away.

A few days later a spring storm covered everything again with a thick blanket of fresh snow. Leta had run out of crochet thread and needed to get the extra ball she had left at her house. Elsie was busy baking bread and could not leave it. All the children wanted to go along but Elsie told her brood they had to stay and finish their lessons. Leta's older four scrambled into their coats while she bundled up Ellen and tucked her into the tiny sleigh Dan had made from a wooden apple box. It had a rope attached to the front so it could be pulled.

Verna and the twins and Howard were running a short distance ahead of Leta pulling their baby sister along behind them in the little sleigh. They quickly rounded a corner, the sleigh skimming along close to their heels. But they turned the corner a little too fast and the sleigh dumped over and out tumbled the baby. Afraid of an impending spanking they quickly picked her up, brushed her off and tucked her back in her little sleigh before Leta came into sight. They swore each other to secrecy and were grateful the baby never even woke up.

With 11 children and two men to take care of, Leta and Elsie had their hands full. Like all large families, the older children had to watch out for the younger ones. When anything happened to one of the younger children all the older ones received a spanking. The Keogh and Johnson children learned this the hard way. They were all playing in the barn squealing with joy as they slid down the haystack. They were having a great time until Howard became buried in the hay and they could not get him out. And they all received their respective spankings when Alice tried playing underneath one of the horses and it stepped on her foot. The older children soon learned if cajoling did not work to control their siblings, they would resort to threats.

Early in June the Keogh clan moved back into their one room house but still spent most of their time at the Johnson's. The hard work seemed easier with someone to share the load and the fun times were more festive. The only money Leta and Dan had to live on was the $25.00 a month Dan received from the government due to his war injuries. It kept both families in staples during the long winter months.

Chapter Thirty Three

Spring gently turned into summer. The wheat crops and a large
vegetable garden were planted. The children were thriving and
Leta was blissfully content. She felt Dan was too until he
received a letter from the United States Government. Along
with the letter was a large settlement check for his war
injuries. The letter explained that every veteran from the Great
War that had suffered injuries in the line of duty would receive
a settlement check. Leta knew before Dan said a word that
they would be leaving Canada again. With a heavy heart she
slowly began gathering their belongings and started to pack.
"It will be all right. It will be all right," she kept telling herself,
holding back the tears.

On a cool August morning the stars still glittered in the sky
like diamonds scattered over cobalt-blue velvet. The children
piled in the heavily burdened Essex as Leta said her final
tearful farewells to Elsie. By the time the sun came up
Valbrand would be far behind them. Leta knew they would
never be back.

Following the same route they had the year before, the Keogh
family traveled south through Shellbrook, Prince Albert,
Saskatoon, and Regina. They continued west through the
Cypress Hills, across Alberta, through the southeast corner of
British Columbia and down into Idaho and on to Deerpark,
Washington. After nearly three weeks of exhausting travel

they reached their destination. Dan quickly located a small house to rent and Leta set up housekeeping.

One evening after supper, Dan read the paper aloud. "It says here, Communist Russia advertised 6,000 jobs in the U.S.S.R and over 100,000 Americans applied; there are no jobs in the U.S, banks have closed, and thousands have lost all their life savings." Slowly folding the paper he laid it on the table. "It's bad all over, Leta."

"Maybe we should have stayed in Canada," Leta ventured.

"We will move into Spokane. I know I can get some sort of job there." They had only been in Deerpark six weeks and Leta was packing up again. In Spokane they rented a clean four room house with the tub and toilet on the back porch. Leta was glad to have indoor plumbing and running water in the kitchen again. A letter from Leila caught up with them soon after they got settled.

Leila wrote..."Asa was killed in December of '29 in a hunting accident. The sheep we were raising made us a good living but without Asa to work the farm I had to sell the land and sheep. I have been living with my mother-in-law but now she has passed away and I can not stay here any longer. I am in hopes of coming to stay with you for a while. I just can't stay with Mama. Please write soon..."

Two weeks later Dan picked Leila up at the train station. He was not pleased that she was moving in with them. He just hoped it was not for long. When she began putting on the helpless grieving widow act he wanted to throw her back on the train.

Leila seemed to have more ailments now and kept the children waiting on her hand and foot. She spent her days tatting fancy doilies, cuffs for blouses, and collars for dresses. Leila tatted beautifully and Leta was happy to have the fancy work to spruce up her old dresses, covering the frayed places. But she wished that just once in a while Leila would help with some of the work.

By this time motion pictures had replaced most of the country's vaudeville acts. Leta missed going to the theater and wished she could see the new picture shows that were playing. In the movies of the 20's and 30's, Hollywood made sure the sympathy of the audience would never be on the side of crime, evil, or sin. And Hollywood enforced its volunteer production code. It banned excessive and lustful kissing, seductive embraces, and suggestive postures or gestures. Vulgar expressions and profanity were also forbidden.

The Public Enemy starring James Cagney was playing at one Spokane theater and *Captains Courageous* starring Spencer Tracy was playing at another. Posters of coming attractions advertised *Frankenstein* Starring Boris Karloff. These early movies were pure family entertainment.

But there was no money for such things as picture shows or vaudeville, so Leta never mentioned her desire to go. There were eight mouths to feed and what little they did have was needed for food. Leta wished Leila would offer to buy a few groceries now and then, but she never did.

Their first winter back in Spokane was a bad one for the Keogh family. Baby Ellen had to have mastoid surgery and was in the hospital for two weeks. With no money for street cars, Leta walked the two miles to the hospital in the cold wind and rain to breast feed the baby. She did this twice a day every day until the doctor told her that her milk was no good. Once she was bottle feeding, Ellen began to improve rapidly.

During this time, Leta was thankful Leila was there to stay with the other children.

While Ellen was still in the hospital, Dan came down with acute tonsillitis and had to have his tonsils removed. After she had fed Ellen, Leta would go down the hall and visit Dan a few minutes before walking back home. To make matters worse, both Keith and Kenneth had ear infections which developed into abscesses. Instead of sleeping and getting the rest she needed when she was at home, Leta was up most of every night with her sick twins. Before Dan and Ellen were discharged from the hospital, the Twins had to have their tonsils removed also. Verna and Howard were the only Keogh children who had managed to stay well the entire winter.

While most of her family was in the hospital, a blind colored man came every day to cut wood for Leta even though she could pay him very little. His granddaughter brought him every morning and waited for him while he chopped wood and filled the wood box on the back porch. Then she would drive him home.

In December the twins were well enough to start school at the Bryant Elementary School. There were eight sets of twins that had started school in September. Leta told Dan, "It's like seeing double."

Skilled mechanics were again in demand and as soon as Dan recuperated, he found a part-time job in a garage not far from their house. It paid just fifteen cents an hour but with the Depression still plaguing the nation, he felt very fortunate to have any work at all.

Leta knew it would be another lean Christmas, but for her, it was enough her family was well and no one was in the hospital. Before spring however, all the children contracted the measles and now Howard had to have his tonsils removed. Leta silently wished more than once that they had never left Canada. Even with the bitter cold winters everyone seemed to stay well.

The cool spring rains had finally given way to the warm summer sun. Leta barely took notice of the scent of honeysuckle and roses riding on the soft warm breeze that brushed her skin like a whisper as she bent to retrieve another dripping shirt to hang on the line. Her back ached and her hands were raw from scrubbing clothes on the rub board. Dan had promised her a washing machine but whenever they got the money saved for one it had to be spent for something else. But she was grateful she could hang the wash outside to dry instead of inside the house as she had done all winter.

"Leila should be out here helping," Leta muttered to herself. "I am just about fed up with her and her ailments." Leta's patience had come to an end when Leila decided she could not even get up to go to the bathroom by herself. Dan had to carry her. But he drew the line when she wanted him to sit her on the stool. "Oh, well," Leta said aloud, pinning another dripping shirt on the line, "It won't change anything to get all riled up over it."

After dumping out the wash tub and hanging it on a nail on the side of the house, she saw Howard sitting on the porch step alone. He usually played alone but she wondered why he wasn't playing with his Canadian Flyer wagon Dan had bought him for Christmas. Dan had worked extra odd jobs in order to buy something special for each of his children that year.

"Are the twins and Verna playing tricks on you again?" she asked Howard, stepping past him to open the screen door. "No, Mama," he answered. Letting it go at that, Leta went on in the kitchen to start supper.

For the rest of the day, every now and then, Howard would mutter, "This darn arm." That night Leta heard Howard wake up several times in the night which was very unusual for him. He was such a sound sleeper he still wet the bed.

The next morning while Leta was fixing breakfast, Howard came in and wanted to help stir the oatmeal. He liked to help her cook. Lifting his arm to pick up the wooden spoon off the table he winced and said, "This darn arm."

Setting the pan of oatmeal on the back of the stove she turned her attention to Howard. "What's the matter with your arm?"

"I don't know, Mama. It just won't work."

On closer examination she discovered he was hurt. Dan had already left for work. Leila was in her usual place reclining on the couch. A few days before Dan had lost his patience and had told Leila she could get up and go to the bathroom herself or lay in her own wet. She quickly recovered just enough to dramatically drag herself to the bathroom so Leta knew she would be no help.

"Verna, I have to take Howard to the doctor. You will have to feed Ellen. When the oatmeal is done the Twins can dish it up. If Auntie Leila wants to eat, take her a bowl." Verna felt very grown up being in charge.

Leta gently bundled Howard up, sat him in his Canadian Flyer and pulled him the two and a half miles to the doctor. After a quick examination the doctor told her, "He's broken his collar bone."

As the doctor was setting the bone he asked Howard, "What happened, son?"

"I was riding my wagon down the bank from the railroad tracks behind our house. I hit a rock and fell out." It was a steep bank and the doctor surmised that the boy must have been going extremely fast when he was dumped out of the little red wagon.

Securing the sling on Howard's arm the doctor carried him outside and helped Leta settle him back in the small wagon. "For a five year old this child has the highest pain tolerance I have ever seen." The doctor was amazed Howard had not even shed a tear. When he had asked about the scar on Howard's other arm Leta explained how he had burned himself with the iron and had hardly complained then.

"Well, with such a high pain tolerance, you will have to keep a close eye on him. I can see why it is difficult to know when he is really injured. Most children would be squalling their heads off." Handing her a packet of tablets the doctor instructed, "But if he does get a little fussy and uncomfortable just give him one of these." As he watched her go, he muttered, "Amazing child," then quickly returned to his waiting patients.

Howard healed quickly and all the Keogh children were managing to avoid illnesses. Ellen was still so good natured that nothing seemed to bother her. She just accepted everything and anything that happened to come along. She could play with the others or play by herself. She was content no matter what. They were all good children but somehow Ellen's older siblings always seemed to get themselves into some kind of mischief. The Twins were expert pranksters.

A few days after the Fourth of July Leta received a letter from Elsie Johnson. Leta was elated when she read aloud the good news. "We are moving to the States and will be in Spokane sometime in early August." Leta had always been closer to

Elsie than her own sisters. Even though it had been only a few months since they had left Canada, Leta missed her terribly.

The moment Dan walked in the door that evening, Leta excitedly told him about the letter. The children could hardly wait to see their cousins again. "Write and tell them what they need when they cross the border so they won't have any trouble. I will mail it on my way to work tomorrow." Leta knew Dan was as thrilled as she was that the Johnson's were coming even though he did not show it outwardly. What she did not know was it also stirred the wanderlust in him.

When the long awaited day arrived, Dan drove to the train station alone to pick up the Johnson family. Four adults and 11 children were just too many for the Essex. On the way to the station he thought how he would give anything to be putting that troublesome Leila on the train. He accepted her only because she was Leta's sister. She was such a faker and a whiner, and he hated these traits in anyone. To Dan it was dishonest. And he hated dishonesty. A smile came to his lips as the thought came to him how Elsie would take care of Leila. "My patient Leta puts up with a lot more than Elsie will. She will not tolerate such nonsense," he mused as he parked the Essex in front of the train station.

As the Johnson's spilled into the Keogh house they were greeted with squeals of delight and hugs and tears of happiness. The aroma of savory stew simmering on the stove and bread baking in the oven filled the house. The small house was bursting with sounds of love and laughter. Even Leila suddenly recovered and joined in the merriment.

After supper. when all the youngsters were put to bed with wall-to-wall girls in the bedroom and the boys camped out on the back porch, Frank told Dan that they were moving on to Riverside, California. His mother and sister lived there and had encouraged them to leave Canada. Dan decided then and there that California would be a good place to take his family too. His brother Bill lived in Los Angeles which was only about 50 miles from Riverside. When Dan told Leta they would be going with the Johnson's, she knew this move would be a good one. It would be good living closer to Elsie again.

Chapter Thirty Four

A few days after the Johnson's arrived at the Keogh's, Frank bought his first car, a Hudson Teraplane. It was an old touring car with a hard top. With his large family and all their belongings, he needed one big enough to hold it all. He also bought a small trailer with two big wheels that looked more like a big cart. But it was large enough to hold part of the Keogh's belongings as well as their own. He didn't know how to drive and would have to learn before the long trip to California.

The next week was spent in a flurry preparing for the long journey. Dan checked his tools and the tire repair kits, making sure they had everything they might need. Being a good mechanic he wasn't worried about break-downs, but he made sure he had extra parts just in case. With the older children's help, Elsie packed the Keogh's belongings while Leta taught Frank how to drive his new car. Leta chuckled when she overheard Elsie telling Leila, "If you don't get your behind off that couch and help, we will leave you here."

The day to begin their journey had finally arrived. Trailer and both cars were packed full. All eleven children were crammed into their respective cars. Leila settled herself in front beside Dan. "If I ride in the back, I'll get car sick," she insisted. Dan knew it was just another put-on but he also knew she could make herself vomit and for spite she would probably do it in his back seat. Leta wedged in the back with her children, holding four month old Ellen on her lap. As the two heavily laden automobiles, with Frank following close behind Dan, the two families began their long journey. As the two cars headed south, a faint strip of gray tinged the horizon promising daylight soon.

Driving south through Ritzvill and Pasco, they turned west along the Columbia River, crossing at Plymouth into Oregon. Leta thought the country along the Columbia River was beautiful. She imagined explorers, Lewis and Clark, traveling by canoe on the broad river 200 years before. She imagined they must have looked like tiny dots on the wide river as they slowly glided toward the Pacific Ocean.

After crossing the Columbia River, the small caravan headed west to Portland. At Portland, they turned south toward Eugene, continuing their long journey south, again passing through the small towns with strange names like Drain, Yoncalla, Myrtle Creek, and Riddle. At Medford, they started across the Siskiyou Mountains covered with huge Douglas fir, cedar, and manzanita, with scrub oak here and there. Leta had never seen so many shades of green. The mountains were so high Leta feared they would slide off the narrow graveled road down into a ravine.

The roads were rough and there were long stretches grooved by deep ruts. Frank and Dan fixed more flat tires than they cared to count. Money being scarce between the two families, they camped out at night rather than stay in an auto court. The two men were busy each night patching inner tubes. Leta and Elsie were busy with the cooking, washing diapers, and wiping noses.

All their meals were cooked in an old black cast iron skillet and a Dutch oven over an open fire. The men killed small game birds, a rabbit now and then, and would catch some fish in the streams they camped along. Leta and Elsie kept a pot of beans cooked. For their noon meal they usually had cold beans. Everyone slept on the ground, rolled up in quilts on a large tarp to keep out the dampness. That is everyone except Leila, who insisted she could not sleep on the hard, uneven, cold ground. So she slept in Dan's car.

Leaving the Siskiyou Mountains behind them the landscape seemed to roll by in slow motion. California was a big state and the temperature seemed to soar with every mile. The merciless sun had baked every blade of grass brown. Seldom did Leta see a cloud in the sky. On a good day, with no car trouble or flat tires, they could leave 100 miles behind them.

The relentless heat baked down on the nearly treeless San Gabriel Mountains. As the travelers slowly climbed over the Tejon Pass they had to stop several times with radiators boiling over and flat tires. This steep, narrow gravel road was known as The Grapevine. They stayed a couple of days at Gorman to repair a hole in Frank's radiator and to patch tires.

Somewhere between Gorman and Newhall, the Keogh's and the Johnson's became separated. The Johnson family went on to Riverside and Dan's car broke down just before they reached Tujunga. Their money was gone and they had eaten the last of their food. Swallowing his pride, Dan contacted the Salvation Army for help. They fed the destitute family as well as giving them a place to sleep.

The next morning Dan telephoned his brother Bill in Los Angeles. Bill and Spike arrived that afternoon and took the family to a house they owned in Tujunga. Both Bill and Spike hoped Dan would finally settle down. "Dan, you know you and your family can stay here as long as you like," Bill told him. It was a two story frame house with a large screened porch across the front as well as across the back.

Leta was delighted to find three small bedrooms upstairs. "I can section off the back porch to make two more bedrooms," Dan told her. They quickly settled into their new home and Dan went to look for work.

Leta had learned early in her marriage to adapt quickly to each new environment. Once settled, she was thrilled to learn of the many free craft classes that were offered in Tujunga. She wasted no time signing up for sewing - even though she already knew how to tailor and was a good seamstress - millinery, and leather-working classes. She could tat, crochet, knit, and embroider, but she wanted to learn more. When an oil painting class was offered, Dan encouraged her to sign up.

After a week of painting classes, Leta brought home her first effort. She had painted a bouquet of Violets in a milk-glass vase. Dan looked at it with a twinkle in his eye and a slight grin on his face. "Well, that looks like hell." After eight years of marriage he still liked to tease her about her work. But she knew he liked it and was proud of her accomplishments.

The day after Labor Day Howard started his first year in school. Every morning Verna, the Twins, and Howard walked the mile to school. In the hot afternoons as they walked the dusty road home, dawdling Howard would be left behind. He didn't seem to mind walking alone. There were too many things to discover along the way for a curious five year old.

The relentless heat continued day after day. The brown, rocky hills were covered with thick brush and tall grass scorched tinder dry by the sun. One hot afternoon Dan was tightening the clothes line while Leta was filling the wash tub on the back porch and she saw black smoke billowing up on the horizon. "Dan! Dan! There's a fire coming!" Leta was terrified. Dropping his hammer he shouted, "I'll get the truck!"

As Dan jumped in the old Buick pickup he had traded several hours of work for, he saw Verna, the Twins, and Howard making a bee-line for home. Pulling the truck up close to the front door, he shouted to them, "Quick! Help your mother!" With all of them grabbing food, clothes and anything else Leta thought they would need, the truck was loaded in record time. With all five children in the cab with Dan, Leta climbed in the back and lay across the load trying to hold everything on. There was no time to tie it down.

With her heart pounding, Leta hung on for dear life until Dan stopped the truck at the American Legion Hall in town. "You stay here with the children. I'm going to help fight fire," he told her. Leta prayed that the house wouldn't go. Dan was gone all night with the men fighting the fire. It swept through the canyon and around the town. When the fire was finally out they had amazingly lost only one house.

As the weeks wore on the Keogh family's financial situation seemed to worsen. The entire country was still in the clutches of the Great Depression. Stories of desperate people filled the newspapers. Less expensive than coal, Iowa farmers burned grain for fuel. Farmers in South Dakota could only get three cents a bushel for their corn. Once-prospering dairy farmers were out of business as milk was only a penny a pint. In Washington State, woodsmen set fire to the forests to get jobs as firefighters. Oregon sheep ranchers, unable to give their sheep away, slaughtered them.

In this Hoover regime, shack-towns called 'Hooverville' contained hundreds of homeless people. Many were sleeping under newspapers dubbed 'Hoover blankets'. The armadillos Texans ate were known as 'Hoover Hogs'.

Known as the 'Do Nothing' President, Herbert Hoover believed in the natural order of letting things take care of themselves. The year before, 1931 to be exact, a newspaper quoted him, "What the country needs is a good big laugh. There seems to be a condition of hysteria. If someone would get off a good joke every 10 days, I think our troubles would be over." Hoover had even asked Will Rogers to think up a joke that would make people stop hoarding. Hoover also offered Rudy Vallee a medal if he could sing a song that would make people forget their troubles and the Depression. He was so far removed from the real world he could not understand the desperate struggle of the people just to survive in these hard times.

Chapter Thirty Five

It was New Years Eve, 1932. Dan had hoped to take Leta to the dance at the American Legion Hall but it had been pouring down rain for several days and all the roads were a quagmire. "It's just as well we stay home. You know Leila will insist on going too. She won't stay with the children," Leta told him.

Having finished their supper of chili beans with hot biscuits, Verna and Keith cleared the table then washed and dried the dishes. Leta stacked them in the cupboard when they had finished. Ellen had fallen asleep in her father's lap as he smoked a cigarette and listened to the radio. Tobacco was a habit he had picked up since moving to Tujunga.

After laying the sleeping baby on the bed, Leta went back to her knitting. Leila was snoring loudly on the couch. She had read a story to Howard and Kenneth and the three of them had fallen asleep. The boys had worn themselves out running along the edge of the canyon watching the muddy water running where only dry arroyos had been before. Brown water streamed down the steep hillsides in rivulets.

The quiet peacefulness of the evening was suddenly broken by the sound of a distant rumbling. It was getting louder and louder. Suddenly there was a loud cracking sound and the house shuddered. Leta froze in mid-stitch, her face ashen. She wanted to scream but her mouth would not open. Dan leaped to his feet and quickly jerked open the door. The porch was gone. A huge boulder had rolled down the hill ripping it from the house. The rapidly rising, debris filled, brown water was roaring past the house in torrents.

"We've got to get out of here!" he shouted. "Hurry, get the youngsters!" Leta dropped everything on the floor and grabbed Ellen off the bed. "The water seems to be swinging around the Saunders' place. We'll go up there."

"Get your coats on! Hurry!" Leta told Verna and Keith as she shook Leila and the boys awake. "Leila! Get up! We have to get out of here! Now!" Holding Ellen in one arm, Leta helped Howard and Kenneth get into their coats. They were still groggy from sleep and were trying to make out what was wrong. Leila was in an instant panic and started to go into one of her 'spells'.

"You straighten up and get out of the house! Now!" Dan bellowed at her. She obeyed instantly.

With his family crowded behind him, Dan tried to open the back door. It was already blocked with mud and debris. Picking up a chair, he broke out the pantry window and started pushing everyone out. After Leta crawled out, he handed Ellen back to her then climbed out himself. Ushering his family ahead of him, they trudged up the slick muddy hill to the Saunders small house. The drenching rain quickly soaked them to the skin.

Watching the family struggling up the hill, Mr. Saunders stood in the doorway waiting for them. Mrs. Saunders had mugs of hot coffee and hot chocolate poured. After the sodden coats were hung by the stove to dry, Mrs. Saunders seated the children at the table. With wide, frightened eyes, water still dripping from their little blonde heads, they quietly sipped the steaming liquid. Hot chocolate was a rare treat for the Keogh children.

When the children had dried out and their cups were empty, Mrs. Saunders helped Leta put them to bed. Verna, Keith and Ellen were tucked in the bed. Howard and Kenneth wrapped in a quilt, fell asleep on one end the couch with Leila curled up on the other end. The rain was still pounding on the roof but it was warm and dry inside small house and Leta finally started to relax a little.

Every now and then, Dan and Mr. Saunders would step outside to check on the rising torrent that was sweeping past the house. Coming in shaking the water off their coats Dan said, "The debris is piling up making dams in several places and the water is backing up behind us." They all knew it was a very dangerous situation. Mrs. Saunders continued to keep the coffee pot full.

Just before midnight the rain seemed to lessen. "It seems to be letting up a bit." Leta said stepping to the door. When she opened the door the strong odor of gas nearly choked her. "Dan! I can smell gas out here." Her eyes widened, "Dear God, the water is up to the house." Leta shouted, horrified. Instantly both men were at the door. The pressure was so strong the three of them could not shut the door as the muddy water swirled in quickly spreading across the floor.

Dan glanced up and saw a forty foot wall of water and debris roaring down the canyon straight toward them. "Get out! Get out and up the hill, quick!" he yelled as he turned and raced for the bedroom where the children were sleeping. Quickly getting Verna and Keith on their feet, he shouted, "Run! Run out the back door!"

Leta grabbed Ellen shouting, "Leila! Get up and get the boys out of here!" Mr. Saunders was shouting for everyone to get up the hill to the chicken house. For once Leila responded in an instant. She grabbed Howard and Kenneth each by a hand and bolted for the back door. The Saunders' were racing out the door pushing Verna and Keith in front of them along with their daughter Greta. The ground was so slippery the children kept falling and sliding back down the hill. Mr. Saunders grabbed Verna and hoisted her up on the chicken house steps. Quickly regaining her footing, she scrambled up the slick wooden stairs.

Realizing they could not make it out the door, Dan grabbed Leta with Ellen clutched in her arms. He quickly threw open the kitchen window and began climbing out pulling, Leta with him. Suddenly they felt the house move. A wall of water tore the walls away and the roof collapsed on top of them. The force of the water that now filled the house pushed them over the library table and out another window. Leta knew in that instant they were going to die.

Leta, still clinging to Ellen, disappeared under the swift, swirling torrent. Dan pulled her back up shouting, "Hang on to her, Leta! Hang on to her!" He was struggling to stay afloat himself but he was not about to let go of them.

Buffeted by debris, they were swiftly swept down stream several hundred yards. People that lived across the road on the other side of the canyon could see them floundering in the debris choked muddy water, but could not get to them to help.

A man standing on the bank hanging on to a small tree grabbed Dan as they swept by him and managed to pull them out. As they were being pulled out of the water, Leta thought how odd it was that even though it was night, it was still light enough that she could see the people standing on the bank

315

across the canyon. *Everything is too clear. We must be dead,* she thought.

The Saunders and the children huddled in the chicken house, dripping wet and shivering. The children were barefoot and clad only in their underwear. Verna wore only her bloomers and a black and white checked flannel petticoat her mother had made her. Mr. Saunders looked around alarmed, "Where's Leila and the boys?" Shaking her head, Mrs. Saunders feared for them. She also feared Dan and Leta were drowned along with baby Ellen. She had seen the house collapse. Her heart broke for the little ones that would be orphaned.

Leila had been swept down stream and flung against the side of a house. She managed to get to her feet and stood, streaked with mud, screaming for help. A man found her and wrapped his rain coat around her naked body. Every stitch of clothing had been ripped off her in the raging current. She was so hysterical she did not realize she was naked. The man took her to his house farther up the hill and his wife wrapped her in a blanket. Leila kept babbling, "The boys...where are the boys?" Most of her ranting was so incoherent they were not sure whose boys she was raving about, her's or someone else's.

With sodden clothes and barefoot, their hair plastered to their heads with bits of leaves and twigs entangled in it, Dan and Leta slowly made their way back to the chicken house hoping the Saunders were still there. With her tiny arms wrapped tightly around his neck, Dan carried Ellen in one arm and held on to Leta with the other. When they reached the chicken house, Leta's joy was quickly extinguished when she learned Leila, Howard, and Kenneth were not there.

Mr. Saunders knew Mr. Wallace who lived in a one room cabin just up the hill from the chicken house and suggested they take the children up there. Mr. Wallace lived alone most of the time because of bad health. His wife visited him once a month and she had come to spend New Year's Day with him. Watching the bedraggled group struggle up the hill, Mrs. Wallace quickly ushered them inside the moment they stepped on the porch. Grabbing the few towels she had she began to dry off the children.

With the heat from the wood stove and the kerosene lamps they soon were dry and warm. But they were all still in a state of shock. Mrs. Wallace wrapped Keith and Verna in her husbands flannel shirts. Not uttering a sound they sat on the foot of the bed wide-eyed, white faced, and trembling. Leta sat in the rocking chair at the foot of the bed rocking Ellen who was wrapped in a borrowed sweater. As Leta silently rocked back and forth, she could feel a strong Presence behind her. With a blanket wrapped around them, Mrs. Saunders and Greta sat on the edge of the bed clinging to each other. Dan and Mr. Saunders, along with some other men, as well as the police, were out looking for Leila and the boys.

Mr. Wallace kept the fire blazing. His wife put a kettle of soup on the stove and kept the coffee pot full. The lady whose husband had found Leila came over and told them Leila was at her house but there was no word about the two boys. Mrs. Wallace kept pouring coffee, and shoved the searchers out the door that kept stopping in to warm themselves every hour or so. She kept insisting, "I can hear a little voice saying, 'I want my Mama.' If you find a dead child out there in the morning, I will go crazy." The men were convinced she already was, but they took their flashlights and kept searching.

After warming himself, Mr. Saunders went out to search again. As he came around a building not far from the Wallace cabin, he saw Kenneth face down in the mud. As he rushed over to the small boy, Kenneth raised his head up and whimpered, "I want my Mama."

Farther down the canyon, Art Brown, the Police Chief, and another man were walking slowly a few feet apart scanning the ground with their flashlights. "Did you say something?" Art asked. "No." The man replied. "There." Art pointed the beam of light. "Listen." "I hear something now." Standing motionless they scanned their lights in every direction. Suddenly Art's beam shone on a small hand, a mouth, and a nose barely sticking out of the mud.

"Oh, God," he breathed, afraid to move and afraid not to. He was sure this child was dead. As the men approached, Howard uttered, "I want my Mama." Both men jumped into action. Frantically digging down in the mud just far enough to get hold of him they pulled him from the debris. His legs were tangled in barbed wire and broken 2x4s. As they pulled him, out the boards and wire ripped the backs of both little legs open from knees to heels. Quickly wrapping the boy's small limp body in a blanket someone had handed him, Art, with Howard in his arms, started walking to the doctor's house which was nearly three miles away. Every road was impassable by car. They were all full of boulders, parts of homes, broken trees, and other debris.

Doc King had been having a New Years Eve party and ladies still dressed in evening gowns were rushing around taking care of injured flood victims. When Art arrived with Howard, the doctor quickly put the injured child in a tub of warm water. He used the vacuum cleaner to suction mud and gravel out of the boy's stomach. His mouth was so full of dirt his lips were turned inside out. One of the ladies gently began cleaning the mud out of his eyes. He had no skin or hair left on one side of his head.

Shortly before Art arrived with Howard, someone had brought Kenneth in. He was as full of mud and gravel as Howard. He was skinned, scraped and barely conscious. Two other ladies in beaded gowns were busy trying to clean his wounds.

The two boys had been washed down among trees, boulders, and other debris, and had been found more than a mile from the canyon where the Saunders' house had been.

About daylight Mr. Saunders came back to the Wallace cabin and told them the boys had been found but Doc King didn't have much hope for the little one, Howard. Clutching Ellen to her breast, Leta's face paled, numbing fear enveloping her body. Rocking a little faster she suddenly felt that same strong Presence behind her again.

Glancing worriedly at Leta, Saunders told his wife, "You stay with her. I'll find Dan."

Meanwhile back at his house, Doc King was working frantically on Howard. The boy wasn't breathing. After injecting two shots of adrenaline straight into his little heart there was still no heartbeat. Doc McCafferty, who had come in to assist, kept saying, "He's dead. There's nothing more we can do." The druggist had just finished wrapping the splint on a man's broken arm, looked over and said, "Yes, I'm afraid he is dead. You might as well send him to the morgue."

When Mr. Saunders found Dan they rushed to the doctor's house. He stood waiting anxiously outside the room where they were working on his youngest child. Doc King would not allow him to come in to see the boy. The doc finally sat down in defeat. "You might as well let Dan come in." He said wearily wiping his brow with his handkerchief. As Dan came through the door Doc King told him sadly, "I'm sorry Dan. I've done all I can."

319

Tears welled up in Dan's eyes as he approached the tiny limp form of his son. Gently laying a hand on Howard's small, skinned forehead, Dan said, his voice breaking, "How you doing little man?" Howard answered with a weak, "Fine."

Before Dan could respond Doc King leapt to his feet. "My God in Heaven! It's a bloomin' miracle! Out of the way, man. Let me get to work!" He quickly brushed Dan aside.

When Dan left Doc King's he knew both Howard and Kenneth were going to be all right. "The doc is right," Dan muttered to himself. "It is a miracle both boys survived." On his way to tell Leta the good news he learned the Legion Hall which was a block from the Doc's place had been used for a shelter and rescue house for those caught in the storm with nowhere to go. When the flash flood hit the building, the raging water went in one corner and out the other. The building had been teeming with people and they were all swept away. Most of them were never found. The tremendous force of the huge wall of water had completely torn the building apart and washed it away with everything and everyone in it. The only thing left was a small part of the floor with the piano still standing on it.

When Dan stepped inside the Wallace cabin, Leta stopped rocking, tears of dread pooled in her eyes. Laying his hand on her shoulder, Dan said quietly, "It's over, Leta. Our boys are going to be all right. They're at Doc King's." Tears of relief streamed down her face.

Totally exhausted and drained, Dan scooped up his other two terrified children and sat on the foot of the bed holding them close to him. As Leta began slowly rocking Ellen again she silently thanked God for sparing her children and felt the pervading Presence slip away. Even though they had lost everything she knew they were going to survive. The children were going to be all right. That was all that mattered.

Looters had been prevalent during the worst part of the flooding the previous night. Police had to be posted in the canyons to keep them out. People's belongings were scattered everywhere, tangled in brush and trees and wedged between boulders. When Leta and Dan could finally make their way back to what was left of their house they discovered the several cases of beer bottles that had been stored under the staircase were missing. The children had gathered the empty bottles from along the roadside for their mother. Leta had canned tomato juice on a wood cook stove in 110 degree heat using the beer bottles to put the juice in as fruit jars were scarce. Dan had a bottle capper and he had capped each and every bottle for her.

Laughing, Dan said to Leta, "Someone is going to get a big surprise when they start drinking your 'beer'."

Later that evening after getting Leila, Verna, Keith, and Ellen settled with their friends the Campbells, Dan and Leta went to see about their two injured children. Since there was no hospital, all the injured were taken to a nursing home for recovery. Leta was not prepared for the shock when she saw Howard. He was so swollen, skinned, and bruised she nearly didn't recognize him as her own. His legs were elevated on pillows with just a sheet over them. A large bandage covered half of his head. Doc King had given him a sedative so he would sleep.

Kenneth was in the bed next to his brother and woke as his parents came in. Leta wanted to pick him up and hold him but was afraid to touch him for fear of hurting him. "I want to go home, Mama." He said weakly.

Gently brushing his blonde hair from his brow, she said with a lump in her throat, "When you get better. Then we'll all go home."

Chapter Thirty Six

Kenneth and Howard spent several weeks recuperating in the local nursing home. Mrs. Campbell kept the other three children so Leta could stay with Howard and Kenneth. She stayed with her boys night and day. The large wounds down the backs of Howard's legs could not be stitched up because no matter how they tried to wash out the dirt they could not get it all out. She had to change the dressings on Howard's legs twice a day as Doc King was afraid that infection or gangrene would set in.

Before the boys came home, the Red Cross rented a house for the Keogh family with the rent paid in advance for 8 months. To furnish the house, Dan had gathered scraps of lumber to build a table and a couple of benches. He also fashioned a bed with pieces of an old bed frame he had found in a junk pile. He obtained mattresses and a small coal-oil stove from the Red Cross and built bunk beds for the children from the wood left over from the table and benches.

The Essex was lost in the flood and all they had left was the old Buick truck. Leta had driven it to get her first driver's license. She hadn't needed one anywhere else. After they brought the two boys home, Leta drove Howard to the doctor every day for six months in the rickety old truck. She carefully laid him on pillows in the seat beside her for the bumpy ride to Doc King's.

Through his connections in the Los Angeles Police Department, Dan's brother Bill was able to send them a large basket of food that Spike had filled to the brim. Grateful tears filled Leta's eyes. "Oh, Dan. We need this food so badly but I have no way to cook it. It will only spoil." The coal-oil stove they had was used for heat as well as cooking, and she had run out of coal-oil. And they had no money to buy more.

"I think they might have a wood cook stove down at the second hand store," Dan said as he pulled on his coat. "I'll go down and see if they will let me work for one." The roads were still barely passable in places and Leta knew it would take him awhile. Wrapping the basket up in a sheet to keep the bugs out, she had Dan set it under the house to keep it cool.

In a short while a man with white hair and a full grey beard drove up to the house. He had a stove and an ancient battered washing machine in the back of a beat-up old truck.

"This the Keogh place?" he asked.

"Yes," Leta answered from the porch.

"Well, I got a stove and washing machine for you. Your husband is helping me out down at my store and said you needed these right away." Leta felt as though she had been given a million dollars. She could now cook all the food before it spoiled. It was just a small wood burning stove but it looked grand to Leta. The old washing machine was operated by pushing and pulling a side lever back and forth. They were both battered and dirty, but to Leta they were beautiful.

After the kind, aging man set up the stove and left, Leta tucked Ellen in her crib and told Howard and Kenneth to stay in their beds. Not bothering to wake Leila, she took Verna and Keith up the steep hill behind the house to help her gather any wood she could find. After they had gathered what they could, she took strips of rags and tied the bundles of wood together and they packed it down on their backs. She cleaned up the stove, started a fire in it, and spent the rest of the day cooking. Verna and Keith were kept busy cleaning up the old washing machine.

After several weeks Howard's legs healed nicely. Deep ugly scars remained down the backs of both legs all his life. The family was slowly getting their life back to normal. Work was scarce and Dan took any odd job he could find to get the items they needed. Leta was grateful for the $25.00 a month he still received from the government. Most families had nothing at all.

It had been several weeks since the flood and there were still many families that badly needed help. Dan had went in to attend a committee meeting that was being held in town to try to get some relief funding from the government. He had been gone for hours and it had been pouring rain all day.

Leta and the children had quickly gathered up every scrap of wood they could find before dark. Even Leila pitched in to help. She was scared too. Leta became more and more afraid as the water that had begun as a trickle rapidly became torrents rushing down the canyon walls forming a muddy, debris-filled river roaring past the front of the house. The edge of swirling brown water was nearly up to the porch. Looking out the kitchen window, Leta was horrified to see mud oozing against the back door, blocking it shut. They were trapped. Leta could not let the children, or Leila, know how terrified she was.

Afraid to put the little ones to bed, she let them sit up with her. They all sat huddled in the small house listening to the rain pounding on the roof and the terrifying rush of water as it swept past the house.

As the hour grew late, the children dropped off to sleep. Leta paced the floor all night praying the water would not get any higher. It was nearly daylight when Dan finally made it home. He and several other men had hiked miles around the rim of the canyon to reach their homes. The water had receded but Dan still had to wade in knee deep muddy water to reach the front door.

When she heard the door open, Leta grabbed a stick of firewood. "Leta, you here?" Dan called as he entered the dark house.

Dropping the stick on the floor with a bang, she said in relief, "I thought you were a looter." Her knees were shaking so bad she dropped into the nearest chair. She thought she detected a faint smell of liquor on his breath. Dan had never been a drinker, so she dismissed the thought completely.

A few weeks after this last flood, when the roads were passable, the Keoghs and Leila were on their way to visit Bill and Spike when the old car Dan had traded the truck for broke down. Dan walked to the nearest garage and asked the owner if he could borrow some tools. Instead of just loaning the tools to Dan, Charlie Lovejoy towed Dan's car to his garage and helped him fix it. As the men were busy repairing the car, Dan learned that Charlie was a widower and needed a live-in housekeeper. And he needed one as soon as possible. Overhearing the men's conversation, Leila quickly offered her services. "I can start right away but I'll need to go back to Tujunga to collect my things." A widower with his own home and business was very appealing to Leila.

"We're going on to Bill and Spike's, Leila. We won't be going back home for a few days," Leta reminded her.

"Well, if you can start today, I will be glad to drive you back to get your things." Charlie offered. "Now that I have hired you, I think introductions are in order." He added smiling. "I am Charlie Lovejoy."

"Leila Corsair." Charlie shook Leila's limp extended hand sealing the deal. "I'm a widow," she quickly added.

Leta watched them in amazement. Leta was happy for her sister in spite of her misgivings about Leila's capabilities. She wondered how Leila was going to cook and clean for this man when she never seemed well enough to help her.

Waving goodbye, and promising to visit often, the Keoghs continued on to Bill and Spike's, leaving Leila behind. Dan silently wished Charlie good luck. He liked the man.

Bill and Spike were thrilled the family could stay several days. The children spent their days playing and exploring the neighborhood. The adults discussed the dreadful condition of the country. Crime was increasing. Desperate people were doing desperate things.

"Okies are streaming into California by the thousands," Bill told them. Miles of over-burdened Model-T's brought desperate, frightened people to what they hoped would be a better life. The great dust storms in the mid-west and severe poverty had driven them out of their homes.

In the cities and towns men, stood on street corners shining shoes or selling apples for a few cents a day to feed their families. Soup kitchens and bread lines became more prevalent.

The country now placed their hopes in a new President, Franklin Delano Roosevelt. He introduced his 'New Deal', creating thousands of government jobs. The Agricultural Adjustment Administration paid farmers to kill their livestock and plow under their crops, limiting the supply which would control prices. The Civilian Conservation Corps put young men to work, building fire trails, planting trees, and making hiking trails; the Tennessee Valley Authority built dams; Civil Works Administration built highways.

The Keoghs visit seemed to end all too soon. As Dan and his family drove away, Bill and Spike waved goodbye from the steps of their house, promising they would come to Tujunga soon.

Summer turned to fall and the children returned to school. Except for the rains in winter, all four seasons were about the same in southern California. Every now and then Leta found herself missing the brilliant Canadian Fall colors and the winter snow. At least in Canada she never worried about floods or mud slides.

After Leta had sent the children off to school with sandwiches of oleo and brown sugar, lunchmeat being a luxury, she checked the pots and pans simmering and boiling on the stove. Spike had sent another large box of food for them and Leta was thankful she would be able to can most it this time. After searching her cupboard she realized she had no salt. She began searching through everything: button cans, pockets, drawers and gathered up all the pennies she could find.

With two year old Ellen in tow, Leta walked the three miles to the store. To her great disappointment she discovered the salt cost more money than she had. Then she saw a sack of salt that was torn. Taking it up to the clerk and laying the pennies on the counter beside the small sack of salt, she asked, "Since this sack has a hole in it, can you let me have it for what I have here?"

"Looks like you have just the right amount." Knowing how families struggled these days, he put it in another sack for her so none of it would spill out. On the way out of the store she saw a gallon of cooking oil that had been used to fry potato chips in for twenty-five cents. When Dan's government check came in she would come back for a gallon. This oil was slightly brown but still fresh enough for her to use for cooking.

In October Dan put a down payment on a larger house situated farther down the canyon on higher ground on Valmont Street. It was a long narrow house with a wide cement porch across the front. Leta loved the house. At last they would have a place of their own. The monthly payments were $11.00, but they would manage even though any kind of a job was still scarce.

Dan had looked for work for weeks but had no luck. "You need to find something, Dan. I don't want to lose this house and have to move again," Leta finally told him. Surprised at her sudden assertiveness, he assured her, "Well, I'll go up to Sacramento and stay with Uncle Jule. Maybe get some work in the orange groves. Don't you worry, I'll get the money to pay for the house." The next day he climbed into his old car and headed north.

Dan quickly discovered there were no jobs in or around Sacramento. When he returned home a few weeks later he had made very little money. But he surprised the children with a black and white Fox Terrier. Never having owned a dog before, the children were delighted. "We're going to teach her tricks so we'll call her Trixie," Kenneth announced. Leta was disappointed Dan's trip had not been as successful as he had hoped but she was happy the youngsters had a pet.

The 1933 school year had barely begun when all the Keogh children contracted the mumps, one right after the other. As soon as one was well enough to go back to school, Leta had another sick child.

Soon it was Halloween night and like most every night, the family gathered around the radio to listen to their favorite programs; Jack Benny, George Burns and Gracie Allen, Kate Smith, Lum and Abner. But tonight there was a news program already in progress as Dan tuned in the station. The announcer was saying something about Martians landing somewhere back east. The dramatic news report scared the youngsters half to death. Dan assured them and Leta that it was just a drama program. And as it turned out it was Orson Well's *War of the Worlds* which terrified half the country with its realism.

Before the program ended a couple of men from the American Legion hall stopped by. Dan went with them telling Leta he would be late. She had an uneasy feeling about these new friends of Dan's. They seemed to spend most of their time down at the Legion Hall and lately whenever Dan would come home from the Hall he always had liquor on his breath. Leta was confused and concerned as this was not like the Dan she knew.

Life in the house on Valmont Street was never dull. The wide porch was used for roller skating, jacks, hopscotch, and many other games the Keogh youngsters were constantly thinking up. One hot afternoon as the Keogh children were playing in the shade of the wide porch, a chubby, redheaded boy walked by and began throwing rocks at them. One large rock hit Howard in the eye causing it to hemorrhage. When Leta couldn't stop the bleeding, she ran over to a neighbor's house with Howard in her arms. They rushed him to the hospital.

The next day at school, when the principal learned how Howard had been injured, he asked the Keogh children to point out the boy responsible for throwing the rocks. They had difficulty convincing him the boy did not attend their school. As they walked home that afternoon, they swore between themselves if they ever saw that boy again he would be taught a lesson he wouldn't soon forget. The Keoghs would take care of their own.

The full, busy weeks passed quickly. Leta was thankful there had been no more mishaps with her children. On this particular warm evening after dinner, the family was gathered around the radio. Leta was mending, Verna was embroidering pillow cases, and the boys were playing cards. The night after the Twins' eighth birthday Dan had chosen to stay home rather than go down to the Legion Hall. Holding Ellen on his lap he tuned in the news. The May 28 broadcast came statically over the wire announcing the birth of the Dionne quintuplets on a small farm in Callander, Ontairo, Canada. The children were puzzled at the big fuss about some babies being born. After all, their mother already had five. "Quintuplets," Dan explained, "means when five babies are born at the same time. Like you Twins, only three more." The children listened in amazement. Leta silently thanked God that she had no more than twins at one time. She thought twins were difficult enough and could not imagine having five babies at once.

In the days that followed, Dan began spending less and less time at home. When he did come home he always had liquor on his breath. Leta was getting concerned." We have little enough money for groceries, Dan. I wish you wouldn't be out spending at the Legion Hall."

Dan brushed her off impatiently, "I never have to pay for drinks. Someone's always there buying for everyone."

Lately he seemed to have no patience with her or with his children. Leta had never known Dan to lose his temper with his children before. The only time she had seen him lose his patience was with her mother and she had deserved it. He seemed to be changing somehow, and she knew it was the drink. She tried to keep quiet hoping he would realize what it was doing to him and quit drinking.

Now most every evening Leta and her children listened to the radio alone. They listened to the newscasters telling of the great dust storms that hit the Great Plains blowing tons of dirt from one state to another. And they were saddened at the news that Will Rogers had died in a plane crash near Point Barrow, Alaska. On one of his rare evenings at home, Dan had told Leta the men down at the Hall were worried about Hitler denouncing the Versailles Treaty and reoccupying the Rhineland. Dan had already fought a war over there and he feared there would be another if someone did not stop Hitler.

Now most of the news on the radio upset and frightened Leta. She was glad when it was finally over and the humor programs started. She really enjoyed Jack Benny. Dan's favorite was Kate Smith and the youngsters liked Lum and Abner. But these days Dan was seldom home to listen to Miss Smith.

Late in the Spring Ellen brought scarlet fever home to the family. Leta had allowed her to go across the street and play with the neighbor children while Verna and the boys were in school and she had contracted the disease from them. Keith and Verna were next to come down with it, followed by Howard and Kenneth. Moving all their beds in by the stove, Leta turned the front room into a small, private hospital.

Gruff old Doc King had Leta and all five children in quarantine for eleven weeks. As well as caring for her five children, Leta pieced nine quilt tops, tended to the dog and a black cat. Dan had to sleep in the room in the back of the house. It had a door that opened to the outside so the Doc said it was all right. "But you are not to have any contact with your family whatsoever," the doc warned Dan. Ignoring the doctor's advice, Dan went in to talk to them everyday anyway. When Leta also became ill, Dan stayed home to help. He stayed home every evening, even forgoing his regular American Legion meeting.

Everyday before he left, Doc King would play a few songs on Leta's upright rosewood piano that Dan had traded work for not long after they had moved into their house. Leta wished she could play but didn't know when she would ever have the time to learn. The doc told Leta that when the children's hands and feet quit peeling, they could go back to school.

Not long after everyone had recuperated from scarlet fever, Howard was coasting his bike down the hill in front of the house. Leta had warned him, "Howard, that bike is still too big for you so don't be riding it in the street." Losing control, he rammed the bike between the fender and bumper of Bert Howell's truck. Bert was a friend of Dan and Leta's and, seeing Howard racing down the hill straight toward him, he had screeched to a stop. Howard flew up on the hood, smashing his face into the windshield and breaking off four lower front teeth. Bert quickly loaded Howard up, bike and all, and took him home.

Howard went directly into the bathroom, climbed up on a chair and inspected his bleeding swollen mouth. Broken nearly in two at the roots, his bottom front teeth were laying flat under his tongue. Dan had come home very late the night before and was still sleeping. He started to get angry when Leta woke him but quickly got his wits about him when she told him Howard was hurt again. He got up and drove to them to the hospital while Leta held Howard on her lap holding a wet towel to his mouth. Howard had to have surgery to remove what remained of the roots. He grew up with no lower front teeth.

Chapter Thirty Seven

During the winter of 1935, all the Keogh youngsters were involved in a small local dance troop. Leta did not have the money to pay for the dancing lessons so she asked the troop leader, Mrs. Wendy, if she could make the costumes and do dishes for her in order to pay for the children's dance lessons. Mrs. Wendy was delighted that Leta could sew. She was 72 and walked with a cane so it was difficult for her to stand and do her dishes. "My Dear, you don't know what a big help that will be to me. You can start right away. And let me show you what kinds of costumes we will need."

Mrs. Wendy was amazed and considered herself very fortunate to have a seamstress with Leta's extraordinary skills.

After showing Leta what types of costumes that were needed for each dance recital, the two women would sketch them on butcher paper. Leta took the drawings home with her as well as the material Mrs. Wendy provided and sewed costumes most of the night while she waited for Dan to come home.

Each night as she sat and sewed costumes and watched the hour grow later and later, the anxiety Leta felt would build to near panic fearing something terrible had happened to him. When Dan would finally stagger home in the wee hours of the morning, Leta would be asleep in her chair, needle and thread still in her hand. Mixed feelings of anger and relief washed over her when she knew he was safe. Whenever she reproached him about his drinking, he became belligerent and defensive.

Everyday after Leta had finished her own work at home she walked with her children the seven long blocks to Mrs. Wendy's. The aging instructor had turned her large living room into a dance rehearsal hall. It was the joy of her life to take in youngsters and train them for plays and other types of entertainment. While Leta was washing dishes in the kitchen, she listened to the children practicing their steps over and over. After rehearsal the children would set on the floor entranced as Mrs. Wendy animatedly told stories of her daughter who was in silent films.

Mrs. Wendy enlisted her son Paul to help with the dance troop. He was a Drill Sergeant in the Army and played the saxophone. When the children were rehearsing to perform the *Dance of the Wooden Soldiers*, Paul put them through all sorts of drills until they could do them to perfection. Leta sewed the white shirts and red pants while Mrs. Wendy made the tall hats. Paul made the wooden rifles.

Their first performance was at an Old Soldiers home with an audience of six hundred. Before the performance, some of the elderly veterans came backstage while parents were helping the children into their costumes. Paul's girlfriend had a daughter that looked so much like Verna the old gentlemen thought the two tiny towheads were sisters.

With everyone milling about backstage, Leta caught snatches of conversation here and there. Dan, Paul, and a few of the aging veterans were quietly discussing the latest news from Europe. Hitler had invaded Austria. Not everyone was concerned. But Paul was. So was Dan. They all agreed that Hitler was a very dangerous man. Leta did not like talk of war. It frightened her. Even though her boys were still too young to be in the Service and the Army would not take Dan again, it gave her a feeling of foreboding.

A few weeks after the *Dance of the Wooden Soldiers*, the troop performed at Exposition Park to an audience of nine hundred. Mrs. Wendy had twelve children in her troop at this time and five of them belonged to Leta. On this particular night, Ellen was to go on stage by herself and sing, *The Old Spinning Wheel*. "I'll buy you a new dress if you will sing it real pretty," her father had promised her. She was only four and had practiced her little dance and song until she could do it perfectly. She proudly wore her new pink organdy dress to the recital.

When it came time for Ellen to go on stage she stepped from behind the curtain, saw all the people and froze. All the cajoling and prompting from backstage could not get her to move. She looked just like a little pixie in her fairy costume with her short, dark brown hair framing her small round face. Her big blue eyes quickly filled with tears. She sat down in the middle of the stage and bawled. Quickly gathering up the distraught child, Mrs. Wendy prompted her son to go out and play his saxophone.

After the performance, while the children were dressing to go home, Ellen began to cry again. She could not find her underpants. Her costume had little ruffled panties that were made to match and Leta had told her she did not need to wear her under pants with the costume. Ellen knew she had wore them and refused to go home without them. After everyone had searched and searched, Mrs. Wendy discovered Ellen was still wearing them underneath the ruffled ones.

The years were slipping by so quickly, Leta could not keep track. A few days after Howard's 10th birthday he was helping the neighbors across the street build a rock wall and smashed his hand between two large stones. When the neighbor brought him home with his mangled hand wrapped in a wet towel, Leta nearly fainted when she saw it. Seeing that Dan was not home, the neighbor quickly offered, "I can take him to the Doc's." During the dusty, bumpy ride to the doctor, Leta said, almost to herself, "Of all my youngsters, why is Howard the one always getting hurt."

Within a few days Howard's hand became infected and developed proud flesh. "If gangrene sets in he could lose his arm if we don't amputate the hand," he told Leta.

"No." Leta said, her voice quivering, "I will take care of him."

For the next several weeks Leta soaked Howard's hand in Epsom salts every fifteen minutes around the clock. When his wounds had healed, with the exception of a few scars and one stiff finger, Howard had full use of his hand.

When his mother finally allowed him to venture out of the house, the Twins and Verna took Howard to the movies to see *Love finds Andy Hardy* with Mickey Rooney. The three had saved money they had earned doing odd jobs around the neighborhood. It was a nickel each to go to the movies at the neighborhood theater. Neither Keith nor Kenneth particularly wanted to see a "mushy movie", as they called it, but Verna persuaded them by offering to buy the popcorn. Anyway, they decided, they liked Mickey Rooney.

The next year Hitler occupied Czechoslovakia. In 1939 he invaded Poland. Italy's Mussolini was conquering his own part of Europe. The talk at both the American Legion Hall and the V.F.W Hall was of the war in Europe and what it could mean to the United States. Dan was gone more and more with his cronies now. The family wouldn't see him for two or three days at a time. Leta still kept making excuses for him. But the liquor was turning him into someone she no longer knew. Her Dan, the Dan she had married, seemed to have disappeared in a bottle.

The four oldest children began to resent their father and hated his behavior. When he was home, which was seldom these days, he was always ill tempered with them. Verna, the twins and Howard soon learned to stay clear of him when he was around. But Dan favored Ellen and she missed him terribly during his long absences.

For a special treat for their mother, the children had saved their hard earned money to take her to see *Gone with the Wind.* Verna and Ellen helped her change clothes, fixed her hair and rushed her out the door before she could protest. They did not tell her where they were taking her until they arrived at the movie theater. She was so touched she almost cried. She knew they had all spent their own hard earned money for this treat.

Chapter Thirty Eight

Spring of 1940 the Keoghs moved from Tujunga to Bell Gardens, a small community near Los Angeles. "I know a man there who can get me a good job," Dan told Leta. He had not made the payments on house in Tujunga for several months and the bank was repossessing it. It just about broke Leta's heart to lose her home but she hoped if they got away from Tujunga, Dan would quit drinking and be himself again.

Within a few days of arriving in Bell Gardens, Dan bought a large lot with a structure similar to a military tent that was already set up on it. This makeshift building had a wood floor with walls about 5 feet high. The roof and doors were made of canvas. They would have to use kerosene lamps for light as there was no electricity, and no indoor plumbing. There was only an outhouse out back. Leta was devastated when she saw it. When Dan had told her that he had bought a place, she had envisioned a nice little house of their own and had looked forward to the move. In spite of it all, she went about scrubbing the place clean and unpacking without a word, holding back the tears.

Within a day Dan and the boys had a tiny bunk house built directly behind the tent house for them to sleep in. Dan had managed to find two old army bunk beds for the bunk house and two cots for Leta and the girls. Verna and Ellen would have to share a bed. Verna did not like the idea she would have to share the small bed with her little sister, but she knew better than to voice her disappointment.

For the first time in her marriage Leta wished with all her heart she was back in Canada. She was so tired of all the moving. Her greatest disappointment came when Dan's friend, who had promised him a job, turned out to be another drinker.

Between drinking bouts, Dan managed to build cupboards in the kitchen area of the tent and found a used sink and draining board to put in it. A large bucket was kept under the sink to catch the water. When the stove and the table and chairs were all in the tent house it seemed homier, but it was very hot and stuffy. The front half of the tent served as the kitchen, the back half the bedroom.

Now in high school, Verna rode the bus to Montebello High. Ellen and the boys walked a mile to Bell Garden's grammar school. The Keogh's had moved so often they weren't accustomed to forming friendships with their school mates. But they never lacked ways to amuse themselves.

Against her better judgment, Leta allowed the twins to keep two white pet rats they had traded a sling shot for to a neighbor boy. When the boys brought the rodents home, Leta had warned, "Make sure they don't get out of that pen." But somehow the rats escaped and took up residence under the tent house where they quickly multiplied.

For several weeks, every night after the supper dishes were done, the twins would set a lamp on the drain board, turn it down low and sit in the middle of the large plank table. As the rats sneaked out in the open, the twins would shoot them with a sling shot. Both boys were excellent shots but this method was not working fast enough for Leta. So she set out poison and they saw no more of the rat population.

Very early one morning, before any of the children were stirring, Leta raced to the outhouse barely making it inside before she became violently ill. At first she thought she was coming down with the stomach flu. As she walked shakily back to the tent house she remembered the day Dan talked her into going to the bunkhouse with him before the youngsters got home from school. They had not shared a bed in a long, long time. Fear, like a sharp pain, stabbed her in the stomach as the memory of the difficult time she had with Ellen came flooding back. Tears flooded her eyes, "It can't be. It just can't be."

Dan continued to spend more of his government check on liquor and each month he gave Leta less and less of it. Selfishness, along with other negative traits never seen in Dan before, increased along with his drinking. The four oldest Keogh children kept busy doing odd jobs wherever and whenever they could find them. But their combined efforts barely put potatoes on the table.

The older children were working so hard to help keep food on the table Leta could not tell them there would be another mouth to feed in February. But when she told Dan, he started right to work on a baby bed. Leta knew he loved his children in spite of the drink and bad temper at times. With this baby, she was sick morning and night. She knew she was too old to be having another baby; after all she was thirty-seven, well past child-bearing age.

As the days and weeks wore on, Leta became well acquainted with all her new neighbors. But she was not fond of the woman, or her wild bunch of youngsters, who lived directly across the street. No one ever saw a man around the house and there were rumors about the children's parentage. The house was a pigsty with rotting, rusty junk piled in the yard and on the porch. This woman would not send her bunch to school claiming it was too much trouble. So all day long they roamed the neighborhood as they pleased.

One hot September afternoon when this unruly bunch knew there was no one home at the Keogh's, they went over to see what they could find in the bunkhouse. It was dark inside so one of the boys lit a match and tried to light the lamp. The match burned down before he could get the chimney off the lamp, burning his fingers. Yelping in pain, he dropped the match on a stack of newspapers. The dry paper immediately exploded into flames. The boys ran out of the bunkhouse and up the street as though they themselves were on fire.

The fire quickly spread to the tent house, consuming everything. The few nice pieces of furniture that Leta had managed to hang on to, the china that had been a wedding gift, silverware, and other dishes she had collected over the years, were gone in minutes. The silverware and china pattern matched and she had been very proud of it.

Leta was down the street visiting a neighbor who had wanted to show her a quilt she was making. The two women smelled the black smoke and ran outside to discover that it was Leta's house. Leta stood in stunned disbelief as everything she owned disappeared in the flames. It was five days after Verna's seventeenth birthday. The fire was so hot and dry it did not take it long to consume everything. The fire department never appeared as the Keogh house was outside of the fire district.

One of Leta's neighbor's went to meet Verna at the bus stop. Stepping from the bus Verna greeted her in surprise, "Hello, Mrs. Short." Suddenly a stab of fear shot through Verna. She knew by the expression on Mrs. Short's face something was terribly wrong. "Something's happened to Mama," Verna squeaked, on the verge of tears.

Trying to control her own tremulous voice Mrs. Short told her, "Your mother is fine. She is at my house. It's your house. It burned to the ground. Everything is gone. I've come to take you home with me."

Relief and shock washed over Verna. All she could think of was the new formal her mother had made for her to wear at her Job Daughter's initiation that was to be held in two weeks. "My formal is gone? My beautiful formal?" She started to cry as she thought of losing the most beautiful dress she had ever seen let alone owned. Leta had spent hours on it. The chartreuse taffeta was cut with a gored skirt so the bottom was very full. The bodice was fitted with short puffed sleeves. Leta spent hours sewing tiny jet black buttons down the back to the waist, making every tiny button hole by hand.

For the next several days the family was scattered. Howard and Verna stayed at their Uncle Bill and Auntie Spike's in Los Angeles. Since they both had been going to Children's Hospital, Howard for his kidneys and Verna for the muscle that ran from hip to knee, Leta and Spike agreed the two youngsters needed to stay in Los Angeles. Howard still had bed wetting problems and the muscle in Verna's leg was too short. Both Verna and Howard loved staying with Bill and Spike. There was always something fun to do at their house.

When the Wrigley Company sponsored a day long trip to Catalina Island for the children at the hospital, Bill and Spike made sure Verna and Howard could go. The morning of the scheduled day, Uncle Bill dropped them off at the pick-up point in Long Beach, assuring them he would be there to pick them up when the boat returned. Later that evening on the return trip home Uncle Bill and Auntie Spike smiled and listened as Howard and Verna chattered excitedly about all they had seen and done.

"And we rode a glass bottom boat all around the island," Verna told them.

"You could see everything in the ocean. The fish. The seaweed. Just everything." Howard chimed in. It had been a wonderful, memorable day for them both.

When the time came for Howard and Verna to go back home, they had had such a great time, neither of them wanted to go, but they knew their mother needed them.

People from everywhere came to the Keogh's aid after the fire. A man told Dan that he could have the lumber from his old chicken houses. "I have two of them that haven't been used in years. Need to get them torn down and off the place anyway."

Dan and his boys wasted no time in taking the two buildings apart and hauling the lumber to their vacant lot. Another man gave them cement for the foundation. Dan was an excellent carpenter and with the help of his boys, it didn't take them long to build another bunkhouse as well as a small two room house with the salvaged lumber. Leta was relieved that Dan seemed to have quit drinking and was his old self again. He was a big comfort to her in this time of trouble.

While Dan was building the house, the family stayed at Jim and Roberta Campbell's. The Depression still gripped the country and many men took work wherever they could get it no matter how far from home. Jim was working in San Francisco and Roberta told Leta her family was welcome to stay there while she and Jim were away. When the Campbells returned, Dan had the walls up and a roof on the new house so they stayed there nights and ate their meals with the Campbells.

Friend's and neighbors brought clothes, bedding, dishes, pots, and pans. They brought everything that was needed to start house-keeping again as there was no money to replace what they had lost. The neighbor women knew what an excellent seamstress Leta was and brought all the material they could find, even the smallest scraps. An elderly man, whose wife had died the year before, brought over a treadle Singer sewing machine. It hadn't been used in several years, but Leta oiled it up and had it running in no time.

The American Legion Auxiliary gave Leta a baby shower. She received everything she needed to outfit the little newcomer. She was so touched she cried.

Leta was grateful the one thing that hadn't burned was the washing machine she had bought from Sears. Leta kept the washer at her friend Jo Goins place twelve miles away. As much as she hated to, Leta had had to borrow the money from Leila so she could order it while it was still on sale. Leila had so much and Leta had so little, but Leta still had to pay her sister back every penny. Jo knew Dan was unreliable and not home much so she would come once a week, load up Leta and the laundry so she could do her wash.

As soon as the house and bunkhouse were finished Dan started drinking again. Leta could not understand the obsession he seemed to have for the liquor. When he was off the drink, he was her Dan again, the Dan she loved. But after just one drink, he was transformed into a stranger. Leta began to hate all liquor and at times, she hated him.

For short periods, Dan would sober up and be a real help to his family. There wasn't anything he couldn't build or fix and he had taught his boys everything he knew about carpentry and mechanics. As long as he was sober he was patient and a good teacher. But when he was drinking he found fault in everything they did and lost his patience and his temper easily.

Whenever Dan would leave the old Model-T home and drive off with some of his cronies, the Twins and Verna would take it down to the river bed to practice their driving skills. The Keogh property ran from the street to the edge of the Rio Hondo River so it was easy for them to take the car without their father suspecting anything. When they would get it stuck in the sand they spent hours digging it out. But, to them, it was all worth the trouble.

While Verna and the twins were busy teaching themselves how to drive, Howard and Ellen would take vegetables from their small garden to the Hobo camp down by the river. Leta wasn't worried about the youngsters as she knew the Hobo's were just men who had left their families in search of jobs and by a stroke of misfortune had become homeless drifters. The men looked forward to the youngster's visits as well as the fresh vegetables. Ellen and Howard would listen intently to the stories the men would tell while one of the men whittled a small whistle for Howard and another made Ellen a little grass doll.

Their small neighborhood was growing by leaps and bounds. It seemed that every day new people were settling in from out of state.

Chapter Thirty Nine

Early in November a young couple and the woman's younger brother moved in across the street from the Keogh's. Like so many others coming from Oklahoma, they hoped to find a better life in California.

The Twins and Verna soon became acquainted with the younger brother, Jack Payne. He was a tall, handsome young man with a strong resemblance to Henry Fonda. Verna was smitten from the first time she saw him but feigned indifference. Jack did a double take when he saw her. She was petite, with sky-blue eyes and platinum hair that lay in waves around her delicate face. But she wasn't the only one smitten. It wasn't long before Verna, the Twins and Jack had become close friends. They seemed to be inseparable, going everywhere together.

They went to the movies, crawfishing, or stayed home and played cards. Jack was a real charmer and Verna was very flattered by all the attention he paid to her. He wanted to ask her on a real date in the worst way. He knew the Twins were so protective of her he was afraid they would not allow her to go anywhere with anyone alone. Jack had been out of school two years and worked at the same garage with his brother-in-law. He made sure he had the money saved in the event he would get to take Verna out.

One a warm sunny afternoon, Verna was sweeping off the front porch when she noticed Jack coming across the street toward her. Keeping her head down so he wouldn't see her watching him she pretended not to see him coming up the steps.

"Hi," he said, smiling. He had even white teeth set against a tanned face.

"Hello." He had the bluest eyes she had ever seen. Quickly gathering her wits and trying to calm her racing heart. She was seventeen and hopelessly in love for the first time.

"We're going to the movies tonight. Would you like to come with us?" He asked so quickly she wasn't sure she heard right.

"The Twins didn't say anything about going to the movies tonight." She was puzzled, and a little miffed. They always included her in their plans.

"No, I mean I'm asking you to go with me. With my sister and her husband and me," he added quickly.

Verna was euphoric. Jack was asking her for a date! A real date! But all she could say was a cool, "Sure."

"Great! I'll be over around seven." He smiled broadly, jogging back across the street whistling as he went.

It was the first time Verna could remember going anywhere without the twins. They teased her unmercifully the entire time she was getting ready. Ellen could hardly wait until she got older and could go out on dates too. Lying on her stomach on her narrow cot with her hands under her chin, she watched intently as Verna prepared for her first date. Ellen thought her sister looked beautiful in her pleated plaid skirt and the matching angora sweater.

Leta was relieved that Dan wasn't home when Jack came to get Verna. She was afraid he wouldn't let her go on the date and she didn't want a scene in front of company. Since the sister and husband were going along, Leta had given her permission, but she knew Dan would say no because he had not been asked first.

When he arrived to pick Verna up, Jack did not mention that his sister and her husband had changed their minds about the movie and had gone dancing instead. He was afraid that she would want the twins to come along too and he had wanted to be alone with Verna from the first moment he saw her. The twins were Jack's good friends and he enjoyed the time the four of them spent together, but four was getting to be a crowd.

After the movie Jack invited Verna to his house for a cold drink. In her naiveté Verna saw no harm in a little light kissing. She trusted Jack. Then the kissing turned to heavy petting and before Verna realized what was happening, she had lost her virginity. Walking her across the street, Jack told her he was sorry for allowing things to get out of hand. But what was done could not be undone.

Christmas was only three weeks away and this year Leta had managed to put aside a little money for "a rainy day", as she called it. With the extra money they carefully selected a gift for each family member. They also found a tiny tree that they sat on an orange crate in the corner of the living room. Verna wrapped tinfoil around the cardboard caps from the milk bottles to make ornaments to hang it.

Christmas dinner was lima beans, with a quart of Leta's home canned tomatoes thrown in to stretch the bean pot, a stewing hen and hot fresh bread. Having gone out early in the day, Dan had not come home to share in their meager meal or celebration. The pocket knife the youngsters had bought for their father still lay under the tree in its brown paper wrapping with Ellen's hair ribbon tied around it in a bow.

Several weeks later Verna became ill. The stomach flu was going around and she was sure she had been exposed to it at school. For several days she was violently ill before breakfast. Leta wanted to give her a dose of caster oil but Verna told her it would just upset her stomach more. In a few days she began to feel better. Having dressed for school she went into the kitchen for breakfast. Leta was frying eggs and as soon as the smell reached Verna's nose she started to wretch and made a mad dash for the outhouse.

Walking slowly back to the house she knew she did not have the flu. Fear crushed her like a lead weight. Her mind raced. What was she going to do? What would everyone think of her? She had to tell Jack. But he was in Oklahoma. When he left he said he was going to visit his father, but that was nearly two months ago. What if he didn't come back?

When she entered the house the entire family was seated at the table. Her father was reading the morning paper. Leta was spooning scrambled eggs onto a large platter. The baby was due any time and Leta was so large she had to stand sideways to reach anything. The aroma made Verna's stomach knot with nausea. Swallowing several times as she passed through the kitchen and into the small room she shared with Ellen, she could feel everyone's eyes following her. Seeing Verna's pale face and vacant eyes, with a sinking heart, Leta knew Verna was in the family way.

Lying down on her small cot, Verna covered her face with the pillow to block the pungent odors coming from the kitchen. She did not realize she had fallen asleep until her father was shaking her awake.

"Come on now, Miss. Wake up." He pulled the pillow from her face as she slowly opened her frightened eyes. "You gonna tell me about it?" It was so rare that her father was home these days, let alone sober, that it took her a few moments to comprehend what he was saying.

"Come into the kitchen, we need to talk," Dan said. When Verna came out of her room Leta was sitting at the table with an anguished expression on her pale face. The four other Keogh children had been sent on to school. Verna sat down across from her mother. Dan poured himself another cup of coffee and then seated himself next to Leta. "Now Verna, let's hear it," He said.

"What did you tell him?" Verna said in a small voice, directing the question to her mother. She knew Leta had guessed and told her father.

"Your mother did not have to tell me anything. I have seen her in the family way often enough to know the symptoms."

Verna never said a word nor did she look at either of her parents as the tears began to slide down her cheeks. She did not see the tears that filled her mother's eyes.

"It's that Jack Payne, isn't it? He's the one that got you in the family way isn't he?" Hanging her head, Verna said nothing. Her small shoulders were shaking with silent sobs as the tears streamed down her face. She had never felt so afraid, so alone and so helpless in all her seventeen years.

351

"Well, by God, he'll get back here and marry you!" Dan decided, pounding his fist on the table.

That night Leta's contractions started. Throughout the night, between pains, she worked on the quilt she had started for the new baby. Whenever she heard a car coming up the road she hoped it was Dan. The sun was over the horizon when she woke the girls. The pains were unbearable now. Verna jumped up and ran to get Keith. He and Kenneth had bought an old jalopy that only ran occasionally. But, by the grace of God, this morning it started as soon as Keith pushed his foot on the starter.

As with all her births, Leta experienced a long labor. Dan never appeared and the children never went looking for him. They stayed with their mother until the baby was born.

Early on the morning of February 15, 1941, Leta gave birth to a healthy baby girl. Verna and the Twins had chosen a name. Howard and Ellen both agreed it was a fine name. So the newest Keogh was promptly named Reta Elizabeth.

By the time Jack finally returned from Oklahoma another month had gone by. Verna wasn't sure if he had come back because he wanted to or because his father had brought him. Verna liked Mr. Payne instantly. He was quiet, kind, and gentle. His wife had been dead for sometime and Verna could tell that he still missed her very much.

On April 24, 1941, Jack and Verna were married in Yuma, Arizona. His sister, her husband, and Leta, as well as Leta's infant daughter, went with them. To Verna's horror, she later learned that Dan had stormed across the street the very morning he had confronted her about her condition. In a rage, her father had demanded they "get that whelp back to

California because he had Verna in the family way and he was, by God, going to make it right or else!"

Jack's father had rented a small house just down the street from the Keogh's. Verna and Jack moved in with him and on August 8, Verna gave birth to a girl. The baby was born breech and the difficult birth took its toll on Verna's small young body. And she had no idea what to do with this tiny screaming bundle. Leta remembered Olivia De Havilland in *Gone with the Wind.* She liked the actress as well as the name. So it was agreed the baby would be named Olivia Dee.

Leta's heart went out to this red, bald, scrawny baby instantly. This was her grandchild. Her first grandchild. Ellen was thrilled. She had a baby sister and a niece in the same year. When she saw Verna's baby for the first time she said in awe, "She looks just like a little doll." From that day on the baby was called Dolly. Keith thought the baby was great. He was an uncle. He promptly began work on a toy box for her. Kenneth and Howard were not sure what to make of suddenly being uncles. But they were proud all the same.

When Verna and her baby came home from the hospital the Twins and Howard carried the tiny bed Dan had made along with other baby things Verna would need, up the street to Mr. Payne's house. Leta and Ellen had went on ahead to clean it up. Leta knew Jack would not do it and his father was ill and not able.

Two weeks after Olivia was born, Jack told Verna that he had to return to Oklahoma. He had failed to mention the fact that he was already engaged when he had started dating her. Verna listened in shock as Jack rambled on, "Myrtle and I were engaged before I came to California. She's pregnant and I want a divorce so I can go back to Oklahoma and marry her."

Verna was devastated. Her entire world had come crashing down.

Overhearing the conversation, Mr. Payne stormed into their room. "Verna, you and the baby are welcome to stay here as long as you like." Turning his rage on his son he stormed, "And Jack, you can go to Hell! You irresponsible, rutting pup. You have no sense of decency! Get out! Get out of my house! Now!"

The pain Verna felt was so great she couldn't even cry. In stunned silence she watched Jack gather his few belongings and leave the room. Her innocence gone, her heart broken beyond repair, she began to build an invisible protective wall around herself.

Leta helped Verna through the painful divorce. As Mr. Payne paid the lawyer he said, "I'll take it out of Jack's hide later." Verna stayed on with Mr. Payne. The cooking and cleaning was easy for her as her mother had taught all her children the art of housekeeping very young. But the baby was another matter. When Dolly wasn't throwing up she was screaming. She wasn't at all like Ellen had been. Verna was at her wits end. Mr. Payne was such a kind and gentle man he never said a word but Verna knew Dolly's constant crying was unnerving him too.

Not knowing what she was doing wrong, Verna took the baby to her mother. Leta soon discovered that Dolly was starving. Verna had not been able to nurse and Leta was sure the cow's milk was not agreeing with her. So she sent the boys to buy a goat. There was a great improvement right away. Dolly kept the milk down and finally started sleeping all night. And, finally, so did everyone else.

Verna went to work at a local drive-in as a car hop when Dolly was three months old. She had moved back home as Mr. Payne was not well and she felt he could not get the rest he needed with a baby in the house.

When Mr. Payne became seriously ill a few weeks later, his daughter and son-in-law took him back to Oklahoma. Verna knew she would never see any of them again. She would miss Mr. Payne. He had been good to her and she had grown very fond of him.

Chapter Forty

"Mama! Mama! Come quick!" Ellen called from the kitchen door clutching the damp dishtowel. It was her job to do up the day's dishes when she got home from school and she liked to listen to the radio as she worked. Leta quickly turned from the clothesline in the back yard. She had just finished hanging up the last of the laundry. Her back was aching and her hands were raw from wringing out the sodden clothes. The boys had tried to fix the broken wringer on the washer but couldn't quite get it to work. Thinking Reta or Dolly had gotten hurt, she dropped the laundry basket and ran to the house.

"Who's hurt?" Her heart was pounding as she raced up the porch steps.

"No one, Mama. It's on the radio." Ellen held the screen door open for her. "Listen."

"Japan has bombed Pearl Harbor," Keith told his mother when she stepped into the kitchen. His pale and expressionless face mirrored her own fears. They all knew what that meant. Howard and Kenneth stood beside the radio as President Roosevelt was speaking. Verna stood in the center of the room still holding the broom. The unthinkable had happened.

"Will we go to war too?" Ellen asked.

"Yes," Leta whispered, choking back tears. The Twins would be eighteen in two short years and she prayed that it would be over before they were old enough to be in the Service.

From that day on, news of the war was everywhere: the radio, newspapers, magazines, and newsreels at the movie theaters. Young men signed up in droves, anxious to enlist to serve their country.

This year the family celebrated Christmas to its fullest. They went all out decorating nearly every room of their small three room house. Keith and Kenneth found a large cedar tree at one of the Christmas tree lots near where they worked. The tree was flat on one side and no one had wanted it so the man gave it to the twins for a bargain price. They strapped it to the top of their jalopy and hauled it home.

Verna, Howard, and Ellen were busy making decorations for the tree when the twins came in dragging the huge cedar. They could see the decorations they had made were not nearly enough to cover it. Even after the boys sawed off about eighteen inches from the bottom, it still filled the entire corner of the room. They trimmed off limbs to decorate the rest of the room, Leta and the girls made more bows out of scraps of yarn and ribbon. There was no tinsel or lights to place on it, but they all agreed it was the most beautiful tree they had ever had.

Dan surprised them all by coming home early that evening and he was still sober. They all secretly hoped he would stay sober this Christmas Season. When he came in and saw the tree he said grinning, "Well that looks like hell," Leta knew it would be a peaceful and pleasant evening for a change.

A week before Christmas, Verna went by bus to visit her Aunt Leila in Burbank. She didn't go very often as it was not her favorite place to go but Leta had made a jacket for Leila and wanted Verna to take it to her. Soon after she arrived at Leila's, a young man brought his mother to visit with Leila. Leila had met Myrtle Meeks in Naples, Idaho, and they had become friends.

Leila quickly introduced them. "Myrtle, this is my niece Verna. Verna this is Myrtle Meeks and her son Clement." Clem was a handsome young man with black hair, dark brown eyes, and olive complexion. He lived in Inglewood and worked at Lockheed Aircraft.

Leaving Myrtle and Leila inside the house to visit, Clem and Verna sat on the porch step where there was a cool breeze. Even though it was December it was still quite warm in southern California. All too soon, it seemed to Clem, his mother was ready to go home. "After I take Mama home, I'll come back and take you to Bell Gardens so you won't have to ride the bus." Verna happily accepted his offer. He seemed to be a perfect gentleman.

Leta liked Clem the moment she met him. She had known his family in Idaho and remembered him as a small boy. One of his brothers, Russell Meeks, had managed the dress factory in Spokane where Leta had bought scraps of material. Clem began courting Verna the day he met her and he quickly became one of the family. He did not care that Verna was divorced or the circumstances of her short marriage. He accepted Verna unconditionally, baby and all. As far as he was concerned, Dolly was his.

Wherever they went, Clem and Verna took Dolly with them. They would lay her on a pillow on the wide shelf behind the front seat of the Plymouth coupe Clem drove and she was perfectly content on her pillow. Many times in order to get her to sleep they would take her for a drive.

In late March Leta knew she was pregnant again. She was heartsick. And she was angry. Angry with Dan, but mostly angry with herself. He had done so well staying sober for several weeks and they had seemed like a real family again. It had raised her hopes that he would quit his drinking. But it was not to be. After she told him she was going to have another baby he went out to celebrate the news with his cronies.

The following day when Dan came home, his head pounding and sick to his stomach, Leta told him firmly, "I've had all of this I can stand. As long as you keep drinking you can stay away from me. From now on, when you are home, you will sleep in the bunkhouse with the boys." She hoped an ultimatum would make him give up the liquor, but Dan continued to drink heavily, becoming more and more intolerant and belligerent. The family began hating to see him come home at all.

Unknown to Leta, Dan had quit making the payments on the lot in Bell Gardens. The family lost their home again. "It wasn't much of a house anyway," Dan smirked.

He knew a man up north in Lodi, just south of Sacramento, and decided they would move there. Again, Leta's hopes were raised. If he got away from the men he was running with maybe this time he would quit drinking, she thought. Moving to Lodi, they rented a four room house on Railroad Avenue with gas heat and a gas cook stove.

The year 1942 seemed to be gone in the blink of an eye. In July, Clem joined the Navy and was shipped out on a Destroyer, the *Case,* DD370. The war with Japan had accelerated throughout the South Pacific and they went to Enewetak, an atoll southwest of the Marshall Islands.

Leta gave birth to her seventh child, November 22, 1942, in French Camp, California. When she named him Arthur John she knew her mother would not be pleased. But Leta wanted one of her children to bear her father's name.

When Clem came home on leave in December, he told Verna he wanted a family of his own. He wanted her and Dolly to be his family. Not sharing their secret with anyone, they drove to San Diego and were married on December 5, 1942.

Reta contracted pneumonia around Christmas time and the doctor told Leta she would have to move where she could have wood heat. "This gas heat is just too damp," he had told Leta. Reta spent her second birthday in the hospital with a large tube in her back to drain the fluid out of her lungs. Leta stayed at the hospital with her most of the time.

During the long weeks Reta was in the hospital, Dan's drinking binges continued to worsen. Leta now knew nothing, short of death, would stop him. He was on a self destructive collision course and had no desire to get off. She had lost the fine man she had loved and married. She didn't know what she was going to do but she knew she could not go on living this way.

The doctor had told Leta before he could let Reta come home she had to find a house with wood heat. Kenneth and Verna started looking right away and soon located a large farmhouse not far from town on Kettleman Lane at a rent they could afford. The owner told them it had a wood heater in the living room and an electric cook stove. Not bothering to take a look inside the house they rented it on the spot. The next day when the two proudly drove Leta out to see it they were all shocked at the condition of the house. Leta almost cried. She had never seen a house so filthy. A barn was cleaner. "How will we ever clean this up?" She said tearfully.

"Don't worry, Mama." Verna assured her mother. "The Twins and Howard and I will clean it up." And clean it they did. The four siblings spent every spare minute they had scrubbing and painting. The previous tenants had owned a monkey and they had allowed the primate to spread his filth all over the walls and everywhere it could reach. The stains in the wainscoting would not come out. After scrubbing the walls with strong Clorox water, it had to be painted over with several coats of paint.

Dan seldom came home at all now. He would be gone for days at a time, fishing with his new found cronies. Leta knew there was more drinking than fishing going on. It seemed she had not been able to depend on him in years and now she wished he would just stay away. She felt it would be easier on her and the youngsters if he did.

After a month of hard work, the family moved in the day before Reta was released from the hospital. Not having seen the house since the first shocking visit, Leta was overwhelmed with surprise and delight. The house looked like new: clean, warm and roomy. Without the help of their father, the four oldest Keoghs had moved everything while Leta was at the hospital with Reta.

The old farm had a good well, and room for a large garden. A huge, aging walnut tree grew in the center of the backyard. The dirt driveway circled around it. Weather had worn the paint off the outside of the house and the boards were gray, but to Leta the house was beautiful. Her children had made this house on Kettleman Lane into a real home. This is where she would stay. The twins and Verna were paying the rent so Dan could not make her move again.

Reta weighed less than twelve pounds when she came home from the hospital. She was so frail and tiny, Leta still feared for her health. But Reta healed quickly in the fresh country air. Verna, the Twins, and Howard had found jobs at the local winery and Leta took a job in one of the canneries. They all worked different shifts so someone was always home with the little ones. When Ellen got home from school each day she enjoyed her job of tending Reta and Dolly. But, she still did not like doing the dishes.

The months seemed to slip by like leaves floating downstream on a swift current. Dan had become a virtual stranger to his family. Leta wasn't sure if he ever drew a sober breath anymore. The only time he came home now was when he knew the twins and Verna were getting paid. They worked hard for their money and it angered Leta for Dan to come and demand they give him part of it. If she had any at all left she gave him hers to keep the peace.

The final straw came when Dan came home, drunk, just as the family was sitting down to the dinner table. Staggering in, he sat down heavily in the chair at the end of the table. No one dared say a word for fear of setting him off. Not only had he become belligerent and obnoxious, he would get mean. With an unsteady hand he grabbed the glass pitcher of milk and filled Reta's glass to the brim.

Keith had rolled his new Pontiac the week before with his youngest sister in it and she had broken her collar bone. When Reta reached for the glass she knocked it over spilling milk everywhere and began to cry. Ellen got up to get a towel and Dan exploded in a fit of rage. He slammed the pitcher down on the table so hard it shattered, showering glass over the entire table of food. A small piece of glass hit Reta in the forehead and blood was running down her tiny face mixed with her tears.

Everyone froze for an instant. Leta quickly grabbed the towel from Ellen, holding it to Reta's head as she picked her up and left the table. Then pandemonium hit. Verna started yelling at her father. Dan jumped up and slapped her hard across the face. When he hit Verna, the twins jumped up and grabbed him and the fight was on. Howard quickly jumped in to help his brothers. Reta, Art, and Dolly were all squalling by now. Ellen stood against the wall with tears streaming down her face. Wrestling their father outside, the three boys threw him off the porch.

"Now get out and stay out! Just stay away from us! We don't need you anymore!" the boys screamed at him as he lay sprawled in the dust.

Verna had called the police and they came and took Dan away. Leta knew now there was no choice in what she had to do.

The day she had to go before the judge to finalize the divorce, Leta was terrified he wouldn't grant it. In these days it was very difficult for a woman to obtain a divorce. When she walked into the courtroom and saw Dan standing there alone, a mere shell of the man he once was, it broke Leta's heart. Steeling herself against a painful searing emotion, she knew divorce was the only answer.

The judge pored over the petition and as a man he sided with Dan on every issue. Leta's heart sank as the judge told her that drinking wasn't enough reason to divorce a man. "All men have a drink now and then," he told her. Bolstering her courage, she quietly told him the names of the men Dan had been keeping company with.

The judge frowned and grumbled, "Well, why didn't you say so. Every one of these men has been in front of me more than once. They are a no good lot. Divorce granted."

Leta turned and left the room without looking in Dan's direction. She knew if she did, it would be her undoing. It was all she could do to keep herself from flying apart in a thousand pieces. Part of her died as she walked down the courthouse steps into the hot California sun. It was as though a light had been snuffed out deep inside her. For so long she had held the hope that Dan would quit the drink and become a loving husband and father again. But he had not. She knew he never would as long as he lived. She had lost that wonderful man she fell in love with and married, forever.

Soon after the divorce, putting all the unhappy times behind them, Leta and her family began living a normal, happy, fun filled life together. They all worked hard but could now truly enjoy the fruits of their labor as well as each other. Every day when the mail came, Leta would hold her breath until she knew the dreaded letter from Uncle Sam was not there. Now that the twins were eighteen her greatest fear was that they would get drafted. The war had intensified throughout the world with no end in sight.

Two months after Leta's divorce, Keith and Kenneth each received a "Greetings" letter from Uncle Sam. Kenneth was rejected due to a perforated ear drum and a heart mummer. Keith, however, was accepted. When the time came for him to report for basic training, Elsie Johnson was visiting Leta. Elsie drove Keith out to highway 99 so he could catch a ride to Fort Ord. She never told Leta that, when she drove away and looked back at Keith standing there looking so small and alone, she had cried all the way back to Leta's.

Howard had joined the Navy a few weeks before and was still in basic training. There seemed to be an emptiness in the house with the two boys gone. Kenneth missed his twin brother more than he knew how to tell anyone.

Howard received a medical discharge and was sent home within six months. But before he came home, the Navy put in permanent partial dentures so now he had a full set of bottom teeth. Leta was grateful to have two of her boys out of the war. She prayed every day that Keith and her son-in-law Clem would come home safe and sound, in mind as well as body.

In the spring, Leta and her brood planted a large garden and Howard bought a calf. It had the scowers and the farmer was certain it would die anyway so he let Howard have it for $2.00. But Leta scorched flour in an iron skillet to put in its milk and she soon cured it. In about a year they would have good beef on their table. A few weeks later Kenneth bought a suckling pig. They didn't have much money but their little farm was flourishing and Leta knew no matter what, they would eat.

Japan surrendered on August 14, 1945. The war was finally over. People were celebrating all over the world. Hitler was dead. Mussolini was dead. And Japan had finally been beaten.

Leta thanked God that Keith and Clem were safe and would be coming home soon. She had her seven children, a granddaughter, and a son-in-law that was as good to her as he was his wife. Her vegetable garden was thriving. Her rose garden sported huge, fragrant cabbage roses. The old walnut tree was laden with maturing nuts. Leta had her farm and her peace of mind at last. And for the first time in her life she felt she was her own person.

Her father had been right. She had survived the many blackberry winters through her life. And they had made her stronger. She just hoped with everything in her that there would be no more blackberry winters. But deep in her soul, she knew there would be.

www.ingramcontent.com/pod-product-compliance
Lightning Source LLC
Chambersburg PA
CBHW070716280326
41926CB00087B/2169